Contents

THE IRIGARAY READER

Luce Irigaray

Edited and with an introduction
by

Margaret Whitford

✓

B

Introduction, editorial matter and organization copyright © Margaret Whitford 1991

First published 1991
Reprinted 1992, 1993, 1994, 1995, 1996, 1997, 1999, 2000

Blackwell Publishers Ltd
108 Cowley Road
Oxford OX4 1JF, UK

Blackwell Publishers Inc
350 Main Street
Malden, Massachusetts 02148, USA

British Library Cataloguing in Publication Data
A CIP catalogue record for this book is available from the British Library

Library of Congress Cataloging in Publication Data
Irigaray, Luce
[Essays. Selections. English]
The Irigaray reader / Luce Irigaray; edited and with an
introduction by Margaret Whitford.
p.   cm.
Translated from the French.
Includes bibliographical references and index.
ISBN 0–631–17043–X (pbk.)
1. Women—Psychology. 2. Women and psychoanalysis. 3. Femininity
(Philosophy). 4. Sex (Psychology). I. Whitford, Margaret.
HQ1206.173213   1991   91—9540
305.42—dc20   CIP

Typeset in 11 on 13pt Plantin by Best-set Typesetter Ltd
Printed and bound in Great Britain by MPG Books Ltd, Bodmin, Cornwall

This book is printed on acid-free paper

Acknowledgements

I would like to thank Luce Irigaray for her support for this project and for her patient replies to queries over several years. Thanks also to Marie-Christine Press for generous help at the outset, and to Toril Moi for her enthusiastic encouragement. My biggest debt is to David Macey for his remarkably accurate and painstaking translations; this *Reader* would not have been possible without him.

Margaret Whitford

The editor and publishers are grateful for permission to reproduce the following material:

Chapter 1 this translation © 1991 David Macey. Originally published in *Je, Tu, Nous*, Grasset, 1990. **Chapter 2** this translation © 1991 David Macey, reprinted from Luce Irigaray, *Sexes et parentes*, © forthcoming Columbia University Press. Used by permission. **Chapter 3** this translation © 1991 David Macey. Used by kind permission of Luce Irigaray. **Chapter 4** retranslated by David Macey from Luce Irigaray, *Speculum of the Other Woman*, translated by Gillian C. Gill. Translation © 1985 by Cornell University Press. Used by permission of the publisher. **Chapters 5 and 6** this translation © 1991 David Macey, from Luce Irigaray, *Parler n'est jamais neutre*, © forthcoming the Althone Press. Used by permission. **Chapters 7 and 8** reprinted from Luce Irigaray, *This Sex Which Is Not One*, translated by Catherine Porter with Carolyn Burke. Translation © 1985 by Cornell University Press. Used by permission of the publisher. **Chapter 9** this translation © 1991 David Macey, reprinted from Luce Irigaray, *Sexes et parentes*, © forthcoming

Columbia University Press. Used by permission. **Chapter 10** this translation © Seán Hand (from Toril Moi, (ed) *French Feminist Thought*, Basil Blackwell, 1987). Reprinted by kind permission of Cornell University Press. **Chapter 11** reproduced by kind permission of Luce Irigaray. **Chapter 12** this translation © 1991 David Macey. Used by kind permission of Luce Irigaray. **Chapter 13** this translation © 1991 David Macey, reprinted from Luce Irigaray, *Sexes et parentes*, © forthcoming Columbia University Press. Used by permission. **Chapter 14** this translation © 1991 David Macey. Originally published in *Je, Tu, Nous*, Grasset, 1990. **Chapter 15** this translation © 1991 David Macey, from Luce Irigaray, *L'oubli de l'air*, reproduced by kind permission of Les Editions du Minuit.

Introduction

Irigaray can be considered from many different aspects, and any selection of her writings must choose what to emphasize. Nonetheless, it seemed to me that her most essential audience was the feminist one – those who are involved, like her, in the project of bringing about fundamental social and symbolic change. An alternative *Irigaray Reader* was considered and rejected – one which would have presented her primarily as a philosopher in dialogue with a range of contemporary philosophers and philosophers of the past. That *Reader* has yet to be constructed. Readers of this *Reader* will, however, get a glimpse in this collection of Irigaray the philosopher, Irigaray the psychoanalyst, Irigaray the researcher in linguistics, and Irigaray the visionary. (It should also be noted that the choice of texts was dictated partly by constraints of copyrights.)

The reception of Irigaray

In an interview in 1983, Irigaray explained how much she hated being asked personal questions:

> Let [people] take what they will out of my books. I don't think that my work can be better understood because I've done this or that. The risk is that such information will disrupt people when they read.[1]

This is not just a personal stance of suspicious defensiveness, but the well-founded realization that one way of neutralizing a woman thinker whose work is radically challenging is to 'reduce' her to her biography – which is what has tended to happen to Irigaray's most celebrated predecessor, Simone de Beauvoir. In her book on Simone de Beauvoir (1990), Toril Moi exposes with devastating clarity the kind of gauntlet that the brilliant woman writer or philosopher may have to run. The topoi of Simone de Beauvoir's reception include: reducing the book to the woman, by focusing on her appearance or her relation with Sartre; using the personal to discredit the political, by reducing her political commitments to emotional problems; presenting her as a cold and uncaring political woman (read: not really a woman); or presenting her as a bluestocking (again, read: unfeminine) – this topos includes the implicit or explicit contrast between male intellectual creativity and audacity, versus the dutiful, hardworking but intellectually submissive female. The aim of such topoi, argues Moi, is to discredit Beauvoir as a speaker (p. 23). Similarly, Irigaray. As a result of Irigaray's uncompromising anti-autobiographical position, critics have been denied much opportunity to reduce the book to the woman or the political to the personal, although the naivety topos (Moi p. 52) has been exploited to the full. However, there is also an interesting array of more or less dismissive accounts from within feminism, which it is tempting to interpret in terms of the mother–daughter dynamic. As Irigaray suggests in *Speculum* and *Ethique de la différence sexuelle*, relations between mothers and daughters (whether natural or spiritual) are likely to be conflictual, since our culture displays a quasi-total absence of adequate representations of the mother–daughter relationship which would permit women to negotiate new relations with each other. Relations between women are often marked by ambivalence, and never more so than when a woman is outstanding in some way.

It is one of the ironies of reception that stances for or against Irigaray were adopted well before any of her major work was available in translation. Three of these stances in particular are worth mentioning, because they are as inaccurate as they are widely adopted. The first is the fairly widespread view that Irigaray is an essentialist who assumes an unproblematic connection between women's bodies and women's true selves. The second and associated reading is to see Irigaray as one of the high priestesses of *écriture féminine*, along with Kristeva and Cixous. This reading blurs the differences, both theoretical and political, between the three women.[2] But it also reduces the complexity of Irigaray's work to the simplicity of a formula –

'writing the body', and conveniently ignores that Irigaray's brief comments on women and writing in *This Sex Which Is Not One* have been made to represent more or less the totality of her work, most of which is still largely unknown to anglophone readers. The third reading is the view that Irigaray is celebrating the pre-oedipal closeness between mother and daughter, attempting the impossible return to a pre-patriarchal space before language. Together, these three inadequate and not entirely mutually compatible readings have dominated the discourse on Irigaray for quite a long time, while dissenting voices (Burke, 1981; Gallop, 1982, 1983; the numerous articles of Elizabeth Grosz) struggled to make themselves heard. It is only recently that we have begun to see signs of a critical shift. In my view, none of the readings sketched above stands up to scrutiny when compared with Irigaray's oeuvre.

Irigaray's intertexts

Irigaray's first published work was in psycho-linguistics. In a number of papers (some of which appear in *Parler n'est jamais neutre*) and a full-length book, *Le Langage des déments*, she explores the way in which the symptoms of different kinds of mental disturbance can be discerned in the formal features of language – in the breakdown of syntactical structures, in different forms of aphasia, and so on. Initially, she was not looking for speech differences between men and women. However, as she became convinced that identity was enacted at least partly in self-positioning in language vis-à-vis an interlocutor, she began to look for differences between the normal (i.e. non-pathological) speech of men and that of women. It is important to note two points here. Firstly, this is not a question of *writing*, but of response to another speaker or to a stimulus, of which the best experimental situation is psychoanalysis, where the dynamics of speech and response are addressed directly. Secondly, it is not a question of biology determining speech, but of identity assumed in language within a particular symbolic system known as patriarchy, and described by Lacan, in which the only possible subject-position is masculine. Within this system, the only feminine identity available to women is that of 'defective' or 'castrated' men; women are not symbolically self-defined.

Irigaray's thesis, formulated in *This Sex Which Is Not One*, is that there might be the possibility of a different, non-masculine discourse: 'the problem is that of a possible alterity in masculine discourse – or in relation to masculine discourse' (p. 140). Her work on language (see especially *Le Sexe linguistique* and *Sexes et genres à travers les langues*) is an attempt to make visible the deep emotional structures conveyed in discourse: in a nutshell, the underlying Oedipal structure of language and culture, which distributes different roles to men and women. In retrospect, her early statements about *parler femme* (speaking (as) woman) may seem rather optimistic, corresponding perhaps to the political climate of the early 1970s and the initial euphoria of the women's movement. She now makes it clear that big shifts in society and culture will be necessary if transformations in language are to come about.

Precise theoretical references are on the whole absent from her work, but it seems clear that the work of the linguists Emile Benveniste (1966, 1974) and Roman Jakobson has been influential. Kurt Goldstein's work, which was important for Merleau-Ponty's thesis in *Phenomenology of Perception*, appears in the bibliography of *Le Langage des déments*. It seems likely that she is also familiar with the semiotics of Greimas (1966, 1979) and Umberto Eco (1988).

Her most recent project in this area is to set up international research teams to examine the expression of sex in language. *Sexes et genres à travers les langues* is a collection of articles by researchers working in English and Italian; their results are compared with those of Irigaray in French, in order to attempt to establish how the operation of sex in language takes place in different languages. In summary, Irigaray argues that the evidence of the research shows that:

1 men are more likely to take up a subject position in language, to designate themselves as subjects of the discourse or action; women are more likely to efface themselves, to give precedence to men or to the world;
2 the use of the first-person pronoun, 'I', by women, does not necessarily indicate a feminine identity;
3 women are accustomed to being the vehicles of men's self-representation; their own self-representation in language is more or less absent;

4   women are more likely to engage in dialogue; while men privilege the relation with the world and the object, women privilege interpersonal relations;
5   women are not, as is sometimes thought, more emotional and subjective than men when they speak; their speech is likely to efface the expression of their subjectivity;
6   women are less abstract than men, and are more likely to take account of context; they are also more likely to collaborate with the researcher and take the research seriously.[3]

Although the theoretical models are different, these arguments overlap to a considerable extent with Anglo-American arguments about the linguistic perpetuation of oppression. (For comparison, see Dale Spender's *Man Made Language* (1980), or Deborah Cameron's collection, *The Feminist Critique of Language: a reader* (1990), which gives examples of a range of different approaches.) The vision of woman's language that seemed so revolutionary and iconoclastic in *This Sex Which Is Not One* turns out not to be a question of a totally different language, but more to do with socially-determined linguistic practices, sexual differences in the generation of messages and self-positioning in language vis-à-vis the other, all of which are possible sites for transformation, opening up the possibility of women's distinct cultural identity.

The second aspect of Irigaray's work is her critique of psychoanalysis, both of Freud and of Lacan. She became well known as an outspoken feminist and critic of psychoanalysis with the publication of her second book, *Speculum*, in 1974. She immediately lost her post in the Department of Psychoanalysis at Vincennes, and, in her own words, was 'put into quarantine' by the psychoanalytic establishment (Baruch and Serrano, 1988, p. 163). In particular she was censured for being politically committed by psychoanalysts who thought that being a psychoanalyst precluded political commitment. As Irigaray points out (in *Le Corps-à-corps avec la mère* p. 58), such a position is itself politically determined. What is interesting about Irigaray's critique is that it is a critique from within psychoanalysis. She uses psychoanalytic theory against itself to put forward a coherent explanation for theoretical bias in terms of unconscious fantasy, splitting, resistance and defences in the discourse of psychoanalysis.

Thus she is not simply hostile to psychoanalysis; and in fact, she speaks of Freud as an 'honest scientist' who went as far as he could (Baruch and Serrano, 1988, pp. 162–3), but whose limitations need to be identified and not turned into dogma.

In summary, the main points of her critique of Freud are as follows. Firstly, psychoanalysis is unaware of the historical and philosophical determinants of its own discourse. Secondly, psychoanalysis is itself governed by unconscious fantasies which it has not been able to analyse. Thirdly, it is patriarchal; it reflects a social order which does not acknowledge what it owes to the mother. As a consequence of these factors, its phallocentric bias is taken for universal truth; psychoanalysis is blind to its own assumptions. For example, Freud takes the development of the little boy as norm, and assumes that a similar model of development must apply to the little girl; her difference is assumed under male parameters. Irigaray is also critical of the way in which psychoanalysis is transmitted – from father to son – with a premium on identification with the father and devotion to his law (an identification and devotion that her critique of Lacan put into question).

Her relation to Lacan is equally complex. Lacan's structural reading of Freud, the emphasis on the role of language in the formation of the unconscious, and in the acquisition of sexual identity, undoubtedly made her own psychoanalytic readings possible. In addition, Lacan was one of her mentors; she had attended his seminars at the Ecole Normale Supérieure, she was a member of the Ecole freudienne de Paris, and he was effectively in charge of the Department of Psychoanalysis at Vincennes. His rejection of her was particularly painful, but Lacan did not easily tolerate theoretical deviations. Irigaray attacks Lacan for what she sees as his ahistoricism and social conservatism (see especially 'Così fan tutti' in *This Sex Which Is Not One*, and 'The poverty of psychoanalysis' in this volume) and indicts some of the cornerstones of his theory: the primacy of the phallus, and his conceptualization of the imaginary body of the mirror stage as a male body. The title of the book, *Speculum*, refers to the mirror used by doctors for examining the internal cavities of the body. Playing on the idea of the mirror, she points out that Lacan's mirror can only see women's bodies as lacking, as a 'hole'; to see what is specific to women, he would have needed a mirror that could look inside. The mirror, of course, is the mirror of theory or discourse, and although Lacan is not named, *Speculum* is as much a challenge to Lacan as it is to Freud and to western philosophy.

After *Speculum*, she has turned her attention away from psycho-analytic theory to examine other discourses, though it is possible to argue that the psychoanalytic model of dialogue – a *here and now* in which two interlocutors meet, and in which the question of desire or transference is central – continues to reverberate throughout her entire oeuvre (see Whitford, 1991). This model has been replaced to a certain extent by that of the 'amorous exchange', or encounter between the sexes (see 'The bodily encounter with the mother' and 'Questions to Emmanuel Levinas', both in this volume), and that of the parousia, or 'second coming', in which the flesh would be made word and women would no longer be excluded from the divine (see *Ethique de la différence sexuelle* and *Divine Women*). What is constant however, is the stress on sexual difference and the address to the other.

A large part of *Speculum* is an examination of the history of philosophy, 'going back through the masculine imaginary' (*This Sex*, p. 164), to show the workings of patriarchy in western philosophy from Plato onwards. This Derridean-influenced work sets out to show the re-pressed and hidden underside of metaphysical constructions, what they conceal and yet depend on for their existence – what Irigaray refers to as the unacknowledged mother: 'All of western culture rests on the murder of the mother' (*Le Corps-à-corps avec la mère*, p. 81). After *Speculum*, Irigaray wrote a series of further books, engaging with philosopy: *Passions élémentaires, Amante marine, L'Oubli de l'air*, culminating in *Ethique de la différence sexuelle*, which is a series of readings of Plato, Aristotle, Descartes, Spinoza, Merleau-Ponty and Levinas. As she explains in an interview:

> To begin with, I wanted to do a sort of tetralogy, tackling the problem of the four elements: water, air, fire, earth, applied to philosophers nearer our own time, and at the same time, interrogate the philosophical tradition, particularly from the side of the feminine. (*Le Corps-à-corps avec la mère*, p. 43).

This theme is elaborated in the paper *Divine Women*:

When I wrote *Amante marine, Passions élémentaires, L'Oubli de l'air*, I intended to make a study of our relation to the elements: water, earth, fire, air. I wanted to return to these natural materials which constitute the origin of our body, our life, our environment, the flesh of our passions. . . . We still live our everyday lives in a universe which is composed of and is described in terms of four natural elements: air, water, fire, earth. We are made of them, and we live in them. They determine, more or less freely, our attractions, our affects, our passions, our limits, our aspirations. (*Sexes et parentés*, p. 89)

In *Ethique de la différence sexuelle*, it is the Kantian conditions of experience, the categories of space and time, that are re-examined. In each case, Irigaray is tackling, not the explicit arguments of the philosopher, but the sexual subtext, the fantasmatic organization underlying the surface rationality.

In order to tackle the philosophical fantasies, Irigaray wrote, 'one must assume the feminine role deliberately' (*This Sex*, p. 76). This strategy of mimesis has been much discussed. It is an attempt (1) to avoid adopting the position of the male subject and thus perpetuating it; and (2) to avoid recapture within the parameters of a metaphysical system in which the place of/for the feminine is marked out in advance. What I should like to note here is its implications for reading and interpreting Irigaray.

Irigaray goes on to say, in *This Sex Which Is Not One*, that occupying the feminine role means playing the part of the philosopher's wife (or sister, or mother in some cases). The sexual imagery is quite deliberate; she has in mind a kind of 'amorous exchange' in which sexual difference would be enacted in language, and she attempts to suggest this textually, to a certain extent, by mingling her own voice with the voice/text of the philosopher. This can be seen in its purest, unmixed form, in *Speculum*, where one of the sections ('Une Mère de glace'), consists entirely of extracts from Plotinus, judiciously selected. (Irigaray is here only present in the selection of extracts.) Irigaray states specifically at the end of *Speculum* that:

Precise references in the form of notes or punctuation indicating quotation have often been omitted. Because in relation to

the working of theory, the/a woman fulfills a twofold function –
as the mute outside that sustains all systematicity; as a maternal
and still silent ground that nourishes all foundations – she does
not have to conform to the codes that theory has set up for
itself. (p. 365)

But more or less all of the philosophical texts ventriloquize. Whether
one recognizes the sources or not depends on one's familiarity with
the philosopher, since inverted commas are seldom used. Sometimes,
the quotations are obvious: the classical Greek in *Speculum*, for
example. But sometimes there are no indications, and in cases where
Irigaray is using a French translation, and the English translator
reproduces the citations without recognizing their source, they
become unidentifiable, couched in a different form of words so far
from the familiar English version that we know, that they evoke no
answering echo. In practical terms, this means that there is a good
deal of textual scholarship yet to be undertaken on Irigaray's texts if
we are to understand them more fully.

The philosophical texts are dazzling, allusive, deliberately poly-
semic, difficult to unravel, and for the most part still untranslated.[4]
As a result, although Irigaray's debt to psychoanalysis is well-known,
her position in relation to the history of philosophy has hardly been
studied or documented at all. (See Grosz, 1989, Mortensen, 1989,
and Whitford, 1991, for initial exploratory studies.)

If, as Michèle Le Doeuff argues, philosophy is constructed by
exclusion and in particular the exclusion of women, how can women
enter it without contradiction?[5] Irigaray addresses this problem directly. Although she is profoundly critical of a certain kind of philosophy, she situates herself as a philosopher, with a clear sense of
philosophy as 'the work of the universal' (*Sexes et parentés*, p. 162)
with stringent ethical requirements. She is preoccupied by questions
of phenomenology and ethics, subjectivity and identity, death and
desire, rationality and the unconscious. The point of philosophy in
our time is to rethink these questions in the light of sexual difference, as the opening lines of *Ethique de la différence sexuelle* make
clear:

Sexual difference is one of the questions, if not *the* question to
be thought in our age. According to Heidegger, each age has its

issue. One alone. Sexual difference is probably that issue in our own age. which, if thought, might be our 'salvation'?

But wherever I turn, whether to philosophy, science or religion, I find that this question continues to remain hidden, underlying, more and more insistent. A problematic which might enable us to put a check on the many forms of destruction in the universe, the nihilism which affirms nothing more than the reversal or repetitive proliferation of existing values – whether we call these the consumer society, the circularity of discourse, the more or less cancerous diseases of our age, the unreliability of words, the end of philosophy, religious despair or regressive religiosity, scientistic or technological imperialism that does not take the human subject into account, and so on.

Sexual difference would represent the horizon of worlds of a fertility as yet unknown, at all events in the west. [. . .] [I]t would also involve the production of a new age of thought, art, poetry and language: the creation of a new *poetics* [. . .]

For the work of sexual difference to take place, a revolution in thought and ethics is needed. We must reinterpret the whole relationship between the subject and discourse, the subject and the world, the subject and the cosmic, the microcosmic and the macrocosmic. (In Moi (ed.) (1987), pp. 13–14, trans. adapted)

Since about 1985, Irigaray has become and more concerned with having an effect on society and changing existing social forms. The books published since 1985, *Sexes et parentés* (1987), *Le Temps de la différence* (1989) and *Je, Tu, Nous* (1990), are all collections, including papers given at conferences, interviews with other feminists, or occasional publications, primarily in feminist journals. Throughout the 1980s, Irigaray was involved with political groups in Italy, first the women of the *affidamento*,[6] and later with the women of the Italian Communist Party. The direction her work is taking involves a more direct focus on women's civil status, their position as a sex before the law, the need for *woman*kind to be recognized as a genre distinct from *man*kind, and the importance of translating sexual difference into specific social forms, both to mediate relations between women themselves, and also to lay claim to an existence embodied in distinct and concrete instances as a basis for relationships with and negotiations with the world of men. One can discern certain shifts in emphasis resulting from this new preoccupation. The stress on the mother–daughter relationship and relationships between women has to a certain extent made way for a focus on having an effect on and in the world of men. *Parler-femme* has been replaced by the sexuation of discourse and culture. Mythology – a culture's self-image – has become more important than philosophy, perhaps for political reasons, since mythology is more readily accessible to a wider audience and more formative of the social unconscious, but also because Irigaray believes that mythology 'is one of the principal expressions of what organizes a society at a particular time' (*Je, Tu, Nous*, p. 28). There is a clear desire to be more involved in political action, and to put forward concrete and practical proposals to help women to achieve a cultural identity.

Since Chernobyl, in particular, Irigaray seems to have felt with especial urgency a sense of the imminent and threatened destruction of the world by patriarchal society, and her work has taken on a prophetic and messianic note as she appeals to women to save the world of men from catastrophe:

> What we need is a general cultural mutation. . . . Patriarchal culture is a culture founded on sacrifice, crime, war. [. . .] The people of men need others, who are persons in the full sense of the word [des personnes à part entière] who will allow them to understand themselves and to find their limits. Only women can play this role. Women do not belong to patriarchal culture as genuinely responsible subjects. From this arises the possibility of interpreting this culture in which they are less implicated and have fewer interests than men. (*Sexes et parentés*, pp. 200–201; *Le Temps de la différence*, pp. 23–4)

The urgency of transmitting a message to an audience has simplified Irigaray's formerly rather sibylline prose. She now states, rather than evoking indirectly, and spells out instead of alluding (cf., for example, the difference in style and register between the philosophical text of chapter 4 (1974) and the interview of chapter 3 (1981)). The result is, paradoxically I think, that her later work is in some ways as difficult to understand as her earlier work, for the simplified statements cannot simply be taken at face value. Their meaning depends on the complex analysis and infrastructure of the earlier work. In my view, there is a real danger that the rather less subtle and more programmatic elements of the later work could close off rather than open up dialogue with other women. Irigaray has often been accused of being inaccessible and elitist; it would be ironic if her efforts toward greater accessibility led to monologue rather than communication.

Her work is marked by a tension between critique and the vision of a new order. On the one hand, her critique of patriarchy stresses the death drive, and the impulsion towards 'sacrifice, crime, war', though she does not suggest, as a counterpart, that women are innocent, essentially non-violent, victims; on the contrary, she argues that women's death drives have up to now remained completely unsymbolized, and that this can make them destructive both to men and to each other, even if they do not have the power to organize this destruction in any institutional way. On the other hand, she has a more constructive vision of a harmonious future, a revolution in life, thought and culture which would transform and fertilize the rigid and death-seeking patriarchal world, a revolution in which women would have a central role to play. If one admits the death drive, then the bright future can never be a completely realizable possibility; but without the emancipatory and utopian horizon, it is arguable that the point of struggling for a better world would be lost. Irigaray's work is at its best when these two elements are held together in tension. When one or other – the pessimistic or the optimistic – gains the ascendant, the tension is lost, and the danger of ordinary banality is then never far away.

Irigaray's work is of crucial importance, particularly if one regards the modernism/postmodernism debate as the principal intellectual debate of our time (see some of the articles in Linda Nicholson (ed.) *Feminism/Postmodernism* (1990), and Susan Hekman's book *Gender and Knowledge* (1990), which puts forward this argument from a feminist position). For this debate confronts feminists with a dilemma. On the one hand, they share with postmodernist thought the radical critique of the modernist Enlightenment inheritance; on the other hand, the emancipatory thrust of feminism is rooted in the Enlightenment. Feminist politics, up to now, appears to be

grounded in a modernist category, 'woman', with essentialist implications, while the possibility of founding a political programme on a
postmodernist base is, to say the least, still a matter for debate.

Irigaray's contribution here is to point to the dangers for women of
embracing postmodernism too hastily or too uncritically. If, as she
argues, all western theory – including the theories of postmodernism
– fails to recognize sexual difference, then we have to examine
postmodernism for its sexual subtext. She warns against displacing the
male/female binary before the female side has acceded to identity and
subjectivity. To omit the question of the woman-as-subject and her
identity in thought and culture is to leave in place a tenacious and
damaging imaginary structure. 'Woman's time', then, is not necessarily coincident with the chronology of the male subject.

Her work poses the feminist dilemma in one of its clearest forms.
To interpret Irigaray in terms of an exclusive alternative – *either*
as modernist/essentialist, *or* as postmodernist in her deconstructive
strategies – is to perform a drastic reduction of her exemplarity and
centrality. Holding the tension here, walking this particular tightrope,
is what makes her work so challenging and so insistent. In its
enactment of the tension, it does not provide answers; it rather
appeals to the reader to begin to invent the next step(s). Her analysis
of patriarchy is both compelling and revealing, but the question of
'what is to be done' retains all its potential for controversy.

Reading Irigaray

There has always been a visionary aspect to Irigaray's work, a utopian
element that many have felt uneasy with. In Irigaray's texts, the
past, present and future are interwoven, impelling critics to ask:
'Where is she speaking *from*?' (Felman, 1975). However, if we are to
accept her message, then it is the creative power of imagination that
should be stressed. For Irigaray, contrary to much modern thought,
imagination is not inimical to politics;[7] politics is lifeless, sterile
and repetitive without it. I want to argue that it is a mistake to
hypostatize Irigaray, to *fix* her in a single meaning, a single instant of
contemporary history, a single moment of the text. The most productive readings are the dynamic ones, which attempt to engage with

Irigaray. The key words here are 'mobility' and 'exchange'. As Irigaray explains in 'The three genres' (this volume), she is trying to produce writing that cannot be reduced to a narrative or a commentary, but that calls for an interlocutor:

> No narrative, no commentary on a narrative, is enough to bring about a change in discourse. [. . .] Two approaches are important for the establishment of different norms of life: the analysis of the formal structures of discourse, and the creation of a new style. Thus, in *Ethique de la différence sexuelle* . . . there is no basic narrative and no possible commentaries by others, in the sense of an exhaustive deciphering of the text. What is said in this book is conveyed by a double style: a style of amorous relations, a style of thought, exposition, writing. (*Sexes et parentés*, p. 191)
>
> The only reply that can be given to the question of the meaning of the text is: read, perceive, feel. . . . *Who are you?* would be a more pertinent question, provided that it does not collapse into a demand for an identity card or an autobiographical anecdote. The answer would be: *and who are you?* Can we meet? Talk? Love? Create something together? Thanks to which milieu? What between-us [entre-nous]?
> We cannot do that without the horizon of sexual difference. (ibid. p. 192)

The ideal reply to her writing, she says explicitly, is 'who are you?' – the address is to the other. What she wants to do is to 'bring about a change in discourse'. This would account, I think, for the extraordinary variety of responses that she elicits – to this extent she has succeeded in her aim, for the interlocutor/reader is often forced to put him/herself into play in order to read her enigmatic texts, and the reponse is often as much to do with the reader as with Irigaray. At its best, it is a creative response in which there is a productive interaction between reader and text.

Writing this at the end of 1990, with the larger part of Irigaray's oeuvre still untranslated, I would anticipate that we are only just beginning to 'come to grips'[8] with the implications of Irigaray's evocative and provocative writing.

NOTES

1 In 'An Interview with Luce Irigaray', *Hecate*, 9 (1–2), pp. 192–202.
2 Toril Moi, in *Sexual/Textual Politics* (1985), gives accounts of Cixous, Irigaray and Kristeva, which distinguish them clearly from each other. See also Elizabeth Grosz, *Sexual Subversions* (1989) for substantial accounts of Kristeva and Irigaray.
3 I know of only one article in English on Irigaray's linguistic research into sexual difference in language; see Katherine Stephenson (1987). See also Terry Threadgold (1988).
4 Translations are indicated in the bibliography, pp. 219–221.
5 Michèle Le Doeuff, *L'Etude et le rouet* (1989).
6 For brief comments on *affidamento* and suggestions for further reading, see Introduction to section III below.
7 On the suspicion of the imagination in modern thought, see Richard Kearney *The Wake of Imagination* (1988).
8 See Naomi Schor's article: 'This essentialism which is not one: coming to grips with Irigaray' (1989).

Glossary

Certain terms are used by Irigaray in a specific sense. This glossary indicates some of the most salient. A further glossary of Irigarayan terms can be found in *This Sex Which Is Not One*, pp. 219–22.

autre, translated as other. Although 'other' is overlaid with multiple connotations because of its use by other philosophers and theorists (notably Lacan and Levinas), one of its central Irigarayan meanings is 'the other sex'. It can be further subdivided into 'the other of the same', i.e. the feminine as defined within and by patriarchy, and 'the other woman', i.e. the feminine as defined by and for herself. See also *féminin, même*.

discours, translated as discourse. Systemic instances of language use. Cf. *langue, langage, parole* and *verbe*.

échange, translated as exchange. This term covers exchanges both economic, material and symbolic. In patriarchy as analysed by Irigaray, only men are subjects of the exchange; women are among the objects of exchange and are thus a kind of 'commodity'. Irigaray stresses the need for women to become subjects of exchange too; for this, they would need symbolic objects or language, to avoid the danger of confusion of identity between them.

énonciation/énoncé, two linguistic terms which are usually translated as utterance and statement respectively. The grammatical subject, the subject of the statement, does not always correspond either to (1) the speaker or (2) the subject of the action. In linguistics, the subject of the utterance (*énonciation*) may be (1) or (2), but is usually taken by Irigaray to be (1), or the subject position of the speaking subject.

extase, extatique, extasié (also **hors-de-soi**), translated as ecstasy, ecstatic, ecstasied (sometimes ekstasy etc.). Ecstasy refers to the mode of being of the male subject, or transcendence. Transcendence requires that something be transcended; this something is usually conceptualized, according to Irigaray, as feminine. (See also *in-stant*.) When applied to women, ecstasy is more likely to indicate their 'homelessness' in the symbolic order, their place outside (ec/ek) it, and supporting it. *Ecstasy* overlaps with *ek-sistance* or *existence* (see chapter 6, note 1). See also *transcendental sensible*.

féminin, translated as feminine or female, depending on the translator. For the problems of translation here, see *sexe*. The question of nature or culture is an interpretative one, and accordingly the interpretation has been left to the reader.

genre, translated as genre. Genre can mean grammatical gender. It also means kind, sort, race (human race), species (animal), genre (literary or artistic). Irigaray uses all these connotations, but perhaps the most significant is the meaning of *kind*, as in mankind, and the suggestion that womankind should have its own specificity.

indifférent, indifférence, translated as indifferent, indifference. These terms refer to Irigaray's analysis of patriarchy as hom(m)osexual. Within patriarchy, sexual difference is not recognized; women are not the other sex, but the other of the same, always defined in relation to men (see *autre*). Thus Irigaray describes patriarchal culture as sexually indifferent.

in-stant, translated as im-mediate, could also be translated as immanent. It is the other side of *extase*, that which stands inside itself, rather than that which stands outside itself, and corresponds to the non-existent French word *en-stase*. It appears notably in the expression *extase instante*, which appears to be a contradiction in terms, but functions as a way of referring to the horizon of sexual difference, in which male culture will no longer need to transcend the feminine in order to maintain its subjectivity.

langage and **langue**, both translated as language. Whereas *langue* refers to the corpus of language (e.g. French, Italian, English), *langage* refers to the language as it used by a speaker. Thus one can distinguish between *langages* within the same language (*langue*) (register, idiolect, sociolect, etc.).

masculin, translated as *male* or *masculine*, depending on the translator. See *féminin*.

même, translated as same. Patriarchy is defined as the realm of the same, i.e. of one sex. The realm of the same does not recognise sexual difference (see also *autre, indifférent*). Thus love of self (of the same) is impossible for women within patriarchy.

parole, usually translated as speech or word(s), depending on context. Parole refers primarily to the assumption of subjectivity in language (see *énonciation*), hence 'la parole des femmes', not so much women's language, as women speaking as women on their own behalf.

sang rouge, translated as red blood. The red blood refers to the possibility of a maternal genealogy, which would take its place alongside, and in fertile conjunction with the paternal genealogy, which is the only genealogy recognized by patriarchy. Red blood may also refer to the unacknowledged debt to the mother, on which patriarchy depends. See also *semblant*.

semblant, translated as semblance, and sometimes opposed to the *sang rouge*, or red blood (since *semblant* is a homophone for *sang blanc* or white blood). The realm of the semblance is the masked realm of the same (see *même*) in that, although relations between men are governed by love of the same, love between men conceals itself under an apparent heterosexuality, the pretence or guise that there are two different sexes.

sexe, usually translated as sex, although it can also mean something like gender. Because of the theoretical debates over the use of 'sex' and 'gender', it seemed best not to pre-empt discussion by opting for one or the other term in specific cases. Accordingly, *sex* has been kept throughout, except that *sexe* can often just mean sexual organs or genitals, and where appropriate has been translated as such.

sexué, translated as sexuate. The problems with this term are similar to those with the term *sexe*, so again no attempt has been made by the translator to interpret the text.

transcendental sensible, translated as sensible transcendental. Refers to the horizon of sexual difference and the overcoming of the split between material and ideal, sensible and intelligible, female and male. See also chapter 6, note 4.

verbe, translated as verb, or word, according to context. Although *verbe* can mean verb, it can also mean the word of God addressed to men, or God himself as the second person of the Trinity, as in the phrase 'the Word made flesh'. It can also mean language (*langue* or *langage*).

SECTION I

The Critique of Patriarchy

Introduction to Section I

Patriarchy is defined by Irigaray as 'an exclusive respect for the genealogy of sons and fathers, and the competition between brothers' (*Sexes et parentés*, p. 202). What has been absent in western thought and institutions until very recently, claims Irigaray, is any attempt to consider the possibility of a maternal genealogy and the symbolic and institutional forms it might take. This would not be a reversal, the simple replacement of patriarchy with matriarchy, but rather the coexistence of *two* genealogies. It is appropriate then to begin the collection with Irigaray's acknowledgement of her 'mother' or 'elder sister' in feminism, Simone de Beauvoir.

'Equal or different?' ('Egales ou différentes?') was first published in *Die Tageszeitung*, a Berlin radical daily, on 19 April 1986, on the occasion of the death of Simone de Beauvoir. It was reprinted in *Paris-Féministe*, 61, 1–15 April 1988, and in *Fluttuaria*, 6–7, Milan, March-June 1988, and has been collected in *Je, Tu, Nous* (Paris: Grasset, 1990). The latter was not available at the time the present book was being prepared, so the translation has been made from Irigaray's original typescript, which may be slightly different from the final version.

Irigaray pays tribute to the significance of Simone de Beauvoir for modern feminism, but she makes it clear that there are fundamental differences between herself and Simone de Beauvoir. The major intellectual divergence identified by Irigaray is their respective attitudes towards psychoanalysis. Most of the piece is taken up with the crucial difference between the fight for equal rights and Irigaray's alternative conception of sexual difference. For Irigaray, 'equal' tends to mean 'equal to men' and therefore equivalent to the imposition of a male norm, and she warns that, carried to its con-

clusion, this would mean genocide: of women. She puts forward her
view that women need an identity as women, that there should be
*woman*kind as well as *man*kind.

For a glimpse of what Simone de Beauvoir thought of Irigaray, see
the interview published in *The Women's Review of Books*, (March
1986), 3 (6), p. 11. It's a translation of an interview that appeared in
March 1984 in *La Revue Littéraire des Femmes*. The interviewer,
Hélène Wenzel, asks de Beauvoir: 'What do you think of the work of
theoreticians like Luce Irigaray and Julia Kristeva?' De Beauvoir
replies that she finds Irigaray interesting, but that '[a]nyone who
wants to work on women has to break completely with Freud.
. . . But all of them, even Irigaray, they've always begun from
Freud's postulates'. For de Beauvoir, Irigaray adopts too readily the
Freudian account of the inferiority of women. But the issue is
obviously quite complex, since at the same time, de Beauvoir herself
is not always as negative about psychoanalysis. For example, in an
interview with Alice Schwarzer in 1978, de Beauvoir commented:
'there's something else I would very much like to do if I were
thirty or forty now, and that is a work on psychoanalysis' (in Alice
Schwarzer, *Simone de Beauvoir Today: conversations 1972–1982*,
(1984), p. 88). And in *The Prime of Life* (1965, p. 129), she admits
that her attitude to psychoanalysis was not totally consistent: 'One of
our contradictions was that we denied the unconscious.' Irigaray, on
the other hand, is challenging, Freudian theory as an analyst, an
insider, in a way that de Beauvoir never attempted. But whereas de
Beauvoir emphasizes access to the world of men (*equality*), Irigaray is
suggesting the creation of *difference*. She takes up de Beauvoir's idea
of Woman as Other, but develops it further. De Beauvoir's 'other' is,
in Irigarayan terms, the 'other of the same', the necessary negative of the male subject, all that he has repressed and disavowed.
De Beauvoir saw the way forward in terms of women's access to
subjecthood, but she conceived this as universal (and therefore, from
Irigaray's point of view, male). In 1949, in *The Second Sex*, she
subordinated feminism to socialism, and envisaged a totally transformed society in which women would have equal rights to education,
employment and public life. Irigaray, on the other hand, is positing
an 'other' which would not simply be the 'other of the same' (and so
a state to be transcended in the pursuit of 'the same'), but a self-
defined woman who would not be satisfied with sameness, but whose

otherness and difference would be given social and symbolic representation. Each sex would then be 'other' for the other sex. For an account of Simone de Beauvoir and Irigaray which sees Irigaray's work as diametrically opposed to Simone de Beauvoir's, but its necessary corollary, see Naomi Schor's article, 'This essentialism which is not one: coming to grips with Irigaray', in *differences*, 1 (2), (1989), pp. 38–58. See also Judith Butler, *Gender Trouble: feminism and the subversion of identity* (1990, chapter 1), for another recent comparison of Simone de Beauvoir and Irigaray.

In the three texts which follow, we see Irigaray's analysis of the conditions and infrastructure of western culture, and her conclusion that women as mothers are the unacknowledged foundation of the social order.

'The bodily encounter with the mother' ('Le Corps-à-corps avec la mère') is the text of a lecture given at a conference on 'Women and madness', held in Montreal in May 1981 (the fifth in a series on mental health). It was first published in *Le Corps-à-corps avec la mère* (Montreal: Editions de la pleine lune, 1981) and reprinted in *Sexes et parentés* (1987). The latter version has been used as the basis for the translation.

In 'The bodily encounter with the mother', Irigaray puts forward the idea which is the cornerstone of her work: that western culture is founded not on parricide (as Freud hypothesized in *Totem and Taboo*), but on matricide. Irigaray's reinterpretation of the story of Clytemnestra reads the myth as an account of the installation of patriarchy, built over the sacrifice of the mother and her daughters (one daughter, Iphigenia, literally sacrificed by Agamemnon, the other one, Electra, abandoned to her madness, while Orestes the matricidal son, is designated to found the new order). The major cultural taboo is on the relationship with the mother. The stress on Oedipus, on castration, serves to conceal another severance, the cutting of the umbilical cord to the mother. This relationship with the mother needs to be brought out of silence and into representation. The silence perpetuates the most atrocious and primitive phantasies – woman as devouring monster threatening madness and death – that are an indication of unanalysed hatred from which women as a group suffer culturally, bound into archaic projections which belong to the male imaginary; thus they may be more likely to

be incarcerated in mental hospitals than men. Perhaps because contraception and the legalization of abortion have enabled women to
control their reproduction to a certain extent, it is now possible to
see the identity of women *as women* as separate from their identity as
mothers, and to raise the question of women's identity outside
of their role as 'reproducer of children, as nurse, as reproducer
of labour-power'. However, Irigaray warns the daughters against
repeating the murder of the mother. It is necessary, she argues, to
move out of the role of 'guardians of the body' for men, and to put
into words and symbolic representations the primitive relation with
the mother's body. The invention of new ways of speaking about
relationships between women is essential if women are to create a
new identity for themselves within the symbolic order.

These themes are reiterated in 'Women–mothers: the silent substratum of the social order' ('Les Femmes-mères, ce sous-sol muet de
l'ordre social'), which was published as an interview in *Le Corps-à-
corps avec la mère*. The interviewers are Thérèse Dumouchel and
Marie-Madeleine Raoult from the Editions de la Pleine Lune in
Montreal.

The interest of this interview lies in the way in which Irigaray,
from a rather different theoretical stance, displays preoccupations
which overlap with those of English-speaking feminists: women and
madness, the inadequacy or failure of the 'sexual revolution' from
women's point of view, the importance of consciousness raising as a
practice, the analysis of the family as a social device for appropriating
women's labour, the mother–daughter relationship, the attack
on psychoanalysis insofar as it is a discourse which normalizes
patriarchy, and the re-evaluation of hysteria as the unheard voice of
the woman who can only speak through somatic symptoms. Most
importantly, it marks the crucial point in second-wave (post-1968)
feminism when the rebellious daughters, who had turned their back
on their mothers, started becoming mothers in their turn and began
to realize that they must liberate themselves *with their mothers*.
(Irigaray's short text, 'And the One Doesn't Stir Without the Other'
is one of the early accounts of the difficulties of the mother–daughter
relationship.) The early years of the women's movement had been
characterized by demands for *equality* – which meant equality with
men. It was not really until the end of the 1970s that Anglo-American

feminism began to theorize women's *difference* as a source of cultural possibility rather than simply as a source of oppression. (See Hester Eisenstein's introduction to *The Future of Difference* (1980).) Irigaray was never interested simply in equality; from the very beginning of her work, she was examining the mother's function as the infrastructure of Western civilization, and the obliteration of women *as women*. In her preoccupation with women's difference, she was in advance of the movement of Anglo-American feminist thought, which is perhaps why *Speculum* does not seem to have been well understood on its first appearance in 1974. One could speculate that it is in Catholic countries (such as France and Italy) that the importance of attending to motherhood as an institution, sanctioned by the divine, was more immediately obvious (see the article by Mia Campioni and Rosi Braidotti, 'Mothers/daughters/feminists: the darkest continent' in *Refractory Girl* (Australia) 23, 1981, pp. 9–12).

The final text in this section, then, gives an extract from *Speculum*, 'L'Incontournable volume', translated here as 'Volume without contours', although the title is more or less untranslateable. It first appeared in 1974, and is translated in the English version of *Speculum*, published in 1985, under the title 'Volume–fluidity'.

In this extract, Irigaray is specifically addressing philosophy – hence its abstractness and difficulty, and the abundance of philosophical allusions. She is 'going back through the male imaginary', as she puts it in *This Sex Which Is Not One*, looking at woman as she has been defined for/by men, and pointing out that there is something which exceeds all attempts to confine/define her within a system (of discourse, representation etc.), or to appropriate her power(s) within the philosophical logos. One can discern here also a challenge to Lacan (or to any 'subject'/theorist attempting to define woman's sexuality). For the 'woman–mother' is 'torn to pieces' (as Irigaray also explains in 'The bodily encounter with the mother' above). Torn between the sons and the fathers, the stake or sacrifice in disputes between men (for theories are disputes for the ownership of the mother's body: see *Speculum* p. 81, n. 67), she is fragmented into bits and pieces, and therefore 'unable to articulate her difference'. The (male) subject prefers to see her as the maternal–feminine rather than as a woman, because of what woman represents for him: castration and death, the unimaginable heterogeneous other (cf.

some of the phantasies described in 'The bodily encounter with the mother'). For male systems of representation and discourse (translated too into institutions such as the family), woman is the resource or the reserve of the male subject. Within this system, woman has no identity; she is the 1+1+1+ of the *quantitative*, Lacan's 'not-all'. Woman is a 'common noun' for which no identity can be defined. (On Irigaray's critique of Lacan, see also 'Cosi fan tutti' in *This Sex Which Is Not One*. See also *Feminine Sexuality and the Ecole Freudienne*, Juliet Mitchell and Jacqueline Rose, (eds), 1982.)

The dominant fantasy of the mother, then, Irigaray suggests, is as a *volume*, a 'receptacle for the (re)production of sameness' and 'the support of (re)production – particularly discourse – in all its forms'. But man needs to represent her as a *closed* volume, a container; his desire is to immobilize her, keep her under his control, in his possession, even in his house. He needs to believe that the container belongs to him. The fear is of the 'open container', the 'incontournable volume', that is to say, the volume without contours (*sans contours*), the volume which he cannot 'get round' (*contourner*) or enclose, possess and capture in his nets, or master and appropriate. Or his fear is of the *fluid*, that which flows, is mobile, which is not a solid ground/earth or mirror for the subject (see also the section of *Speculum* entitled 'Any theory of the "subject" has always been appropriated by the "masculine"'). To the male representations of woman, Irigaray opposes an 'other woman', a woman 'without common measure' who cannot be reduced to the quantifying measurements by which she is domesticated in male systems, who exceeds attempts to pin her down and confine her within a theoretical system, whose volume is 'incontournable', whose lips touch without distinction of one and two (on this see 'The limits of the transference' in section II below). Against the Lacanian image of woman as *hole*, Irigaray opposes the image of *contiguity*, of the two lips touching, which elsewhere in *Speculum* stands for the contiguity of mother and daughter, or the contiguity of intercourse between mother and father, maternal and paternal genealogies, and the possibility that woman's desire could be represented for-itself, other than as it appears in male representations – a possibility which she describes variously as a volume no longer thought of as a closed or measurable container, as a multiplicity which is not just dispersed fragments, or as the possibility of the divine on the side of women.

We shall come back to the 'divine' in the introductions to sections II and III, but it is worth noting the appearance of the theme already in *Speculum*.

Irigaray is clearly concerned that the interest that contemporary theory displays in the feminine (documented by Alice Jardine in *Gynesis* (1985)), is less an opening to the 'other woman' than a fresh attempt at territorialization of the maternal–feminine body, repeating the familiar gesture of male self-affection. Is the subject's exploration of the feminine a new auto-affection, she asks, or is it perhaps a breach in the self-sufficiency of the subject's logos? The perspective that she offers is that of an *other woman* (the other woman of *Speculum*'s subtitle), exterior to all these masculine metaphorizations, a woman who does not yet exist, but whose advent could shake the foundations of patriarchy.

A note on the translation of 'Volume without contours'. In this passage, Irigaray makes particular play with the words *écart*, *écarter*, *écarteler* and their cognates. The multiple connotations were impossible to translate with a single English word, so we have decided to use a variety of different translations, while signalling the French original in each case.

Margaret Whitford

1

Equal or Different?

What woman has not read *The Second Sex*? What woman has not been invigorated by it? Become a feminist, perhaps, through reading it? Simone de Beauvoir was in fact one of the first women in our century to remind us of the scale of the exploitation of women and to encourage every woman who was lucky enough to discover her book to feel less isolated and more resolved not to surrender or to be taken in.

So what was Simone de Beauvoir doing? She was telling her life story, and at the same time supporting it with scientific data. She never stopped telling her story, bravely, in all its stages. In so doing she helped many women – and men? – to be sexually freer, notably by offering them a socio-cultural model, acceptable for its time, for living as a woman, living as a teacher, living as a writer, living as a couple. I think that she also helped them to situate themselves more objectively in the different moments of a life.

Simone de Beauvoir did more than that. Her relish for social justice led her to support certain feminists in their actions, on their journey, helping them to emerge socially by signing their petitions, going along with their actions, encouraging the existence of a column in *Les Temps Modernes*, prefacing their books, taking part in their television programmes, being their friend . . .

The era of psychoanalysis

Whilst I was one of the readers of *The Second Sex*, I was never close to Simone de Beauvoir. Why not? A question of different generations?

Not only that: she did mix with young women. That was not, or not simply, the issue. There are major differences between our positions, and I hoped that they might be overcome at the level of friendship and mutual help. Concretely, they were not. When I sent her *Speculum*, as though I were sending it to an elder sister, Simone de Beauvoir never replied. I admit that that made me quite sad. I had hoped for an attentive and understanding reader, a sister, who would help me with the academic and institutional difficulties that I was to encounter because of that book. Alas, my hopes came to nothing! The only gesture Simone de Beauvoir made was to ask me for some information about *Le Langage des Déments* (Mouton, 1973) when she was writing on old age.[1] Not a word passed between us about women's liberation.

What are we to make, once again, of this continued distance between two women who could, even should, have worked together? Aside from the fact that I encountered certain difficulties with academic institutions that certain American women, say, encountered, and which she may not have experienced in the same terms, which she did not understand, there are reasons that explain her reserve. Simone de Beauvoir and Jean-Paul Sartre always resisted psychoanalysis. I have trained as an analyst and that is important (even despite existing theories and practices) for thinking a sexual identity. I also belong to a philosophical tradition in which psychoanalysis takes its place as a stage in understanding the self-realization of consciousness, especially in its sexuate determinations.

These two formations mean that my thinking about women's liberation has a dimension other than the search for equality between the sexes. That does not stop me joining and promoting public demonstrations to obtain this or that right for women: the right to contraception, to abortion, to legal support in cases of public or private violence, the right to freedom of expression, etc.

If, however, these struggles are to be waged other than by simply putting forward demands, if they are to result in the inscription of equal (but necessarily different) sexual rights before the law, women – and couples, come to that – must be allowed access to an other identity. Women can only take up these rights if they can find some value in being women, and not simply mothers. That means rethinking, transforming centuries of socio-cultural values.

Women: equal or different

Demanding equality, as women, seems to me to be an erroneous
expression of a real issue. Demanding to be equal presupposes a term
of comparison. Equal to what? What do women want to be equal to?
Men? A wage? A public position? Equal to what? Why not to
themselves?

Even a vaguely rigorous analysis of claims to equality shows that
they are justified at the level of a superficial critique of culture, and
utopian as a means to women's liberation. The exploitation of women
is based upon sexual difference, and can only be resolved through
sexual difference. Certain tendencies of the day, certain contemporary
feminists, are noisily demanding the neutralization of sex [*sexe*]. That
neutralization, if it were possible, would correspond to the end of the
human race. The human race is divided into *two genres* which ensure
its production and reproduction. Trying to suppress sexual difference is to invite a genocide more radical than any destruction that
has ever existed in History. What is important, on the other hand, is
defining the values of belonging to a sex-specific *genre*. What is
indispensable is elaborating a culture of the sexual which does not
yet exist, whilst respecting both *genres*. Because of the historical time
gaps between the gynocratic, matriarchal, patriarchal and phallocratic
eras, we are in a sexual position which is bound up with generation
and not with *genre* as sex. This means that, within the family, women
must be mothers and men must be fathers, but that we have no
positive and ethical values that allow two sexes of the same generation
to form a creative, and not simply procreative, human couple. One
of the major obstacles to the creation and recognition of such values
is the more or less covert hold patriarchal and phallocratic roles have
had on the whole of our civilization for centuries. It is social justice,
pure and simple, to balance out the power of one sex over the other
by giving, or restoring, cultural values to female sexuality. What is at
stake is clearer today than it was when *The Second Sex* was written.

Unless it goes through this stage, feminism may work towards
the destruction of women, and, more generally, of all values.
Egalitarianism, in fact, sometimes expends a lot of energy on re-
jecting certain positive values and chasing after nothing. Hence the
periodic crises, discouragement and regressions in women's liberation
movements, and their fleeting inscription in History.

Equality between men and women cannot be achieved unless we *think of genre as sexuate* [*sexué*] and write the rights and duties of each sex, insofar as they are *different*, into social rights and duties.

Peoples constantly split into secondary but murderous rivalries without realizing that their primary and irreducible division is one between two genres. From that point of view, we are still living in the childhood of culture. It is urgent for women's struggles, for small, popular groups of women, to realize the importance of issues that are specific to them. These are bound up with respect for life and culture, with the constant passage of the natural into the cultural, of the spiritual into the natural. Their responsibility and their opportunity correspond to a stage in the evolution of the world, and not to some more or less lucid and negative competition within a world undergoing a mutation, in which life is in danger for a variety of reasons.

Making friendly gestures towards Simone de Beauvoir means pursuing the theoretical and practical work of social justice she carried on in her own way, not blocking the horizon of liberation she opened up for many women, and men . . . Her vision of that horizon was certainly in part inspired by her long, and often solitary, walks in the *garrigue*, in the wilds. Her enjoyment and her accounts of her walks seem to me to be one of her messages that we must not forget.

NOTES

1 [Simone de Beauvoir's book on old age, *La Vieillesse*, was published in 1970. *Le Langage des déments* was not published until 1973; however, some of the material had already appeared in journals before then (ed.).]

Translated by David Macey

2

The Bodily Encounter with the Mother

I would like to begin by thanking the organizing committee of the colloquium on mental health for having chosen as the theme for this meeting 'Women and madness', that is to say for having helped to bring out of the silence large-scale suffering on the part of women that is all too often kept hidden.

I am astonished – and, unfortunately!, not astonished, but I like to go on being astonished – that so few men-practitioners are here to listen to what women have to say about their madness. Given that the vast majority are the doctors of these women patients, their absence is a sign of their practice, especially their psychiatric practice. What women say appears to be of little importance to them. When it comes to knowing how things stand with women and what treatment should be prescribed them, they are self-sufficient. No need to listen to women. That no doubt explains their therapeutic choices.

But I have so often heard men getting angry about women-only meetings, wanting to penetrate them at all cost, that I find their absence today all the more significant. They have not been excluded from this colloquium, where most of the speakers will be women. How is it that their curiosity has not brought them here to listen? It is up to those men who are here to understand why and in what sense they are the exception!

Could it be something to do with the register of power that has kept away the others, the majority of practitioners? They do not dominate this colloquium. Or is it a matter of shame, given the statistics presented this morning, revealing the impressive number of women interned in psychiatric hospitals (most of them non-voluntary patients committed by families: hospitals function as a place of incarceration for women), and the fact that they are treated by chemotherapy and not psychotherapy? Unless it is a question of scorn because the colloquium is organized by and for women? Or of sexual indifference? I leave the interpretation open.

In any case, this absence is in itself an explanation for the madness of women: their words [*leur parole*] are not heard. What they say is illegitimate in terms of the elaboration of diagnoses, of therapeutic decisions that affect them. Scientific discourses and serious scientific practices are still the privilege of men, as is the management of the political in general and of the most private aspects of our lives as women. Their discourses, their values, their dreams and their desires have the force of law, everywhere and in all things. Everywhere and in all things, they define women's function and social role, and the sexual identity they are, or are not, to have. They know, they have access to the truth; we do not. Often, we scarcely have access to fiction.

As a particularly 'honest' man friend told me not so long ago, not without some astonishment at his discovery, 'It's true, I have always thought that all women were mad.' And he added, 'No doubt I wanted to avoid the question of my own madness.'

That is indeed how the question is posed. Each sex relates to madness in its own way. All desire is connected to madness. But apparently one desire has chosen to see itself as wisdom, moderation, truth, and has left the other to bear the burden of the madness it did not want to attribute to itself, recognize in itself.

This relationship between desire and madness comes into its own, for both man and woman, in the relationship with the mother. But all too often, man washes his hands of it and leaves it to woman – women.

The relationship with the mother is a mad desire, because it is the 'dark continent' *par excellence*. It remains in the shadows of our culture; it is its night and its hell. But men can no more, or rather no less, do without it than can women. And if there is now such a polarization over the questions of abortion and contraception, isn't that one more way of avoiding the question: what of the imaginary and symbolic relationship with the mother, with the woman–mother? What of that woman outside her social and material role as reproducer of children, as nurse, as reproducer of labour power?

The maternal function underpins the social order and the order of desire, but it is always kept in a dimension of need. Where desire is concerned, especially in its religious dimension, the role of maternal–feminine power is often nullified in the satisfying of individual and collective needs.

Desire for her, her desire, that is what is forbidden by the law of the father, of all fathers: fathers of families, fathers of nations, religious fathers, professor–fathers doctor–fathers, lover–fathers, etc. Moral or immoral, they always intervene to censor, to repress, the desire of/for the mother. For them, that corresponds to good sense and good health, when it's not virtue and sainthood!

Perhaps we have reached a period in history when this question of domination by fathers can no longer be avoided. This question is determined, or furthered, by several causes. Contraception and abortion raise the question of the meaning of motherhood, and women (notably because of their entry into and their encounters within the circuits of production) are looking for their sexual identity and are beginning to emerge from silence and anonymity.

And what is now becoming apparent in the most everyday things and in the whole of our society and our culture is that, at a primal level, they function on the basis of a matricide.

When Freud describes and theorizes, notably in *Totem and Taboo*, the murder of the father as founding the primal horde, he forgets a more archaic murder, that of the mother, necessitated by the establishement of a certain order in the polis.

Give or take a few additions and retractions, our imaginary still functions in accordance with the schema established through Greek mythologies and tragedies. I will therefore take the example of the murder of Clytèmnestra in the *Oresteia*.

Clytemnestra certainly does not obey the image of the virgin–mother that has been held up to us for centuries. She is still a passionate lover. Moreover, she will go as far as a *crime passionnel*: she will kill her husband. Why?

He had been abroad for years and years, having gone off with other men to win back the beautiful Helen. This may be the forgotten prototype for war between men. In order to bring his military and amorous expedition to a successful conclusion, he ordered the sacrifice of Iphigenia, the adolescent daughter he had by Clytemnestra. When he comes back, it is with another woman, his slave, and no doubt his *n*th mistress.

Clytemnestra, for her part, has taken a lover. But she had heard nothing from her husband for so long that she thought he was dead. So she kills Agamemnon when he returns in glory with his mistress. She kills him out of jealousy, out of fear perhaps, and because she has been unsatisfied and frustrated for so long. She also kills him because he sacrificed their daughter to conflicts between men, a motive which is often forgotten by the tragedians.

But the new order demands that she in her turn must be killed by her son, inspired by the oracle of Apollo, the beloved son of Zeus: God the father. Orestes kills his mother because the rule of the God–Father and his appropriation of the archaic powers of mother–earth require it. He kills his mother and goes mad as a result, as does his sister Electra.

Electra, the daughter, will remain mad. The matricidal son must be saved from madness to establish the patriarchal order. It is the handsome Apollo, a lover of men rather than women, the narcissistic lover of their bodies and their words, a lover who does not make love much more than Athena, his sister in Zeus, who helps him to recover from his madness.

This madness is, moreover, represented in the form of a troop of enraged women who pursue him, haunt him wherever he goes, like the ghosts of his mother: the Furies. These women cry vengeance. They are women in revolt, rising up like revolutionary hysterics against the patriarchal power in the process of being established.

As you might have gathered, all this is still extremely contemporary. The mythology underlying patriarchy has not changed. What the *Oresteia* describes for us still takes place. Here and there, regulation Athenas whose one begetter is the head of the Father–King still burst forth. Completely in his pay, in the pay of the men in power, they bury beneath their sanctuary women in struggle so that they will no longer disturb the new order of the home, the order of the polis, now the only order. You can recognize these regulation Athenas, perfect models of femininity, always veiled and dressed from head to toe, all very respectable, by this token: they are extraordinarily seductive [*séductrices*], which does not necessarily mean enticing [*séduisantes*], but aren't in fact interested in making love.

The murder of the mother results, then, in the non-punishment of the son, the burial of the madness of women – and the burial of women in madness – and the advent of the image of the virgin goddess, born of the father and obedient to his law in forsaking the mother.

When Oedipus makes love with his mother, it will in fact do him no harm to start with, if I can put it that way. On the other hand, he will go blind or become mad when he learns she was his mother: she whom he has already killed in accordance with his mythology, in obedience to the verdict of the Father of the gods.

This interpretation is possible, but never happens. The event is always related to borrowing the place of the father, to the symbolic murder of the father. Now, Oedipus is no doubt re-enacting the madness of Orestes. He is afraid of his mother when she reveals herself to him for what she is. His primal crime comes back to him like an echo, he fears and detests his act, and the woman who was its object. Secondarily, he has infringed the law of the father.

Isn't all analytically inspired theory and practice based upon Oedipus's ambivalence towards his father? An ambivalence focused on the father, but which is retroactively projected on to the archaic relationship with the body of the mother. When it concerns itself with the life of the drives, psychoanalysis certainly talks to us of the mother's breast, of the milk she gives us to drink, of the faeces she accepts (a 'gift' in which she may or may not be interested), and even of her gaze and her voice. It takes too little interest in them. What is more, isn't this bodily encounter [corps-à-corps] with the mother – and it is probably not without its difficulties – fantasized post-Oedipally, reprojected after the Oedipus? Hasn't the mother already been torn to pieces by Oedipus's hatred by the time she is cut up into stages, with each part of her body having to be cathected and then decathected as he grows up? And when Freud speaks of the father being torn to pieces by the sons of the primal horde, doesn't he forget, in a complete misrecognition and disavowal, the woman who was torn apart between son and father, between sons?

Partial drives appear to be concerned mainly with the body which brought us *whole* into the world. The genital drive is said to be the drive thanks to which the phallic penis takes back from the mother the power to give birth, to nourish, to dwell, to centre. The phallus erected where once there was the umbilical cord? It becomes the organizer of the world of and through the man–father, in the place where the umbilical cord, the first bond with the mother, gave birth to the body of both man and woman. That took place in a primal womb, our first nourishing earth, first waters, first envelopes, where the child was *whole*, the mother *whole* through the mediation of her blood. They were bound together, albeit in an asymmetrical relationship, before any cutting, any cutting up of their bodies into fragments.

Psychoanalysts take a dim view of this first moment – and, besides, it is invisible. A foetal situation or foetal regression, they say, and there is not a lot to be said about that. A taboo is in the air. If the father did not sever this over-intimate bond with the primal womb, there might be the danger of fusion, of death, of the sleep of death. Putting the matrix of his language [*langue*] in its place? But the exclusivity of his law forecloses this first body, this first home, this first love. It sacrifices them so as make them material for the rule of a language [*langue*] which privileges the masculine genre [*le genre masculin*] to such an extent as to confuse it with the human race [*le genre humain*].

According to this order, when a child is given a proper name, it already replaces the most irreducible mark of birth: the *navel*. A proper name, even a forename, is always late in terms of this most irreducible trace of identity: the scar left when the cord was cut. A proper name, even a forename, is slipped on to the body like a coating – an extra-corporeal identity card.

Yet, no matter what use he makes of the law, the symbolic, language [*langue*] or proper names (the name of the father), in practice the psychoanalyst usually sits behind the analysand, like the mother he should not look back at. He should make progress, advance, go outside and forget her. And if the patient did look back, perhaps she would have disappeared? Could he have annihilated her?

The social order, our culture, psychoanalysis itself, want it this way: the mother must remain forbidden, excluded. The father forbids the bodily encounter with the mother.

I feel like adding: if only it were true! We would be much more at peace with our bodies, which men need so badly to feed their libido and, first and foremost, their life and their culture. For the prohibition does not preclude a certain number of exemptions, a certain blindness.

The imaginary and the symbolic of intra-uterine life and of the first bodily encounter with the mother ... where are we to find them? In what darkness, what madness, have they been abandoned?

And the relationship with the placenta, the first house to surround us, whose halo we carry with us everywhere, like some child's security blanket, how is that represented in our culture?

In the absence of any representation of it, there is always the danger of going back to the primal womb, seeking refuge in any open body, constantly living and nesting in the bodies of other women.

And so, the openness of the mother [*ouverture de la mère*], the opening on to the mother [*ouverture à la mère*], appear to be threats of contagion, contamination, engulfment in illness, madness and death. Obviously, there is nothing there that permits a gradual advance, one step at a time. No Jacob's ladder for a return to the mother. Jacob's ladder always climbs up to heaven, to the Father and his kingdom.

And besides, who could believe in the innocence of this bond with the mother when anyone who tries to establish a new bond with her is responsible for the crime that has been committed and perpetuated against her?

The mother has become a devouring monster as an inverted effect of the blind consumption of the mother. Her belly, sometimes her breasts, are agape with the gestation, the birth and the life that were given there without any reciprocity. Except for a murder, real and cultural, to annul that debt? To forget dependency? To destroy power?

The unchanging character of what is known in analytic therapies as orality, infinite thirst, the desire to be gratified by her that we hear so much about and which, it is said, makes some analyses impossible ... the bottomless nature of an infant's mouth – or of a woman's genitals [*sexe*] – ... hasn't that been thought or fantasized on the basis of Oedipus's hatred? There is no reason why either the hunger of a child or the sexual appetite of a woman should be insatiable. Everything proves the contrary. But this buccal opening of the child and all desire become an abyss if the sojourn *in utero* is censored and if our separations from that first home and the first nurse remain uninterpreted, unthought in their losses and scars. So when the child makes demands of the breast, isn't it demanding to receive all? The all that it received in its mother's belly: life, the home in which it lived, the home of its body, food, air, warmth, movement etc. For want of being situated in its time, its space and their exile, that all is displaced on to oral avidity.

The unavoidable and irreparable wound is the cutting of the

umbilical cord. When his father or his mother threatens Oedipus with a knife or with scissors, he or she forgets that the cord has already been cut, and that it is enough to take note of that fact.

The problem is that, by denying the mother her generative power and by wanting to be the sole creator, the Father, according to our culture, superimposes upon the archaic world of the flesh a universe of language [*langue*] and symbols which cannot take root in it except as in the form of that which makes a hole in the bellies of women and in the site of their identity. In many patriarchal traditions, a stake is therefore driven into the earth to delineate the sacred space. It defines a place for male gatherings founded upon a sacrifice. Women may be tolerated within it as non-active bystanders.

The fertility of the earth is sacrificed to delineate the cultural horizon of the father tongue [*langue*] (wrongly termed the mother tongue). But that is never talked about. A hole in the texture of language corresponds to the forgetting of the scar of the navel.

Certain men and women would like to attribute this capture-net to maternal power, to the phallic mother. But when it is attributed to her, it is like a defensive network projected by the man–father or his sons on to the abyss of a silent and threatening belly. Threatening because silent?

The womb, unthought in its place of the first sojourn in which we become bodies, is fantasized by many men to be a devouring mouth, a cloaca or anal and urethral outfall, a phallic threat, at best re-productive. And in the absence of valid representations of female sexuality, this womb merges with woman's sex [*sexe*] as a whole.

There are no words to talk about it, except filthy, mutilating words. The corresponding affects will therefore be anxiety, phobia, disgust, a haunting fear of castration.

How can one not also feel them on returning to what has always been denied, disavowed, sacrificed to build an exclusively masculine symbolic world?

Might not castration anxiety be an unconscious memory of the sacrifice which sanctifies phallic erection as the only sexual value? But neither the postulate nor the name of the Father are enough to guarantee that the penis [*sexe*] of the son will remain erect. And it is not the murder of the father that supports and threatens the phallic erection, as psychoanalysis asserts to us in a sort of act of faith in the patriarchal tradition.

Unless – and this remains unthought – this murder of the father signifies a desire to take his place, a rival and competitive desire, but a desire to do away with the one who artificially cut the link with the mother in order to take over the creative power of all worlds, especially the female world.

No longer omnipotent, the phallic erection could, then, be a masculine version of the umbilical bond. It would, if it respected the life of the mother – of the mother in all women, of the woman in all mothers – reproduce the living bond with her. Where once was the cord, then the breast, there shall come in its time, for man, the penis which binds, gives life to, nourishes and recentres bodies, recalling in penetration, in touching beyond the skin and the will, in the outpouring, something of intra-uterine life, with detumescence evoking the end, mourning, the ever-open wound. This would be a preliminary gesture of repetition on man's part, a rebirth allowing him to become a sexuate adult capable of erotism and reciprocity in the flesh.

This rebirth in necessary for women too. It cannot take place unless it is freed from man's archaic projection on to her and unless an autonomous and positive representation of her sexuality exists in culture.

Woman has no reason to envy either the penis or the phallus. But the non-establishment of the sexual identity of both sexes [*sexes*] results in the fact that man, the people of men, has transformed his penis [*sexe*] into an instrument of power so as to dominate maternal power.

What use can all these descriptions be to us, as women? For us, understanding and describing all that is a way of escaping a world of madness which is not ours, a fear of the dark, of the non-identifiable, a fear of a primal murder which is culturally not ours. I think that it is very important to realize this because, again and again, we are placed in the sites of those projections. Again and again, we become the captives of these fantasies, this ambivalence, this madness which is not ours. We would do better to take back our own madness and return men theirs!

As for us, it is a matter of urgency not to submit to a desubjectivized social role, that of the mother, governed by an order subordinated to a division of labour – man produces/woman reproduces – which confines us to a mere function. Have fathers ever been asked to renounce being men? Citizens? We do not have to renounce being women in order to be mothers.

One other point. I am going to make a certain number in order to open up or institute exchange between us. It is also necessary for us to discover and assert that we are always mothers once we are women. We bring something other than children into the world, we engender something other than children: love, desire, language, art, the social, the political, the religious, for example. But this creation has been forbidden us for centuries, and we must reappropriate this maternal dimension that belongs to us as women.

If it is not to became traumatizing or pathological, the question of whether or not to have children must be asked against the background of an other generating, of a creation of images and symbols. Women and their children would be infinitely better off as a result.

We have to be careful about one other thing: we must not once more kill the mother who was sacrificed to the origins of our culture. We must give her new life, new life to that mother, to our mother within us and between us. We must refuse to let her desire be annihilated by the law of the father. We must give her the right to pleasure, to *jouissance*, to passion, restore her right to speech, and sometimes to cries and anger.

We must also find, find anew, invent the words, the sentences that speak the most archaic and most contemporary relationship with the body of the mother, with our bodies, the sentences that translate the bond between her body, ours, and that of our daughters. We have to discover a language [*langage*] which does not replace the bodily encounter, as paternal language [*langue*] attempts to do, but which can go along with it, words which do not bar the corporeal, but which speak corporeal.

It is important for us to guard and keep our bodies and at the same time make them emerge from silence and subjugation. Historically, we are the guardians of the flesh; we do not have to abandon that guardianship, but to identify it as ours by inviting men not to make us 'their bodies', guarantors of their bodies. Their libido often needs some wife–mother to look after their bodies. It is in that sense that they need a woman–wife [*femme*] at home, even if they do have mistresses elsewhere. This question is very important, even if it seems minor.

It is therefore desirable, for us, to speak within the amorous exchange. It is also good to speak while feeding a child, so that it does not experience feeding as violent force-feeding, as rape. It is also important to speak while caressing another body. Silence is all the more alive in that speech exists. Let us not be the guardians of silence, of a deadly silence.

It is also necessary, if we are not to be accomplices in the murder of the mother, for us to assert that there is a genealogy of women. There is a genealogy of women within our family: on our mothers' side we have mothers, grandmothers and great-grandmothers, and daughters. Given our exile in the family of the father–husband, we tend to forget this genealogy of women, and we are often persuaded to deny it. Let us try to situate ourselves within this female genealogy so as to conquer and keep our identity. Nor let us forget that we already have a history, that certain women have, even if it was culturally difficult, left their mark on history and that all too often we do not know them.

Throughout all this, what we have to do (not that we necessarily have to do one thing before the other) is discover our sexual identity, the singularity of our desires, of our auto-erotism, of our narcissism, of our heterosexuality and of our homosexuality. In that connection, given that the first body they have any dealings with is a woman's body, that the first love they share is mother love, it is important to remember that women always stand in an archaic and primal relationship with what is known as homosexuality. For their part, men always stand in an archaic relationship with heterosexuality, since the first object of their love and desire is a woman.

When analytic theory says that the little girl must give up her love of and for her mother, her desire of and for her mother so as to enter into the desire of/for the father, it subordinates woman to a normative hetero-sexuality, normal in our societies, but completely pathogenic and pathological. Neither little girl nor woman must give up love for their mother. Doing so uproots them from their identity, their subjectivity.

Let us also try to discover the singularity of our love for other women. What might be called (though I do not like these label-words) ' "secondary homo-sexuality" ', with lots of inverted commas. I am trying here to outline a difference between archaic love of the mother and love for women–sisters. This love is necessary if we are not to remain the servants of the phallic cult, objects to be used by and exchanged between men, rival objects on the market, the situation in which we have always been placed.

It is important that we discover the singularity of our *jouissance*. Of course, it is possible for a woman to come [*jouir*] in accordance with the phallic model, and there will never be any shortage of men and pornographers to get women to say that they have amazing orgasms [*jouissent extraordinairement*] within such an economy. The question remains: aren't they being drawn out of themselves, left without any energy, perceptions, affects, gestures or images to relate them to their identity? For women, there are at least two modes of *jouissance*. One is programmed in a male libidinal economy in accordance with a certain phallic order. Another is much more in harmony with what they are, with their sexual identity. Many women are guilty, unhappy, paralysed, say they are frigid, because, within the norms of a phallocratic economy, they do not succeed in living their affects, their sexuality, whereas they could do so if they tried to go back to a *jouissance* more in keeping with their bodies and their sex. This does not mean that they must renounce the other for ever, or immediately. I have no wish to make anyone choose between these alternatives, which could be repressive. But if we are to discover our female identity, I do think it important to know that, for us, there is a relationship with *jouissance* other than that which functions in accordance with the phallic model.

We have a lot of things to do. But it is better to have the future before us than behind us. Let us not wait for the Phallus god to grant us his grace. Yes, the Phallus god, because whilst many repeat that 'God is dead', they rarely question the fact that the Phallus is alive and well. And do not many bearers of the said phallus now increasingly take themselves for gods in the full sense? Everywhere, and also, even – I will end with this question – in the holy Catholic Church, whose sovereign pontiff now thinks fit, once more, to forbid us contraception, abortion, extramarital relations, homosexuality, etc. So when this minister of the so-called one God, of the Father–God, pronounces the words of the eucharist: 'This is my body, this is my blood' in accordance with the rite of celebrating the sharing of food, which is our age-old rite, perhaps we might remind him that he would not be there if our body and our blood had not given him life, love and spirit. And that it is us, women–mothers, that he is giving to be eaten too. But no one must know that. That is why women cannot celebrate the eucharist . . . Something of the truth which is hidden therein might be brutally unmasked.

Humanity might begin to wash itself clean of a sin. A woman celebrating the eucharist with her mother, sharing with her the fruits of the earth she/they have blessed, could be delivered of all hatred or ingratitude towards her maternal genealogy, could be consecrated in her identity and her female genealogy.

Translated by David Macey

3

Women–Mothers, the Silent Substratum of the Social Order

PL: Being a philosopher, a linguist and a psychoanalyst, you are not a conveyor belt for discourses. You retraverse them. You speak. You question the western imaginary through its theories, its philosophies, its myths, always from the site of your difference. So as to hear what is said about us as women in all this patriarchal culture, of which we are the negative. Retraversing, Luce . . .

I: The culture, the language, the imaginary and the mythology in which we live at the moment . . . I say to myself . . . let's have a look . . . this edifice that looks so clean and so subtle . . . let's see what ground it is built on. Is it all that acceptable?

The substratum is the woman who reproduces the social order, who is made this order's infrastructure: the whole of our western culture is based upon the murder of the mother. The man–god–father killed the mother in order to take power. And isn't there a fluidity, some flood, that could shake this social order? And if we make the foundations of the social order shift, then everything will shift. That is why they are so careful to keep us on a leash . . .

PL: And why they gag hysterics . . .

I: Yes. . . . In certain circles, certain forms of madness, especially schizophrenia, are at the moment valorized because of the movement they bear. But I have never heard the word 'hysteria' being used in a valorizing way in these progressive circles. Yet there is a revolutionary potential in hysteria. Even in her paralysis, the hysteric exhibits a potential for gestures and desires. . . . A movement of revolt and refusal, a desire for/of the living mother who would be more than a reproductive body in the pay of the polis, a living, loving woman. It is because they want neither to see nor hear that movement that they so despise the hysteric.

PL: It is the contradiction between our desire to live and the conditions that are forced upon us that is disastrous for us. We have no decision-making power over those conditions. We often feel so guilty about not being resigned, or so powerless, that the only path that remains open to us is madness.

I: It is not certain that we even have the right to madness. Or in any case to a certain type of madness to which one accedes only through language [*langage*]. How can we define the madness in which women are placed? You often need something of language [*du langage*], some delusion [*délire*], to signal that you are living in madness. Women do not in fact suffer much from delusions. If they could, it would protect them. They suffer in their bodies. An absolutely immense bodily suffering.

PI: An inaudible suffering . . .

I: And which finds expression in depressive collapses. But that is not even the blaze of madness.

PL: And the discourse of psychiatry . . . it is a discourse of men about women. Which again puts women in the position of objects. And which returns them to silence.

I: You can take any sector of decision making. They are all in the hands of men. It is they who decide our desire, our pathology, our needs, our rights, our duties. And in psychiatry, it is they who interpret. . . .

You see, I feel like saying here that . . . a conference on 'women and madness' is held to talk about the madness of women and reflect upon it. All the psychiatrists are invited. But they don't come. Because they are not organizing it. Because they are not in a position of mastery. That really is quite serious; the majority of their patients are women . . .

PL: Luce, you say: for men, we have to be their bodies. What do you mean?

I: In the system of production that we know, including that of sexual production, men are distanced from their bodies. They have relied upon their sex, their language and their technology to go on and on building a world further and further removed from their relation to the corporeal. But they are corporeal. They therefore need to re-assure themselves that someone really is looking after the body for them. Their women or wives [*femmes*] are guardians of their corporeal unity. A man can have mistresses or go with prostitutes . . . he needs a legitimate wife. A wife–mother. A body-object which is there, which does not move, which he can go back to whenever he likes. A legitimate wife as a guarantee of the maternal corporeal.

PL: Being guardians of their corporeal unity, we cannot be beings of desire . . . desire is movement.

I: That's right. The *jouissance* they talk about today is in fact basi-cally capitalist. It is an appropriation–exploitation of the bodies of women–mothers, not necessarily reproductive bodies in the strict sense, of women–mothers as guardians of corporeal unity.

PL: In that sense, so-called 'sexual liberation' has done absolutely nothing for women?

I: Precisely. And they lay traps for us. Not that I think that we should hold it against individual men. But all the same, they do lay traps for us. The superegoization of sexual excess: you aren't a liberated woman if. . . . The superegoization of mothering: we men are so unhappy, you don't know the distress we're in, the crisis . . .

PL: On the one hand, the appropriation of the wife–mother, on the other, fear . . .

I: I would say that they also project the infernal (in the Greek sense) element in their desire for the mother on to us. The anxiety they feel in relation to women is also a kind of blindness on their part about relations with their mothers.

PL: An anxiety that stems from the fact that, in our western culture, this origin in the womb has been disavowed . . .

I: Of course. . . . And once the man–god–father kills the mother so as to take power, he is assailed by ghosts and anxieties. He will always feel a panic fear of she who is the substitute for what he has killed. And the things they threaten us with! We are going to swallow them up, devour them, castrate them . . . That's no more than an age-old gesture that has not been analysed or interpreted, returning to haunt them.

PL: And what about our relation with this origin? The mother–daughter relationship?

I: Most women reproduce children. They play no part in social decisions. They have no access to work, and even when they are in the labour market, they are not really on equal terms with men in production. They are restricted to particular sectors of production. They are the first to be laid off, etc. They are not valorized as workers, as citizens, or in political life. Basically, even when they do work, what society demands of them is that they go on being mothers. Machines to serve the man–father in private ownership, and to serve the State. The two things are institutionally connected.

So what is a mother? Someone who makes the stereotypical gestures she is told to make, who has no personal language and who has no identity. But how, as daughters, can we have a personal relationship with or construct a personal identity in relation to someone who is no more than a function?

In a sense we need to say goodbye to maternal omnipotence (the last refuge) and establish a woman-to-woman relationship of reciprocity with our mothers, in which they might possibly also feel themselves to be our daughters. In a word, liberate ourselves along with our mothers. That is an indispensable precondition for our emancipation from the authority of fathers. In our societies, the mother/daughter, daughter/mother relationship constitues a highly explosive nucleus. Thinking it, and changing it, is equivalent to shaking the foundations of the patriarchal order.

PL: And the family . . .

I: . . . is the origin of private property . . .

PL: And the law of the father is the law of the property owner . . .

I: That is what is revolutionary about women's movements. We have begun to say aloud what we each felt privately and individually. We have seen that it can be communicated, has been shared, and can be shared. It is no longer the private pain that once made us guilty. Guilty of suffering. Abnormal because we complained, made demands, were unhappy. They would say to us: 'What else do they need? They have their little homes, their little bits of furniture.' We lacked speech [*la parole*]. And all that it implies . . . such as life, a relationship of/with desire, corporeal relations, love relations . . .

They ask us to promote the values of life . . . those are not silent values. For human beings, life takes place and unfolds through speech. In order to promote the values of life, you have to begin to speak.

PL: And it's complicated for women . . . especially in public. They accuse us of being too emotional . . . of not talking rationally. Men, of course, use speech as a screen. They speak through a rationality quite external to their bodies.

I: We can ask them what defensive systems they are establishing with their logic, their coherence, their rationality. What they are defending themselves against. And what they are cutting themselves off from. Just because we are speaking animals, because we have speech, does not mean that we have to renounce our desires, our affects or our sensitivity. That dimension is very important.

We have to renew the whole of language [*langage*]. Above all, at the level of language we must not turn completely into men. I think it is important to have access to a certain rationality so as to be able to, say, 'play chess' with men. To be able to say: your discourses . . . I've heard them. It cost me dearly, but I understand them. I have an answer to your arguments. But we cannot leave matters at that. To say that means that we have a leeway which is in excess of the system, that we can play on that excess to beat the system. To reintroduce the values of desire, pain, joy, the body. Living values. Not discourses of mastery, which are in a way dead discourses, a dead grid imposed upon the living. Ultimately, machines could speak certain alienated and rational discourses for us. On the other hand, no machine can speak the language of this living mobility that is constantly being modified in accordance with the life of the other, that is undergoing a perpetual transformation.

PI: In *And The One Doesn't Stir Without the Other*, you say 'Mothers feed but do not speak . . .'

I: Mothers, and the woman within them, have been trapped in the role of she who satisfies need but has no access to desire.

Food is a need. It can become desire, but it needs speech for that to happen. So long as women are imprisoned in the reality of need, where is desire? Desire, say the psychoanalysts, is simply a function of the law of the Father: one enters into desire when one enters into the relationship with the father. Disastrous! For men, that represents a massive severance from desire. They are paralysed in their relationship with their bodies, in the living and desiring relationship with the mother, which has been censored.

As for us, the daughters, if our relationship with our mothers is a relationship with need, with no possible identity, and if we enter into desire by becoming objects of the desire of/for the father, what do we know about our identity and our desires? Nothing. That manifests itself in somatic pain, in screams and demands, and they are quite justified. Complaints . . . that is what does remain to us of our relationship with our mothers. A little child complains, cries . . .

But if mothers could be women, there would be a whole mode of a relationship of desiring speech between daughter and mother, son and mother, and it would, I think completely rework the language [*langue*] that is now spoken.

Translated by David Macey

4

Volume without Contours

And so woman will not yet have taken (a) place. A 'not yet' which no doubt corresponds to a *hysterical fantasmatic* but/and which acknowledges a *historical condition*. Woman is still the place, the whole of the place where she cannot appropriate herself as such. Experienced as all-powerful where 'she' is most radically powerless in her indifferentiation. Never here and now because she is that everywhere elsewhere from whence the 'subject' continues to draw his reserves, his re-sources, yet unable to recognize them/her. Not uprooted from matter, the earth, the mother, and yet, at the same time, dispersed into x places which do not gather together in anything which she can recognize as herself and which remain the support for reproduction – especially of discourse – in all its forms.

Woman remains this nothing at all [*ce rien du tout*], this whole of nothing yet [*ce tout de rien encore*] where each (male) *one* comes to seek the means to replenish resemblance to self (as) to same. And so she is displaced, yet until now it was not she who displaced herself. She herself cannot shake that stand-in (place of) she constitutes for the 'subject' and to which a value cannot be assigned once and for all, lest the subject become immobilized in what is irreplaceable in his investments. She must therefore wait for him to move her in accordance with his needs or desires. In accordance with the urgings of the prevailing economy. Patient in her reserve, her modesty, her silence, even when the moment comes to undergo violent consummation [*consommation*], to be drawn and quartered. The unstitched sex [*sexe*] – but of the mother? – through which he thinks he can repenetrate into the interior of her body, hoping at last to lose his 'soul' there. A corruption still too calculated, from which he may re-emerge more of a child, and therefore more of a slave, than ever.

While she wards off, thanks to the sheen of her finery, of her glistening skin, the disaster of being devoured and torn apart inside. And so she is *one* [*une*], at least for the gaze, covering up her lacerations with dazzling make-up, or her mothering persona. Fragments: of women, discourses, silences, of still immaculate white spaces?,.... Splitting apart [*mises en écarts*] through which the 'subject' seeks to escape capture. But in struggling to fracture this specular matrix, this enveloping discursivity, this body of the text where he has constituted himself a prisoner, it is still her that he is wounding. Her, Nature who, unwittingly, nursed his project, his production. And who now fuses for him with that wall of glass, that sepulchre of reflections, her difference from which, in her absence from the imaginary, she cannot articulate. Therefore letting herself be consumed again for new speculations, or rejected as unfit for consumption [*consommation*]. Without saying a word. Scarcely trying to perpetuate the use made of her, or to ensure her exchange against a few gadgets: the latest gleaming novelties put into circulation by men and scarcely distorted by her always somewhat baroque frivolity.

Everything must be (re-)invented to avoid the *vacuum*. And it is in search of the lost roots of the same that the place is always being ploughed over again in this way. Because there was perhaps a distant hint of a 'world' so inconceivable, so other, that it would be better to go back underground than to be present at or assist [*assister (à)*] such a vertiginous event. The mother may signify only a silent ground, a scarcely representable mystery, but at least she is a *plenum*. Of course you encounter opacity and resistance in her, as well as the repellence of matter, the horror of blood, the ambivalence of milk, menacing traces of the father's phallus, and even the hole we left behind us when we came into the world. But she – at least – is not nothing. She is not that vacuum (of) woman. That void of representation, that negation of all representation, that limit to all current (self-)representations. Of course the mother is split open, but by the child that is being born, or that is suckling. That is what he can believe, at any rate. He is therefore familiar with that fissure because he made it and closed it up/shut it up [*re(n)fermee*] in his systematics. Not that fissure (of) woman, against which/whom he can only defend himself by (re-)making her a mother, or by opposing her and interposing between himself and this wholly other the preventive veil of a language [*langage*] that has already transformed her/its splits [*écarts*] into fetishes.

Now woman is neither closed nor open. Indefinite,unfinished/ in-finite, *form is never complete in her*. She is not infinite, but nor is she *one* unit: a letter, a figure, a number in a series, a proper name, single object (of a) sensible world, the simple ideality of an intelligible whole, the entity of a foundation, etc. This incompleteness of her form, of her morphology, allows her to become something else at any moment, which is not to say that she is (n)ever unambiguously anything. Never completed in any metaphor. Never this, then that, this and that. . . . But becoming the expansion that she is not, never will be at any moment, as a definable universe. Perhaps that is what they refer to as her irreducible (hysterical) dissatisfaction. No singular form(s) – form, act, discourse, subject, masculine, feminine – can complete the becoming of the desire of a woman. And for her, the danger of motherhood is that of it/her being arrested in the world of *one* child. If she closes up around the unit(y) of that conception, enfolds herself around that one, her desire will harden. *Will become phallic because of this relation to the one?* Similarly, too adequate an idea of femininity, one that conforms too closely to an idea – an Idea – of woman, over-obedient to one sex – to an Idea of sex [*du sexe*] – or to sex as a fetish has already frozen into phallomorphism. Already been metabolized by phallogocratism. Whereas what comes to pass in the *jouissance* of woman is in excess of it. An indefinite overflowing in which many a becoming could be inscribed. The fullness of their to-come is glimpsed, announced, as possibles, but in an extension, a dilation, without determinable limits. Without any conceivable end. With neither telos nor archè. Unless already phallic. Subordinated to the prescriptions of a *hommosexual* imaginary and its relations to origin, to a logos that claims to reduce the power of the maternal to the same – the Same – in itself and for itself.

But woman does not resign herself to this. Except in her phallosensate capitulations and capitalizations. For woman cannot mean herself [*ne se peut vouloir dire*] and, besides, does not want for herself the power of expressing [*ne se veut d'ailleurs pas ce pouvoir dire*] that would assign her to some concept, that would attribute to her, as her own, some set idea. She cannot relate herself to any being, subject or whole that can be simply designated. Nor to the category (of) women. One woman + one woman + one woman never will have added up to some generic: woman. (The/A) woman gestures towards what cannot be defined, enumerated, formulated, *formalized*. A common noun indeterminable in terms of an identity. (The/A) woman does not obey the principle of self-identity, or of identity with any particular *x*. She identifies with every *x*, without identifying with it in any particular way. Which implies an excess of any identification with/of self. But that excess is (not) nothing: the abeyance of form, the fissure in form, the reference to another edge where she re-touches herself without anything/thanks to nothing. Lips of the same form – yet never simply defined – overlap by retouching one another, referring one (to) the other for a perimeter that nothing arrests in *one* configuration.

Which will already have taken place without the assistance [*concours*] or aid [*secours*] of any object, any subject. Another topo-(logy) of *jouissance*. Foreign to male auto-affectation, which will have seen in it only its own negative. The death of its logic, and not its altering in a copulation yet to be defined. Man's auto-erotism presupposes an individualization of the subject, of the object, and of the instrument appropriate(d) to *jouissance*. If only for an instant, the moment of substitution. (The/A) woman is always already in a state of anamorphosis in which all figures blur. The discontinuity of a cycle in which closure is a slit which merges its lips with their edge(s). And so she cannot *repeat herself* or produce herself as *wholly other* in pleasure, for the other already in her affects her, touches her, without her ever becoming one – masculine or feminine [*un(e)*] – or the other. The intervening space [*écart*] (of) this de-forming contact cannot be formulated in the simplicity of any present. And because she has never attained it, (the) woman remains (in) her indifference. Or what he rapes in his rending operation. With his meaning [*vouloir dire*], touch, here and now in his act. Even in the act of re-feeling. For (the/a) woman is already self-feeling, before any decidable intervention. On this side of any opposition in a couple where the attribution of active or passive, past or future can be distinguished. But this surreptitious auto-affection is not admitted, cannot be spoken. It is *true* that women do not tell all. Even if you begged them to speak, even if he begged them, they will or would say nothing but the meaning of the 'subject' in this rape/theft [*v(i)ol*] of their *jouissance*. Already exiled from a more intimate place – which does not collect itself in any 'soul' – in specified propositions. Already subordinated to an intention, a meaning, a thought. To the laws of *one* language [*langage*]. Even in their madnesses: again, his obverse or reverse side. And telling all has no meaning for (a/the) woman, no one meaning, because she cannot utter that nothing which affects her, in which she has always-already been touched, has always-already touched herself [*où elle (s') est déjà touchée*]. That nothing to say which history – History – reduplicates by removing it/her from the economy of discourse.

And so (the/a) woman might, at a pinch, be a signifier – even below the bar – in the 'subject's' logical system of representations or ideational representatives. Which does not mean that she can in any way recognize herself in that signifier. Or even that man, as representative of the power (of the) phallus, corresponds for her to any signification, except perhaps that of her exclusion from herself. For man is so positioned as to re-mark the gap, the space, the distance [*écart, écartement*] in which she finds herself, in which she is a hole again and is holed [*se retrou(v)e*], but the subject's entanglement in the autarky of his metaphorics means that this intervention (only) takes place alongside the contiguity wherein she is contained, retained in her *jouissance*, carrying her off course in the articulation with any phallic *one* [*tout un phallique*]: she will henceforth function as a *hole* [*trou*]. And for her, metaphor will have the efficacity of a non-violating distance [*écart*] only if, *empty of all already appropriated meaning*, she/it keeps open the indeterminacy of the possibles of her *jouissance*: God. A design-plan [*Dess(e)in*] for the intromission of a 'figure' that resists grounding itself in its belonging to an individual. Still inclusive as ever, but without division into/between increasingly denotative forms. God, the science of whose desire no learning [*savoir*] has produced. Left to/in his ignorance. Because He refuses to hate? Yes, if hatred .comes of the particular character of knowledge [*connaissance*]. Each one, male or female, wanting to have the best *bit* of knowledge and striving to tear away the representation of the other from his/her specula(risa)tion so as to preserve the power (of the) truth of the spectacle in which he/she gazes at him/herself. Denying the fiction of the mirror that underpins it. Yet for someone who knew all, rivalry over knowing oneself to have been appropriated, over appropriated knowledge [*(se) savoir approprié*] would be meaningless. Woman certainly does not know (herself to be) all, even knows (herself to be) nothing. But her relationship with (self-)knowledge creates the opening on to an all of what could be known of what she could know herself to be . . . : God. And once again, by reduplicating this speculative condition in a caricature, that is by excluding it – except by phallic proxy – from any singular science, from the appropriation of all (self-)knowledge, 'History' will have perpetuated in the desire of the woman – the operation of an object or, more rarely, a subject – the existence of God as an issue for an omniscience still alien to his determination. A God all the more adored in that He is abhorred in his power. And who, given a new lease in/by female *jouissance*, will have brought down upon the latter the horror and aversion of a not-like [*non-pareil*] that defies with its 'not yet' all comparisons. And if, in the attention the 'subject' now devotes to defining the sexuality of woman, his aim is to become identical to the being – the Being – of the other – the Other? – alterity once more absorbed into the Same, wanting it, id, wanting to see her, wanting to know . . . [*voulant ça, la, sa . . . voir*] in order to be even more like Self, to be more identical to Self, she can only reply: not . . . yet. And as it happens, in one sense, in that sense, never.

For man needs an instrument to touch himself: a hand, a woman, or some substitute. The replacement of that apparatus is effected in and through language [*langage*]. Man produces language for self-affection. And various forms of discourse, can be analysed as various modes of the auto-affect(at)ion of the 'subject'. The most ideal being the philosophical discourse that privileges 'self-representation'. A mode of auto-affect(at)ion that reduces the need for an instrument to *almost* nothing: to the thought (of) the soul. An introjected, internalized mirror, in which the 'subject' ensures, in the most subtle, most secret, manner possible, the immortal preservation of his auto-erotism.

Sciences and technologies also require instruments for auto-affec(ta)tion. And to some extent they thus free themselves from the control of the 'subject' and threaten to rob him of a fraction of his solitary profit. To become his rival by winning their autonomy. But thought still subsists. At least for a time. The time it takes to think (oneself) woman? The last resource for the auto-affectation of the subject as such in/through language? Or a partial opening up of his vicious circle: the logos itself/the logos of the same [*logos (du) même*]. If machines – including theoretical machines – can sometimes set themselves in motion by themselves, perhaps woman can too? The crisis of an era in which the 'subject' is no longer too sure where, whom, what to turn to, now that there are so many foci of 'liberation' not strictly homogeneous with one another and, above all, heterogeneous to his conception. And as he has long been seeking in that conception the instrument, the lever and not infrequently the term of his pleasure, he may perhaps have exposed himself to destruction and loss of pleasure in these objects of mastery. *Striving now, therefore, to be a science, a machine, a woman . . . so that they do not escape his use and their interchangeability.* But unable to do so completely because form will never have found its completion in them, as it does in him, in the interiority of his mind. She/It is always already exploded. And to that extent she/it can take pleasure in herself/itself [*jouir d'elle-même*] – in the retouching of her edges – or sustain that illusion for the other. Whereas the 'subject' must always re-expose (his) form before [*devant*] the self so as to taste its possession once more. In his pleasure, the master has made himself a slave to his power.

Whereas in the self-touching of the/a woman, a whole [*tout*] touches itself because it is in-finite/unfinished, unable or unwilling to close up or to swell definitively to the extension of an infinite. This (self-)touching giving woman a form which is in(de)finitely transformed without closing up on her appropriation. Metamorphoses where no whole [*ensemble*] ever consists, where the systematicity of the One never insists. Transformations, always unpredictable because they do not work towards the accomplishment of a telos. Which would imply one figure taking over – from – the previous figure and prescribing the next: *one* form arrested, therefore, and becoming *another*. Which happens only in the imaginary of the (male) subject who projects on to all others the reason of the capture of his desire: his language, which claims to name him adequately.

Now, the/a woman who does not have *one* sex [*sexe*] – which will usually have been interpreted as meaning no sex – cannot subsume it/herself under *one* term, generic or specific. Body, breasts, pubis, clitoris, labia, vulva, vagina, neck of the uterus, womb . . . and this *nothing* which already makes them take pleasure in/from their apartness [*jouir dans /de leur écart*] thwarts their reduction to any proper name, any specific meaning, any concept. Woman's sexuality therefore cannot be inscribed *as such* in any theory, unless it is

standardized to male parameters. Within which the fortune of the
clitoris was that it was not thought of in the pleasure of apartness
[*un écart*], and from other pleasures too. The same applies to motherhood, among other things. Their meaning, as with anything to do
with female desire, having been assigned them by self-representations
of (so-called) male sexuality. Which, inevitably, serve as models,
units of measurement and guarantors of economic progress for
anyone sensible. Its necessarily *trinitarian* structuration included:
subject, object, and the copula-instrument of their articulation.
Father, Son, Holy Ghost. The bosom of mother–nature permitting
the conjunction of the (male) one and the (so-called) other in the
matrix of a discourse. By playing with varied skill and good fortune on
negativity, one can even extend this sensible [*sensé*] family circle to
four terms, four members. The fourth, in its absence, its silence or
its unreason, its death, its *glass* ensures an easier exchange between
the other three. But it is always the same discourse that is being
developed, more and more brilliantly, even at the cost of some
inflation. The (male) subject gathering up and regrouping the plurality of the female commodity, scattered in its silence, its in(con)sistent
chatter or its madness, into coins that have a value on the market.
Whereas, if 'she' is to begin to speak (herself) and, above all,
understand (herself), one should first of all suspend for recasting
the systems of credit. In every sense. Investigating the credits and
credence that support monopolies in all their present forms. Otherwise, why speak of 'her', given that it is only in/through her silence
that she circulates, helps them circulate?

But, there again, is this really anything to do with her? Or, rather,
is it the mother once more? Is this revival of interest really anything
more than an anxious search for something that is still good to eat in
a 'world' starved by the imperatives of increased productivity and
the threat of less ground [*sol*] being allotted to everyone? Is this
ultimately a return to her nourishing breast, to the generosity of
her blood and to the eminently territorial wealth of her womb?
Regression? To extract new profits from it. New modes of subsistence. Or is it the mystery of a sex that takes pleasure in nothing
[*un sexe qui jouit de rien*] – except when it too clings to an oral–anal
fantasmatic, consuming the 'phallus' it nourished to reproduce it –
which finally parts [*entr'ouvre*], for an all too often disappointed
desire, the 'veil' that masked this strange 'thing': the pleasure of

endless exchange with the other in a (self-)touching that no privileged identification arrests by re-absorption. Neither one nor the
other [*ni l'un(e) ni l'autre*] being taken as a term, nor the supplement
of their passing one into the other, which is nothing; the less than
the circularity of a movement that loops back on itself, the space
[*écart*] that always refers back to an other (male or female).

Who can intervene in multiple ways, provided that he/she does
not impose the rigidity of his/her forms: of being, having, saying,
thinking.... For that inflexibility will always break off the exchange; fixing and immobilizing the space [*écart*] between the two
into *one*. That this *one* can now identify, repeat him/herself, be
modified as a result, count, serialize him/herself ... add him/herself
up in a finite One will do nothing to remedy that. When its non-
formulatable space [*écart*] has been defined as *one*, the sexual relation
will have lost the *jouissance* of its in(de)finite exchange in the other.
Other pleasures can of course be substituted for it, notably those of
exchanging truths or witticisms with one's peers. For, if the assertion
of the *one* is supported only by this formal rigour, what still *other*
could (cor)respond to so absolute an implantation? Castration will
have been no more than a (de)negation of the other of sexual difference which, in the form of screens, prisons, partitions, stases of
relations, will return from its repression. Including, of course, in
discourse. There, every atom of meaning finds its force of truth
by being unique in both extension and intension; defining in the
self-identity of this assertion the spaces between [*espacements d'avec*]
itself and other meanings, but at the same time decisively [*découpant
et du même coup*] cutting up all the matter of language, the whole of
speculation, and also the 'spaces between' [*blancs*] in discourse. Its
unsaid, its taboos/its between the lines [*inter-dits*], having already
received their signification from it. Even in the silence of the other,
who says nothing (except) what the 'subject' has already had him/her
say. The subject can therefore use, explore, fragment, speculate the
other ... and always find the same in the other. This (male) other
will have served only to reduplicate his self-identity differently.

Which will also have been demanded of woman. A reduplication
postulated, now in a still chaotic substance to which he claims to give
form, now in the efficacity of a negativity, a representative of all
that hollowness from whence determination is still to come, now in
the repetition of an assertion which, instantaneous as it would like

to be, still needs to pass again in/through the other. Yet, in this increasingly subtle duality of meaning in all its properties, *the reduplication that has already taken place, in quite a different way, in the woman, will have been evaded.* The extraterritoriality of the feminine vis-à-vis language will earn her a somewhat ambivalent respect for her virginity: the taboo on frontiers that gape on the horizon of meaning, having the power to express everything. Opening (itself up) on to an other 'world' of which nothing is known (but) that gaping slit [*fente qui s'écarte*]. Triggering the anxiety of transgressing without a password, without any conceivable interpellation, without any right inscribed anywhere, without any taxes to pay, without any strict boundary between before/after, outside/inside, own/alien . . . sayable/unsayable. Should the father, once more, take charge of customs clearance in the expectation of receiving the *extra* that is owed him, he will have reduced the feminine to the maternal, the between [*entre*] not belonging to the antrum [*antre*] contributing to his wealth. Which, as we know, can take the form of a family, a horde, a community, a people. The between-two has already been exported *into* his territory. And there the closeness of a (self-)touching without reserve, even unto ecstasy, has already been excluded from (the) conception (of the proper). Here, the two is reduced to the self-same one in the various modes of its differences. Here, the very close no longer refers to the irreducibly distant in its inappropriability [*dans un rien d'appropriable*].

Except perhaps, again, in God. A beyond-heaven whose qualities, powers, names . . . one has attempted, without reducing its duplicity, to enumerate – the condition for this being chastity . . . God (of) that horde which surreptitiously turns up at the opening [*entr'ouverture*] of a diabolical pleasure? In order to fill the gap [*écart*], according to one, to enjoy it [*en jouir*] according to the other. To enjoy/take pleasure in the other – the Other – in his/her reduplication in nothing that is known, that knows itself. Again . . . God, that entity *par excellence*, that radically autarkic unit, that universality and eternity now and forever, that begetter of all nature, that holy name of names, they say. That sex (of) nothing at all in its absolute fluidity, its plasticity to all metamorphoses, its ubiquity in all its compossibilities, its invisibility . . . who has not stopped being entreated, but without a word being said, by women, in their most secret covering. And who, because he knows them so well, has never touched them directly, except in the forever provisional stealth of a fantasy removed from all representation: between two non-unities which thus imperceptibly take pleasure in themselves/enjoy themselves [*jouissent d'elles mêmes*]. And that 'God' should have been conceived as a perfect volume, a closed completeness, an infinite circle in the fullness of all extension, is presumably not the doing of their imagination. For this passion for a neatly tied up origin, even at the cost of biting the end (of) its tail, for a well-locked (whore) house [*maison bien close*] in which the 'thing' may possibly happen, for a matrix coiled back on/in its interiority, is not women's. Except sometimes in their maternal phallicism, or in their impotent mimicry. Their 'God' is quite other, like their pleasure. And, his death already having taken place, at least for this 'world', is not likely to come about. But of course they will not say so, because there is nothing there that can be exposed. Or known (and this can be written differently, depending on what one expects of its impossible [re]production).

For the/a woman, two does not divide into ones. Relations preclude being cut up into units. And when 'she' clings so desperately to the one, even to the capital of *one* god made Man, it is so as to repeat the value to which 'she' has a right on the exchange market: none. The non-entity, the zero that founds and seals any settlement of accounts by its displacement. Which is not to say that she has no price for each individual male, unless we understand her to be impossible to valuate because she underpins the validity of this economy. Always threatened by the splitting of its commodity atom, by that tiny rise or fall [*ce rien en plus ou en moins*] that upsets all share prices. The fact that until now its privileged locus has been the child no doubt results from the necessity to represent things to self in the same terms. More or less. To reduce them to the *same units*, even if the accounts immediately become more complicated as a result: two producing one so as to merge and cancel one another out in their couple. Reproducing one more, and beginning not to know where he is. This second (of the) one belongs to the mother? Then they may call him Polynices[1] and see to it that he will be reprojected out of the legally recognized polis. And if the one who comes into the world in this way is a girl, it is a thing so inconceivable that a brutally drastic choice has to be made lest value-ratings be thrown into disorder: either she is (only) her mother, or she is another boy to be reduced to the juvenile condition of asexuality [*asexe*] – held in reserve to shore up values in case they fall – or she is nothing. Or in any case nothing that can be shown to the people except in her death, (or) her confinement behind the door of the house.

Where almost nothing happens, except the (re)production of the child. And the discharge of some shameful flow. A horrible sight: bloody. *Fluid* must remain that secret, sacred, *remainder* of the one. Blood, but also milk, sperm, lymph, spittle, saliva, tears, humours, gases, waves, airs, fire . . . light which threaten him with distortion, propagation, evaporation, burning up [*consumation*], flowing away, in an other difficult to grasp. The 'subject' identifies himself with/in an almost material consistency which is repelled by all fluence. And even in the mother it is the cohesion of a 'body' (subject) that he is looking for, the solidity of a land, the foundation of a ground [*sol*]. Not that whereby, wherein, she recalls woman: the fluent. Which he cathects only in a desire to invert it into the self (as) same. All water must become a mirror, all seas, a glass. Otherwise he will have to get around them from behind. Enclosing their chasms with a girdle that fastens at the back: the sewing up of a hole through which the 'subject' ensures a re-birth in matter pure and simple, which the form of the spirit of the Father will already have modelled, will model, in accordance with his logic. And so he is protected from that indecent contact . . . woman. From any possible assimilation to that undefined flow that dampens, wets, floods, conducts, electrifies the gap [*écart*], makes it glow in its blazing embrace. Without common measure with the one (of the subject).

Who, to keep himself from total deliquescence, may also resort to the *speculum*. Abandoning his flat surfaces, his clear contours, his unambiguously framed form, his calculations of proportions established once and for all, his immutably reflected unity, he will try to come to terms with the curves of the mirror. Which complicates relations with the self (as) same. But perhaps it is not impossible to analyse them, with the help of all the instruments he is now armed with? Everything, then, should be rethought in terms of volute(s), helix(es), diagonal(s), spiral(s), curl(s), turn(s), revolution(s), pirouette(s). . . . An increasingly dizzying speculation which pierces, drills, bores a volume still assumed to be *solid*. And therefore violated in its shell, fractured, trepanned, burst, sounded even unto its most intimate centre. Or belly [*ventre*]. Caught up in faster and faster whirlings, swirlings, until matter shatters and falls into (its) dust. The substance of language? The matrix of discourse? The 'body' of the mother? Taking them apart to examine them, gaze at them/himself in their smallest atoms, and antra of atoms. Looking everywhere for the probability of some concealed gold, some surplus power. Guarantees of the value of the 'subject', and therefore of the perpetuation of his exchanges in property. The child may have a lower rating here: it takes too long to (re)produce him. The mother–woman worked over in detail by the specula(riza)tions of the 'subject' no longer has the leisure to shut herself up for the duration of a pregnancy.

But if the reserves of that volume should run out too, would it be necessary to return, this time, towards the instrument that opened up the passage? And indeed forged it? And say that he was already so heterogeneous to what he claimed to be seducing that he has touched nothing so far? Nothing not already known, that did not already know itself. That, when he produced the opening [*écart*], the open-ing that – already – existed was left out of his task. That at best he has traversed the obverse, the reverse of his projections. Been, perhaps, beyond the symmetry of a reflection? Of an inversion? Finding in the impasse of specular, speculative negentropy the need for a growth which, at every moment in its reproduction in the same, must bore deeper, or higher.

The/A woman is never closed/shut (up) in one volume. That this representation is inescapable for the figure of the mother makes us forget that the woman can become all the more fluid in that she is *also* pregnant/enclosed [*enceinte*], in that, unless the womb is reduced – by him, by him in her – in phallic appropriation, it does not seal up the opening [*écart*] of the lips. And that it is the 'subject' who is responsible for bringing the other back to the (male or female) one by reducing their contiguity in his desire. For if she/they was/were at once two, but not divisible into one(s), how could he know where he was? How could he interfere between her/them, in her/their womb(s)? The other must therefore speculate [*spéculer*] the (male or female) one, reduplicating what man supposedly already knows as the place of (his) production. 'She' must be no more than the path, the method, the theory, the *mirror* for the 'subject' that leads back, via a process of repetition, to re-cognition of the unity of (his) origin.

But the mother and the woman do not speculate one another in the same way. A double specularization already intervenes in her/them, between her/them. And more. For the sex [*sexe*] of woman is not one. And as *jouissance* explodes in all these/her 'parts', so they can reflect it differently in their bedazzlement. More plenary than in the whole? Tantamount to saying that this plurality of pleasure is reducible to shards or pieces of *one* mirror. That this may sometimes, or also, be the case in polymorphous plays of reflections, inversions, perversions, is not impossible, and not without its satisfactions. But that is still a play on *hommology*, not a sexuality in which heterogeneous multiples fuse, re-fuse and confuse shards of glass by lighting fires of/in their openings [*écarts*]. Bringing them together in some unity of specula(riza)tion, summoning their pleasures to appear has nothing – yet – to do with what burns and glows in the infinitely rekindled blazing embraces of these incendiary facets.

The/A woman cannot be gathered into *one* volume, except on pain of being removed from her *jouissance*, which demands that she remains open to nothing that can be said, but which contrives the non-closure of her edges, the non-suturing of her lips. And no doubt the history of this turning back on herself has dispossessed her. She remains external to the circularity of thought which, in its telos, reappropriates for itself the cause of her desire: the unconscious support of an attempt to metaphorize a primal matrix into the sphere of intimacy with self, of proximity to self, of a 'soul' or a spirit. She remains the whole of the place that cannot be gathered into a space because it is no more than a receptacle for the (re)productions of the same. At the same time dispersed into functions whose multiple distancing, tearing apart [*écartement, écartèlement*], are subject to the specific unity of a field, of a meaning, of a name, of a sex, of a *genre* . . . and denied their retouching(s). The opacity of matter, the evanescence of a fluid, the vertigo of a vacuum between two: a glass for the 'subject' to gaze upon himself and re-produce himself in his reflection, a shutter allowing the eye to frame the project of its spectacle, a sheath–envelope for the penis [*sexe*] to ensure that its solitary pressures and prints are masked/hidden, a fertile ground for it to plant its seed . . . Never one, male or female.

Unless she competes with the phallosensate *hommologue* that even today fills itself with gold by spawning as quickly as possible off-spring capable of occupying, filling, exploiting for his advantage the space [*écart*] productive of nothing. Nothing that is yet known/knows itself *in truth*. And in *one sense*, never.

NOTES

1 [Son of Oedipus and Jocasta, and brother of Eteocles and Antigone.
   After the death of Oedipus, the brothers were unable to decide who
   should rule Thebes, but eventually resolved to rule in alternate years.
   Polynices went into banishment and became one of the Seven Against
   Thebes. In the ensuing battle, the brothers killed each other, thus
   fulfilling the curse laid upon them by Oedipus (trans.)].

Translated by David Macey

SECTION II

Psychoanalysis and Language

Introduction to Section II

'The poverty of psychoanalysis' ('Misère de la psychanalyse') was first published in *Critique*, 365, in October 1977, and reprinted in *Parler n'est jamais neutre* (1985). Despite its importance, it has remained untranslated until now.

The tone of this piece is caustic and angry; as Irigaray explains in the notes, it was motivated by the suicide of a woman friend, a psychoanalyst. (This suicide was also the occasion of Jeanne Favret-Saada's article criticizing Lacanian practice: 'Excusez-moi, je ne faisais que passer' ['Excuse me, I was just passing'] (1977).) The analyst had failed the 'passe', Lacan's controversial 'rite de passage' qualifying analysts as theoreticians of his School. (For further details of the 'passe', see Sherry Turkle, *Psychoanalytic Politics* (1979); Stuart Schneidermann, *Jacques Lacan: death of an intellectual hero* (1983); and Elisabeth Roudinesco, *Jacques Lacan & Co.* (1990).) 'The poverty of psychoanalysis' is a scathing indictment of the institution of Lacanian psychoanalysis (from which Irigaray herself suffered when she was expelled from her teaching post at Vincennes in 1974). The Lacanian School, she argues, refuses to admit its historical and cultural determinations, or to see that '[t]he unconscious is revealed as such, heard as such, spoken as such and interpreted as such within a tradition'. In this way, the doctrine evades any challenges that might be put to it by treating the challenge as a symptom. Irigaray compares Lacanian analysts with the early analysts who did not know in advance what they would find, and were still capable of listening and of being surprised by what they heard. For Irigaray, the Lacanian analysts impose a rigid grid on the unconscious which makes it virtually impossible for them to hear anything – any unconscious – which does not fit a set of pre-established determinations. In true analytical fashion, she interprets this Lacanian 'imperialism' as an indication of unconscious resistance and fantasies which remain uninterpreted in contemporary psychoanalytic discourse itself: 'The symbolic, which you impose as a universal, innocent of any empirical or historical contingency, is *your* imaginary, transformed into an order, into the social.' One might pick out three points in particular. Firstly, Irigaray suggests that psychoanalysis is governed by a particular economy of repetition or of the death drive (in philosophical terms, nihilism), in which the 'benevolent neutrality' of the analyst apotropaically wards off the violence of their own drives by attributing them to the analysand. Secondly, Irigaray identifies a monosexual (or hom(m)osexual) imaginary, in which woman does not exist, and which therefore leaves women 'in exile', 'like ghosts' in the masculine phallic imaginary. In this phantasmatic system or topo-logic, woman (and as a result women) has been made into the material support of male narcissism, the condition of men's subjectivity. Thirdly, Irigaray points out that it is no doubt not accidental that we are currently seeing a proliferation of 'normalizing' psychoanalytic discourses around the subject of female sexuality; she interprets this as an indication of attempts to contain feminism, and resistance to facing up to its implications for the male narcissism invested in the social order. 'The poverty of psychoanalysis' is also one of the rare places in which Irigaray speaks of bisexuality. She points out that in a monosexual economy, bisexuality is not a genuine option.

The indictment of the Lacanian School, however, is balanced by Irigaray's own more positive account of the possibilities of psychoanalysis for women. We can see this both in 'The poverty of psychoanalysis' and even more clearly in 'The limits of the transference' which follows. Irigaray is often thought of simply as a disciple of Lacan, but it is clear when reading her in a psychoanalytic rather than in a philosophical context, that there are other influences on her psychoanalytic writing. Traces of Melanie Klein and Winnicott can be seen, for example, in 'The limits of the transference', and in Irigaray's remarks on the mother–daughter relationship in *Ethique de la différence sexuelle* one can also discern affinities with the work of feminist object-relations theory. Reading *Women Analyze Women in France, England and the United States*, Elaine Hoffman Baruch and

Lucienne Serrano, (eds), (1988), a series of nineteen interviews with women analysts from several countries, including one with Irigaray, it is clear that Irigaray's preoccupations are in many ways similar to those of non-Lacanian analysts. *Women Analyze Women* puts her work into a psychoanalytic context which gives an instructive glimpse of an alternative reference group, less familiar perhaps than that of contemporary critical theory.

For Irigaray, the unconscious is a *'reservoir of a yet-to-come'*, a creative and regenerative source. She imagines a possible female imaginary which would correspond to the morphology of the female body (the 'two lips', for example), with its own space–time modalities, in which women would be nomads (but no longer in exile), mobile and dancing, taking their own 'house' with them. (See below on the 'house of language'.) Even in 1977, Irigaray is already placing psychoanalysis under the sign of ethics. In these articles we can see early versions of her later work on the ethics of the passions, and the ethics of sexual difference.

'The limits of the transference' ('La Limite du transfert') was first published in 1982, in issue 19–20 of *Etudes freudiennes*, entitled 'L'Amour du transfert' ('Love in/of the transference'); it was reprinted in *Parler n'est jamais neutre* (1985).

The explicit theme of 'The limits of the transference' is the question of women analysands in analysis with a woman analyst. For Irigaray, contrary to a certain psychoanalytic view which she opposes, the modalities of analysis are different for women (and men) depending on whether their analyst is male or female. (This is also discussed in 'The gesture in psychoanalysis' in *Between Feminism and Psychoanalysis*, Teresa Brennan, (ed.), (1989)/'Le Geste en psychanalyse' in *Sexes et parentés*.) However, its implicit theme is the ethics of analysis, and 'The limits of the transference' should ideally be read in conjunction with *Ethique de la différence sexuelle*. Psychoanalysis, which has the passions for its material, has a responsibility to consider the ways in which it colludes with a life-threatening symbolic order. Thus woman, or more strictly, the maternal–feminine, is said to be the sacrificial object, 'forgotten, repressed, denied, confused'. The debt owed to her is never acknowledged. Since women have no language (*langage*) or words (*parole*) of their own, which would give symbolic representation to relations between mothers and daughters, relations between them 'take place in a deadly immediacy.' (On the absence of symbolic representation, see the section in *Speculum* entitled 'The blind spot of an old dream of symmetry'.) In psychoanalytic language, women do not become separate or have an autonomous identity, they remain merged with the mother. As a result, most women are dependent; they live in *dereliction* (abandonment) and their greatest terror is that of being abandoned, since they have no self-identity which would provide them with their own 'home'. Without an imaginary and symbolic home of their own, they live in the world of the *quantitative*, and so find themselves in competition with each other. The imagery which Irigaray uses is a way of speaking of and symbolizing the sexuate woman's body in non-phallic and non-maternal terms: the mucous (membrane), the threshold, the lips which touch or re-touch (see 'This sex which is not one' in the book of the same name). Women too need a 'divine', so that they can measure themselves against an *ideal* (the qualitative) instead of against each other (the quantitative).

The danger in relations between women is that the daughter will eat the mother alive, as it were, use her insides, her body, her mucous, her membranes, to form her own outer, protective skin; in the process the mother, devoured and sacrificed, disappears, and there is no longer anyone there – no mother, and particularly no sexuate and sexual woman who desires. The daughter cannot identify with a desiring woman; there is nothing there for her to identify or have a relation *with*, so it is then impossible for her to articulate her own desire. The woman analyst should be aware of this danger, warns Irigaray. By analysing her own transference, she should make sure that *neither* woman uses the other to 'house' and protect herself. In analysis between women, the task is to create boundaries, not through 'rejection, hate or mastery', but through the separation of mother and woman. These boundaries may be crossed, but they provide an identity to which each woman can return. The two women need to create, in other words, a symbolic object of exchange, to mediate an otherwise fatal immediacy. The analyst needs to be aware that she is creating/providing for the analysand a skin, a container, a space–time within which the analysand can live, move and breathe freely. But to avoid sacrifice, the 'gift' of the analyst must not remain in silence and darkness, in 'a night in which the other has no face'. This article is a little-known contribution to the feminist and psychoanalytic literature on relations between mothers and daughters, and problems of separation and merging, which have been a feminist preoccupation since the end of the 1970s, particularly since the publication of Adrienne Rich's *Of Woman Born* (1977) and Nancy Chodorow's *The Reproduction of Mothering* (1978). Marianne Hirsch gives an account of the feminist literature of this period on mothers and daughters in her 'Mothers and daughters: a review essay' in *Signs*, 7 (1), (1981), pp. 200–222.

One of Irigaray's central ideas is the reworking of the Heideggerian theme of the 'house of language'. The 'house' which women need should be a symbolic one – language, representation, imagery, etc. It is therefore interesting to go back to two of her earlier pieces on language and discourse, and re-read them in the light of her less well-known writing on psychoanalysis.

'The power of discourse and the subordination of the feminine' ('Pouvoir du discours/Subordination du féminin') is an interview which was first published in *Dialectiques*, 8 (1975) after the publication of *Speculum*, and reprinted in *Ce Sexe qui n'en est pas un* (1977) – *This Sex Which Is Not One* (1985). The name of the interviewer is not given.

'The power of discourse and the subordination of the feminine' opens with some specific remarks on psychoanalytic discourse. Freud, Irigaray says, revealed for the first time that science and discourse are sexually indifferent, that is to say, the difference between the sexes has never been symbolized or represented. This section summarizes the pages on Freud in *Speculum*. The strength of Freud is that he brought to light the state of affairs regarding relations between the sexes (and it is clear elsewhere that Irigaray has considerable respect and admiration for Freud). His weakness is that 'Freud himself is enmeshed in a power structure and an ideology of the patriarchal type', which leads him to attribute a historical situation to 'nature' or anatomy. The norm of the male, the one sex, in psychoanalytic discourse, reproduces the economy of the Same in philosophical discourse. It is not surprising, then, that women have traditionally appeared to have no place in philosophy. But although Freud himself reproduces metaphysical presuppositions, Irigaray suggests that Freudian theory has provided the tools to disrupt the order of philosophical discourse. As in the psychoanalytic essays described above, Irigaray looks for the conditions of male subjectivity: 'the "matter" from which the speaking subject draws nourishment in order to produce itself, to reproduce itself', and which constitutes the *space–time* of the subject, or his *mirror*, or the *red blood* which stands for the sustaining maternal-feminine. The essay describes Irigaray's method of approach to philosophy as seeking 'the way the unconscious works in each philosophy and perhaps in philosophy in general', and proposes the strategy of a self-conscious *mimicry* in order to bring to light the mechanisms which maintain sexual indifference in place. In the light of this specific analogy with psychoanalysis, one could perhaps hypothesize that Irigaray is taking up, in relation to philosophy, the position of the *psychoanalyst* who receives the projections of the analysand, and occupies his/her unconscious positions *in order to* interpret them and give them a symbolic and linguistic existence.

Irigaray concludes with reflections on the feminist question of equality or difference. She suggests that equality exacts an enormous price; it means becoming-a-man. Although she is not opposed to women's struggles for equal rights, she does not believe that equality can be achieved so long as women remain objects of exchange within a masculine sexual imaginary. Women need to become speaking subjects in their own right. At this stage of Irigaray's work, there are only a few indications of how she imagines this possibility might come about. There is an early reference to the 'god', defined here as the place of woman's self-affection. In this essay, it is female pleasure or *jouissance*, later called 'love of self on the side of the woman', or a female homosexual economy, which is the condition of challenging the order of sexual indifference. (See also 'L'Amour du même, l'amour de l'autre' ['Love of the same, love of the other'] in *Ethique de la différence sexuelle*, and *Divine Women*/'Femmes divines' in *Sexes et parentés*.)

The question of the female speaking subject is taken up again in 'Questions', an extract from a longer series of questions which were put to Irigaray by an audience at Toulouse University in 1975. The complete series appears in *Ce Sexe qui n'en est pas un* (1977) – *This Sex Which Is Not One* (1985).

Although she expresses some reservations about the way in which feminist groups may simply reproduce masculine structures, it seems to have been the women's movement, i.e. women speaking to each other about themselves, which provided the model for *parler-femme* or 'speaking (as) woman', the topic of these remarks. The questioner appears to have in mind the Derridean equation of the feminine with writing, which Irigaray rejects as a discourse of mastery. She focuses on the 'double syntax', that is to say, a possible articulation between conscious and unconscious, male and female. Unless the self-affection of woman exists within the cultural grammar, the woman's body will continue to be *used* as the material or instrument for male self-affection, thus cutting women off from the articulation of their own desire (see 'The limits of the transference' above). The masquerade for women, then, is a way of providing themselves with a protective skin, in the absence of a language specific to their bodies and their own desires. They 'envelop' themselves in the 'needs/ desires/fantasies of men'. If a woman cannot express her relation to her mother and to other women, she may become 'hysterical'; but Irigaray sees hysteria as a culturally-induced symptom. Although Irigaray's statements about women's language and their self-affection have often been taken to imply a direct unmediated relation between woman's language and women's bodies, it is clear from the psycho-analytic essays in this section that for Irigaray, *un*mediated relations are a source of pathology and dereliction, and in particular lead to women's exile in the male imaginary. It has often been argued against Irigaray that desire (or libido) is masculine (pace Freud and Lacan), and that there can be no desire specific to women. However, contextualizing these essays on language m kes it clear that what Irigaray is elaborating is the possibility of love of self on the side of women, and the recognition of the debt to the mother, thus freeing the mother to be a sexual and desiring woman, and freeing the daughter from the icy grip of the merged and undifferentiated relationship.

The final essay in section II, 'The three genres' ('Les Trois genres') was first given as a lecture in Florence on 11 May 1986, at a conference organized by the *Centro documentazione donna* and the *Libreria delle donne: Il Viaggio*. It was published in *Sexes et parentés* (1987). It is a much later paper than the other two on language, and I think must bear the traces of many of the questions that had been put to Irigaray in the meantime by audiences in different parts of the world. One can imagine English-speaking audiences asking her about the relation between sex and gender, and how to interpret her term 'corps sexué' (body sexuate): was it natural or was it social? The term Irigaray now foregrounds is 'the sexuation of discourse', rather than 'speaking (as) woman', though it should be noted that 'the sexuation of discourse' is also referred to as early as 1977 in *This Sex Which Is Not One*.

In 'The three genres', Irigaray summarizes and discusses her work on linguistic gender, and the question of the position and sex (or gender) of the subject of enunciation. Here too, Irigaray insists that this is an *ethical* question. The indifference to the question of the sexuate positioning of the speaker or message is one of the factors responsible for social and cultural pathology. (For further reading, see *Le Langage des déments* (1973), *Parler n'est jamais neutre* (1985), *Le Sexe linguistique* (1987) and *Sexes et genres à travers les langues* (1990).) Irigaray suggests that as a general rule in our culture, women do not assume the 'I' in discourse; their messages are usually addressed for validation to the 'you', the interlocutor. Men, on the other hand, live within the closed universe of the first-person pronoun; their messages are often self-affirmations which leave little place for co-creation with an *other* sex. What is important is to shift the position of the subject in discourse, the subject of enunciation, and find ways and 'styles' to bring about changes in discourse. Once again, Irigaray stresses that women's masks or decorations cover a void: the absence of their self-love, of the desiring woman-as-lover. Women are still objects of exchange, instead of partners in love. The sexual relationship (the 'amorous exchange' mentioned above in 'The bodily encounter with the mother') is offered here as the paradigm, or figure, for human culture in general. This paradigm is expanded in 'Questions to Emmanuel Levinas' (see section III).

Margaret Whitford

5

The Poverty of Psychoanalysis

On Certain All Too Topical Considerations

Juliette L.: In Memoriam

Gentlemen, psychoanalysts . . .

Why only 'gentlemen'? Adding 'ladies', as is the custom now-adays, would not change anything: in language [*langue*], the masculine noun always governs the agreement. The subject always speaks in the same gender (unless it exposes the flaw in its truth?). The phallus – indeed, the Phallus – is the emblem, the signifier and the product of a single sex.

So, gentlemen psychoanalysts, most of you – if I read you and believe you – will be unable to understand this title, what it evokes, what it refers to, what memory gives it meaning, in which history it is inscribed, in which discourses it has already had a place, what desires it speaks or counterfeits. And so on. Most of you will therefore be unable to interpret it. And you will be prevented from listening by at least two systems of screens, of censorship or of repression.

– A psychical reaction, at first individual, then collective: repudiation. The poverty of psychoanalysis? What next? The phallonarcissism you have duly invested in your function as analysts will not tolerate such a statement, though it is in fact a question. So you will protest, more or less consciously, just like those who want to preserve something of their desire in the repressed: in no way does psychoanalysis suffer from poverty [*la misère*], nor is it wretched [*une misère*]. Your protests will even strengthen your resistance. Let us hope that this is simply a matter of 'time for understanding', and that your very institutions themselves are not founded upon the misrecognition of your poverty . . .

– An urge to know, at least on the part of those who still feel such urges. In which case you might go and ask some *agrége(e)* in philosophy or mathematics, or perhaps some (male or female) political militant or former (male or female) political militant, what all this is about [*de quoi ça cause*]. And they, being 'supposed to know', will enjoy the benefit of your transference.

Know what, precisely? Something about the philosophical? The political? Or something about the workings of the unconscious? You claimed to be able to keep the two separate, and here you are, implacably engineered by the fact that the two are inextricably mutually determined within a history of knowledge. You refuse to admit that the unconscious – your concept of the unconscious – did not spring fully armed from Freud's head, that it was not produced *ex nihilo* at the end of the nineteenth century, emerging suddenly to reimpose its truth on the whole of history – world history, at that – past, present and future. The unconscious is revealed as such, heard as such, spoken as such and interpreted as such within a tradition. It has a place within, by and through a culture. If you fail to resituate it there, you reduce it to a . . . ? To a question or an object of your desire, to an object whose truth constantly escapes you, to some 'O' or 'o'[1] which keeps your drives in a state of effervescence, keeps you on the go, fascinated, terrorized, turns you on/makes you band together [*vous mettre en bande*], flock together, birds of a feather. An economic solution, in every sense of the word, to the general crisis of indifference that broods over the west. But perhaps you don't know that?

As a result of this scorn for culture, from which you reap such profit, you criticize certain men and women for questioning the values sanctified by psychoanalysis. According to you any psychoanalyst, man or woman, who questions the history, culture or politics in which psychoanalysis is inscribed is not or no longer a psychoanalyst. There must be nothing outside psychoanalysis, it must have no limits, no determination other than itself, and its authorization – a matter of existence or essence? – must come from itself alone. To put it in a nutshell: it must be *whole*, absolute and without any historical foundations. Its theory and practice rest upon historical nothingness.

All you have to do to be a real psychoanalyst, woman or man, is read Freud or Lacan – and you'd be better off sticking to the latter.

But what authorizes you to decide if so and so is an analyst, when you yourselves say that the 'analyst's only authorization comes from himself'? Could it be to the *him*self that we should look for an explanation for your criticisms? As it happens, they are always rejections: 'He or she is not an analyst'; 'That isn't analysis'. What determines this proscription, and this 'foreclosure'? Your foreclosure? In accordance with what law? In the name of what name? The name of a father of psychoanalysis to whose unconscious any unconscious should be made to conform? The imperialism of an Unconscious of/to which all men and women have to become subject(s)? Then say so: he or she is not, or no longer, the subject of this Unconscious. And listen to what the unconscious still has to say. Now, either the unconscious is no more than something you have already heard – and is therefore never 'that' [*ça*: id]: what men or women may say that has never been heard before – or the unconscious is desire which is trying to speak of/to itself and, being analysts, you have to listen without excluding anything, even if listening to everything does call *your* desire into question, even if it does mean that *you* risk death . . .

Now don't you think that anything that functions by the name of history, and psychoanalysis, speaks of the economy of your death? Or of *your* economy of death? How can you go on being an analyst without constantly admitting that there's no avoiding that question? Without constantly asking yourself whether the analyst might not be protecting himself from death by making the other a support for death? Whether he might not be defending himself against his violence or hate by imputing it or leaving it to the other? Whether the analyst might not be an analyst so that the other lives the relationship with death in his stead, while he stands by, neutral, benevolent, silent as the grave, a realistic, objective, impartial, scientific observer of tragedies which have nothing, or nothing more, to do with him. Must we interpret the reality known as 'the analyst subject' as a means of warding off death? Or as its effect? As a transition to some beyond? And what arises in the beyond? A ghost? A mechanism? An incorporeal, at all events. What does it mean for a subject with such a status to emerge or persist within our history? How can we know unless we question and retraverse that history?

In other words, how do you interpret the *effects* of a culture on the unconscious? Yours and that of your analysands, male and female. And if the unconscious were *both* the result of the acts of censorship, of repression forced upon us in and by a certain history, *and also* a yet-to-come-into-being, *the reservoir of a yet-to-come*, your repudiations, acts of censorship and misrecognitions would seem to fold the future back into the past. You would constantly reduce the yet-to-be subjected to the already subjected, the as yet unspoken or unsaid of language [*langage*] to something that a language [*langage*] has already struck dumb or *kept silent*. And so – perhaps unwittingly? – aren't you the products and the defenders of an *existing order*, the agents or servants of repression and censorship ensuring that this order subsists as though it were the only possible order, that there can be no imaginable speech, desire or language other than those which have already taken place, no culture authorized by you other than the monocratism of patriarchal discourse? Unwitting culturalists? Some of your statements *symptomatically* bear this out.

Now it so happens that you enjoy prestige, power, love and transference because desire's yet-to-come-into-being is projected on to you. If you are not there to listen to that [*ça*], if that is not your job, and if all that matters to you is the unvarying reduction of all speech to the already-said or written, and its reinsertion into your economy of repetition, your economy of death, then say so, spell it out *clearly* in so many words. Let everyone know. Don't keep certain women and men waiting for you to give them – at a price – something you cannot or will not give them, making demands to which you cannot or will not respond.

You should be boasting about the fact that you have marketed an extraordinarily profitable 'life-trap' (the expression is R. M. Rilke's), a life-trap which no economy ever dreamed of offering or dared to offer its customers–consumers. One has to spend a fortune on it before one realizes that there's nothing there. Something in whose name one is obliged to tell everything, and pay accordingly, so that, when that demand has exhausted all one's resources, your only answer is 'nothing' and 'dis-being' [*désêtre*]. You can say so quite openly. Trade [*échange*] is now in such a state that you will still have clients. But not all men, and certainly not all women. Some men, and certainly some women, want nothing more to do with your 'nothing'. Despite all the seduction, the simulation, the ornaments, the veil, the semblance and the *belief* in which you deck them out.

So stop saying, with mock (?) innocence, that the analyst 'clings to the most particular of the desire of the subject – the particular which is defined at every point by his history and told by his symptom' and that 'it is thus from this most particular symptom that the universal of a possible science is introduced' (Lemoine-Luccioni, 1976, p. 11; 1987, pp. 4–5).[2] Because, quite apart from the fact that you could well be asked what the relationship might be between a *science*, your science in particular, and the universal, it rapidly becomes apparent to anyone who reads you that you establish that relationship in purely deductive and above all normative terms. In other words, given *your* universal – the Lacanian code – one knows *a priori* how you will interpret 'the most particular of the desire of the subject'. To put it a different way: your ears are already fitted with suitable grills or mesh, open or closed in the right places, appropriately damaged or fitted with their orthodoxical prosthesis even before your analysand begins to speak. His or her particular is no more than a *proof* of the cogency of your universal.

Freud and the first psychoanalysts did not act quite like this, or at least not for some time. For them, every analysis was an opportunity to uncover some new facet of a practice and a theory. Each analysand was listened to as though he or she had some new contribution to make to that practice and that theory. But once psychoanalytic 'science' begins to claim to have discovered the universal law of the workings of the unconscious, and once every analysis is no more than an application or a practical demonstration of that law, the only status the now complete 'science' can possibly have is that of an era of knowledge already over. It can therefore be the object of academic diplomas and theoretical qualifications backed by sanctions.

But what if psychoanalysis could only take place if it never sub-ordinated itself to a theory or a science? What if its singularity stemmed from the fact that it can never be complete? Never be reduced to a pre-established corpus, a pre-existing knowledge, a pre-determined law? That it remains 'interminable'? What if every analysis were an elaboration of practice and theory, just like those which have already been written up; what if no model for analysis existed because it would make further analysis impossible? Will you object that we would be straying into the realm of anything goes? Then you are admitting that you have forgotten that any living body, any unconscious, any psychical economy brings *its* order to analysis. All you have to do is listen. But an order with the force of an a priori law prevents you.

And if you claim that desire is always 'particular', how can you force analytic material into a lexicon or a syntax, with schemata, graphs and mathemes which have nothing to do with this particular analysis? What gesture is implicit in subordinating the language of the analysand to a system of signifiers which is not his/her own? In other words, whilst there may well be a bible or a dictionary of Freudian or Lacanian discourse, there can be no grammar or dictionary of psychoanalysis as such, on pain of adapting the analysand to a language [*langue*] which is not the language he or she speaks. Interpretation, or merely listening, comes to mean an act which gives the analyst mastery over the analysand, an instrument in the hands of a master and *his* truth. The psychoanalyst himself is subordinate to it; and he reproduces his subordination.

If a pre-established system – a code which has already been articulated, put in place and set – determines what you expect from/hear in the language of the analysand, woman or man, how, in practice, can that system fail to channel the needs–desires of the analysand and suspend them in a formal, empty ec-stasy? No one can escape its hypnosis and suggestion, now that its medium is a certain mode of the workings of language [*langue*], whose effects must be sustained in the long term. Anyone who attempts to analyse them is automatically declared to be outside the ethics of psychoanalysis.

The role of 'patients', then, is to go on breathing new life and strength – their lives and their strength – into the system, especially if they want to become or remain 'analysts'. The benevolent, and now strictly silent, neutrality of the duty analyst functions as a fascinating appeal to fill in the signifiers–containers–recipients of the discourse of the other. Sorry, the Other. Not the other of the analysand – or the analyst – or his/her unconscious, if you like, but an Other (you insist on capital letters), an *a priori* agency – and an *a posteriori* agency, come to that – always-already and still there, the snare-law of an omnipotent and omniscient father–mother God (the capital covers both) wherein the Truth of every unconscious keeps itself decently veiled. Analysis would 'end', then, in the subjectification of all men and women, who now tautologically become subject(s) – without any real difference between the sexes – to (of) an order bringing their needs–desires in line with the desire, the ever-invisible desire, of a Master. Might I suggest to them that he is no more than a Master of their own making, the unconscious made School, a sort of micro-culture which is at once primitive in its magical components and decadent in its imposition of the cult of a Truth whose power to terrorize is proportional to its ability to mask ignorance.

Is it not surprising that you should criticize certain men and women for asking philosophical questions, given that your school master literally brought you up on philosophy? *Not in the form of questions*, true. But aren't you reprojecting on to the other(s) the parts of his discourse you have not digested? What you reproach him for, what you loathe him for? Why should the privileged object of this repudiation be the words of a woman? Isn't that a fairly common mechanism in your society and, more generally, in society as a whole, come to that?

Of course Lacan delights in not quoting his sources or resources, and that does not make him any easier to digest properly. He is only too ready to play the seductive philosophy teacher who 'knows more', and thus secures the love of his young pupils. But he has told you to read *The Symposium* or *De Anima* often enough, so often that you're sick of hearing him. He's enough of a Hegelian to have been credited in certain psychoanalytic seminars at Vincennes with the discovery of the master–slave dialectic! In a number of relatively famous instances of acting out [*passages à l'acte*], he admits to his passion for Heidegger. And so on.

How can you read his *Ecrits*, without having read the texts the *Ecrits* talk about? How can you understand the status of the 'Thing', of 'the thing in itself', of the 'thing' you borrow from him under its 'Freudian' appellation, without knowing that he borrowed the 'Thing' from Kant? How can you understand the difference between 'talking' and 'saying' if you don't understand what he understood about it from Heidegger? To remind you of only two of many points. Because you know little about, or misrecognize, all the 'symbolic' and 'imaginary' components, the whole tissue of knowledges and identifications that go to make up the word of your Master, his word inevitably looks like the Truth to you.

And when you leave uninterpreted the difference between the knowledge – the knowledges – of your Father–Master and your own, what effect does that have on the way you listen as analysts defined as being 'supposed to know'? What effects of suggestion, what trances, ecstasies, and what convulsions and deaths, are transmitted in this way? Of course Lacan has a desire to know. No doubt that is why he commands your admiration, even a form of beatitude. He loves knowledge more than he loves the unconscious. Alternatively: he loves the unconscious because of the knowledge it can bring him. Could it be that that makes you a bit backward, like the children of a father who knows 'too much' or who is 'supposed to know everything', whose limitations you cannot imagine except on pain of rediscovering your relation to lack, of having to question the function of the lack in your desire? Would you rather go on being the son of God than be deprived of your lack? So is Lacan the God of your unconscious, your School, your world, the world? The last – psychoanalytic – avatar of salvation incarnate? Don't you know that, when science is in power, God is dead? And that your god is a spectre who haunts you because you cannot discover his nature? Or, according to your science, interpret his provenance or cause in relation to desire? Or therefore, perhaps, in relation to his sex? His *real* sex.

For isn't it because you keep veiled from your own gaze and from that of others the relevance of the genitals [*sexe*] of your father in psychoanalysis that your statements about the status of the phallus, as opposed to the organ or real genitals [*sexe*], are so often contradictory and confused? Isn't that what you desire? To turn the way in which this father is situated in the sexual relation into an unfathomable mystery, a well of invisibility, a capital letter whose tip soars to infinity: because of your *primal psychoanalytic scene*? And the imaginary and symbolic value of the phallus is all the more deserving of a capital in that, in the *real*, there is said to be no sexual relation, and we have to make up for its absence in one phallo-narcissistic way or another. Unless we interpret its effects.

There is no question of underestimating the real if we do so. Just ask yourself whether the real might not be some very repressed–censored–forgotten 'thing' to do with the body.

Alas, according to you the body is always-already engineered by language, by a language [*langue*]. The domination of that language means that the sexual relation is as non-existent as Woman, not that the theoretical impact of such statements is without its effects on the most quotidian banality. On the contrary . . . Attaching more importance to the Truth than to the sex of the body has very unfortunate results . . .

Including such statements as: 'Woman is the figure of this scene of the veil which covers over the primal scene: she dances the eternal and often *ridiculous* dance of the veil. She is alone in knowing what nothingness it is intended to veil, while man, fascinated, looks on. Thanks to which, the sexual act can take place' (Lemoine-Luccioni, 1976, p. 180; 1987, p. 152, my emphasis: in many traditions, the dance of the veil is the sexual and religious rite *par excellence*, a dance with a mystery and a cosmic reality that is at once prior to and beyond any already-constituted subjectivity. The scene is played out by the Mother–Goddess or the Betrothed, the gods and the universe. It does not cover nothingness; it attempts to pass through the veil of illusion to reach the act/gesture creating or begetting the world).

It makes you shudder. But shudder with what? If that is all there is to the sexual relation – man's fascination with the nothingness she veils – then we are defenceless against the most negative elements of nihilism. And you will have nothing to do with its positive implication – the fall of the idols. Isn't psychoanalysis now the practice of a nihilism which unfortunately fails to recognize itself for what it is? In that case, 'benevolent neutrality' towards the 'everything' that is said might just as well be taken to mean the ultimate form of a certain indifference in which everything is equal, with a few little differences that go by various names standing out against a background of oneness: everything comes to the same. How could it be otherwise, if there aren't *really* two sexes, each with its own imaginary and its own order?

And if 'allegiance to castration' (!) is not a precondition for breaking out of the imaginary and tautological circle of the subject to perceive and desire some *other*, but 'the experience for each that their desire is the desire of the Other' (Lemonine-Luccioni, 1976, p. 180; 1987, p. 152), if it subordinates both sexes to the cult of the lack of/in the Other, then psychoanalysis is a prorogation of a religion of privation and frustration in which no incarnation of the divine is possible. Its Law is the law of the imposition of nothingness in the name of Nothingness. It inscribes it in the deepest unconscious of sexed bodies.

There is no longer any point in them even looking at each other because 'there is nothing real to see in the one or the other' (Lemoine-Luccioni, 1976, p. 180; 1987, p. 152). Whence the 'unbearable nakedness'? And 'beauty as ornament, that is to say as weapon and as cover' (p. 181; p. 153). But if there is nothing real in one or the other, why the 'deliberate denunciation, on the part of woman, of her own body, in favour of beauty' (pp. 181–2; p. 153)? If the scopic drive is, as you put it, constitutive of the subject, but if what it turns on is in your eyes a 'nothing to see' which is always 'ornamented', 'armed', and 'covered', what conception of the subject are you talking about? Whatever it is, woman still has to renounce her body to perpetuate it. A body of such ugliness that none can look upon it unless it is covered up . . .

Don't concern yourself with philosophy; philosophy won't mind. Without your knowing it you have been 'caught' in nihilism. And in statements like, 'all discourses are equal' (Lemoine-Luccioni, 1976, p. 11; 1987, p. 4). Which is not true, even 'for a subject in analysis or for an analyst'. Some discourses do more to determine the subject than others, the discourse of mastery, and philosophical discourse being cases in point. After the end of philosophy, philosophical discourse leads those who do not take cognizance of it to adopt discourses which might be described as *cut-price*, discourses in which the truth, duly exploited by professional hacks, comes cheap. You just have to remove the brand name. Not that there's any need to now. You reduce everything to an equivalence where nothing has any value. Your language [*langue*] is nothing but a cheap imitation which is unconscious of its own nature. It seems to be governed only by a relationship with *contradiction* which is innocent of any principle or any vital imperative. This end-of-the-world polemic – that's all it is – plays with the forms of language without any respect or regard for their meaning, order, beauty or generation.

So all that is taken from the truth of men is that which divides women and assigns them their lot? The *effects* on women of an ambivalence without the safety device of a disavowal founding truth? The *effects* on women of the underside of 'masculine' discourse? Do women remain divided and assigned to their lot so that men can remain one [*un*(s)]? Are women the site of an irreparable wound (imputed to their sex [*sexe*]), torn between the yes and the no: the wound of all the 'I want–I don't want, I love–I hate, I take–I reject' which lie below, covered by the Good, the True and the Beautiful of men? When you assert that 'Man is and remains, as man – and assuming that he exists as a man who would not be a woman as well, – one' (Lemoine-Luccioni, 1976, p. 9; 1987, p. 3), that 'knowledge does not divide him' (ibid.) aren't you making women a support for what you call the 'splitting of the subject'? Reducing woman to the *effects* of man's relationship with his unconscious? For if man is not divided in his knowledge, he has no unconscious. Or at least doesn't want to know anything about it. And *his* division can only be understood in terms of what divides women and assigns them their lot. It follows that: 'Woman is not, that is agreed; and yet if she disappears, so does the symptom of man, as Lacan says. And if there is no longer a symptom, there is no longer a language [*langage*], and therefore there is no longer a man either' (Lemoine-Luccioni, 1976, p. 10; 1987, p. 4). And so, all woman can do is retain her (or his?) symptoms, live with 'her share and her suffering', 'the zenith of *jouissance*'(!). (p. 8; p. 2), her only alternative being to 'disappear as woman' (p. 10; p. 4).

And 'no sexual revolution will move these dividing lines, neither that which goes between man and woman, nor that which divides woman' (p. 9; p. 3). Such comments are worthy of note in a book which claims to be 'an analytic work, not a philosophical nor a political one', a book which is not very concerned with 'knowing if woman must make the revolution in order to get the better of a *méconnaissance* which, up to now, may have prevented her from speaking' (p. 11; p. 4).

How can such contradictory statements be put forward in the space of two pages? Isn't the neutrality of the analyst beginning to betray itself, pronouncing dogmas about history from the depths of an armchair?

And when you write (Lemoine-Luccioni, 1976, p. 11; 1987, p. 5): 'My thoughts always merge with what one or another of my analysands say (men *or* women) as well as, through these words, with what the analysand that I am says; since one only hears what one is likely to say oneself, but which would remain unsaid without the other', 'one' is tempted to ask where this 'merging' leads. Might it not sometimes lead you to make the other say – or prevent the other from saying – something that you are unlikely to hear? By what authority do you write that 'he' or 'she' said this or that, had this or that fantasy if you do not spell out where *you* stand in relation to *your* sex, *your* things and *your* fantasies? How do you decide *who* is speaking?

Oh, you can easily object that being an analyst means listening to what the other says without taking sides, but on what basis do you determine who is *you* and who is the *other*? And isn't this other, male or female, the *other of you*? How can you tell if you don't give any interpretation of *your* transference on to the other? Technically of course it's not an easy question. But it seems at best naive to hide behind what your analysands (men and women) say in order to assert that 'what I write in their name is the unconscious, and the unconscious alone, it's not me saying that, it's them, I take no positions – neither ideological, political, nor philosophical . . . neither phallocratic nor sexuate [*sexuée*]? . . . – when I write it up'. Not that naivety prevents you from reaching certain judgements and passing certain condemnations. *Inconscient oblige*, you object. Which unconscious?

And if you 'ascribe' to woman an unconscious she does not have, if you claim that 'It is only insofar as she is all, that is, as man sees her and in that alone that the dear woman can have an unconscious',[3] or worse still if you assert that woman exists only as a symptom of man's language (Lemoine-Luccioni, 1976 p. 10; 1987, p. 4), then certain 'complaints' are less 'untenable' than you like to think. They complain – sometimes in court, as in rape cases, for example – that in your law, they no longer have access to *their* desires. But 'the reasons that are put forward by women are all untenable' (Lemoine-Luccioni, 1976, p. 7; 1987, p. 1), and 'if it is true that no one can or should accept slavery, the only question which remains when it is accepted, even requested, is this: What is it accepted for, for what benefit?' (p. 7; p. 4). It is up to you to provide an answer.

But how could you when your male masters have taught you that 'desire is always the same, regardless of sex' (Safouan, 1976, p. 157), that it is difficult to sexualize it within the field of the imaginary, in a word that one language [*langage*] – and traditionally, it is their language – is the only possible tongue [*langue*]. In the circumstances, all you can do is 'lend' women the benefit of the slavery man enjoys in relation to mastery. Whether or not that helps you to begin to say something about women's desire is a very different question. For what disorientates women is not so much their location – either devalued or over-valued – in object relations as their exile from what might be their place. Ecstasied from their space–time, always 'moving house' in the masculine phallic imaginary, they try to embody themselves in some 'thing' with which man can play, or even through which he might rediscover the value of his world of objects (Lemoine-Luccioni, 1976, pp. 154–5; 1987, pp. 130–1). Why not some element of his *House*? Why not some member of his *School*? Why not some book-'o' [*a–livre*] produced in the field of his language-'O' [*A–langue*]?

There again, for themselves, women are nowhere, touching everything, but never in touch with each other, lost in the air, like ghosts. Dissolved, absent, empty, abandoned, gone – gone away from themselves (Lemoine-Luccioni, 1976, p. 154; 1987, pp. 129–30). Whereas if they could have access to the imaginary of their desires, they would, rather, always be in movement, at home everywhere, finding their security in mobility, their *jouissance* in movement, nomads knowing only the frontiers of their living bodies. But if they are to do that, they cannot stay where they have been put. They must, rather, be able to leave the property in which they have been legally confined, so as to try to find their own place(s). And only an 'eminent Italian criminal lawyer' (*male*) could propose 'a law entitling them to keep their furniture in case of divorce' to save them from madness (Lemoine-Luccioni, 1976, pp. 154–5; 1987, p. 130). Presumably it's to prevent women from going mad that psychoanalysts now confine them amongst their furniture. In any case, once they have been duly confined, nothing more will be heard of it [*ça*], mad or not.

And you will be able to remain within the circle of your imaginary. You yourself say that it is *totalitarian*. That explains why you force the evolution of little girls' desire to fit in with the schemata that explain the evolution of little boys' desire, without taking the precaution of saying that you are talking about children (neuter) or man (in the generic sense). An example – and it is in examples that so many actions are bungled – of what might be going on immediately reveals the bid for power: a 'piece of furniture' (yet again) 'up against a place which is the place of language and of Truth (with a capital T)' (Safouan, 1976, p. 23; 1982, p. 133). Yes indeed, if a piece of furniture does come into the schema you have just applied to the girl's 'mute' demand, you will have a free hand. It will never contravene your schema. Your reference to Marx proves the point.

Commodities can only speak the language [*langage*] of those who produce–exchange–consume them. By the same criterion, your 'piece of furniture' can only speak the words that your desire lends it. But even if 'none of us are dispensed from thinking of ourselves as a piece of furniture'(?) (Safouan, 1975, p. 23; 1982, p. 133), being forced to be a piece of furniture and being unable to think of ourselves as such for want of a language [*langage*] is something else again. And that is what your cult of hollow divinities forces us to be. And what, 'effectively' (Safouan, 1975, p. 21; 1982, p. 131), are we now to take your capital fetishism – Other, Thing, Demand, Truth, Phallus – to mean if not, once again, a nihilistic religion in whose light any living, corporeal, or social reality is as nothing to you?

Oh yes, gentlemen psychoanalysts, desire is 'the daughter of an epoch' (Safouan, 1976, p. 19; 1982, p. 130). Which is precisely why you can *now* invest your desire in psychoanalysis, but also why you find yourselves being questioned by women's desire, whether you are willing to listen or not. And your attempts to reduce what they are trying to tell you to your eternal discourse – and to exorcize it by applying labels which *now* call that [*ça*] *'feminist militancy'*, though that does make you abandon your neutrality as soon as it is called into question – are clear signs of resistance, of your reluctance to acknowledge certain limits. Perhaps because they mark the *limits* of your imaginary?

And you want to keep it *all-inclusive*. To ensure that it remains so, you deny the *facts* by somewhat univocally declaring them to be fantasies. Some examples, perhaps?

Your attempts to demonstrate that your women analysands' anxieties about rape bear no relation to reality are enough to make virtually any woman laugh(?). These/their 'fantasies'(?) have to be seen as memories of various traumatic experiences, as images of events undergone, seen or overheard, or as the effect of a whole series of restrictions, prohibitions, impossibilities, oppressions omnipresent throughout the most day-to-day life of women. But a man who fails to recognize his own desire to rape – perhaps because he hasn't analysed it? – can only disavow the reality of his fantasy-objects in the name of woman.

Yet when you assert that the boy manages from a very early age to distinguish between the sexes by going on all kinds of indications, clothes in particular, without it occurring to him to relate these perceived differences to the body of the other (Safouan, 1976, p. 14; 1982, p. 126), aren't you saying that what matters to you is what hides, masks, displays, renders impossible or prohibits any relation between two bodies, except – sometimes – one of breaking and entering? That the cause of your desire is a veil that has to be lifted – sometimes? A 'semblance' that has to be deflowered sometimes – without knowing it? That it is the attractions of rape that both motivate and disappoint your desire? Because the body is always 'holed'? Only 'holed'? But what about *your language* [*langage*]? Don't your capital letters function as palliatives? Doesn't this parade of letters and master-words arrest speech in deep cavities where words – and their arguments – ring hollow? Hence your fear or anxiety about a certain 'thing'?

Statements like 'The phallic conditioning of narcissism in the subject irrespective of its sex' '*is established in, and only in, analytic practice*', 'a thesis which no direct observation could either validate or confirm', that form of observation being 'as useless here as it is in relation to the Oedipus complex' (Safouan, 1976, p. 15; 1982, p. 127; my emphasis) make it worthwhile to stop laughing long enough to ask you: why do you say things that are so far removed from reality? What good does it do you? Do you really believe this? If so, have you ever set foot outside your consulting rooms? And if not, what do you understand by reality?

On reading you, I find effectively that: 'It is not enough simply not to be a feminist to ensure that one knows one's place in the business of sex'! (Safouan, 1976, p. 12; 1982, p. 125). But if you were feminists – an unlikely hypothesis, given the real difference between the sexes and the fact that you exist outside any historical period – perhaps you would know a little more about your own place. Then you might – perhaps – understand why Freud demands that the woman analysand must come [*jouir*] vaginally. Because *it proves his potency*. 'Hardly an injunction to which it would be easy to respond' (Safouan, 1976, p. 17; 1982, p. 129)? Of course it's easy . . . Left to themselves, women have no difficulty in making themselves/ each other 'come vaginally'. All they have to do is to see themselves as under no obligation to satisfy *your* imaginary. You fail to recognize one simple *fact*: women can come without any help from you. That does not rule out the possibility of them wanting to come with you, though, as a general rule, they find it 'harder to respond' to that

injunction. But even if they do enjoy it with you, most of them say
nothing to you about their *jouissance*, and don't have much to 'show'
you. So as not to be frigidified in your gaze, your discourse, your
desire, your theory? Which might make you *think* that they have no,
or no more, sexual life. And is it not surprising that you should
learnedly decree that 'vaginal frigidity constitutes a definite sympto-
matic disturbance of sexual life in the woman' (Safouan, 1976, p. 18;
1982, p. 129; translation modified) without wondering whether this
might not be the *effect* on women of a disturbance of the sexuality of
men? You never raise the question of the state of your male sex life,
and particularly not of your 'verbal parade' (Safouan, 1976, p. 16,
1982, p. 128).

You also state in the same learned terms that 'in our view, female
homosexuality represents an arrest on the path to the assumption of
symbolic castration' (Safouan, 1976, p. 127), but you fail to recognize this *fact: your fantasies lay down the law.* The symbolic, which
you impose as a universal innocent of any empirical or historical
contingency, is *your* imaginary transformed into an order, into the
social. When you write, on your last page, that 'if we think of
marriage as an exchange between men with women as its object,
we find that women take on the unconscious signification of all
objects of exchange', that 'although we are increasingly free to
choose our own wives, the fact remains that we marry a brother-in-
law or a father-in-law', but that 'these propositions can easily be
transposed into a perspective in which marriage could be seen as an
exchange between women, with men as its object' (Safouan, 1976,
p. 127), 'one' might well ask you if your non-assumption of symbolic
castration – to use your terminology – doesn't lead you to 'transpose'
any social organization into another organization which you *imagine*
to suit your fantasy or your disavowal of homosexuality. Has your
symbolic ever been anything but a legal way of sanctioning *strict
cultural endogamy between men*? Psychoanalysts included.

You remind us that the mother is the first object of desire for both
boy and girl, conclude once more that 'everything happens for the
girl exactly as it does for the boy' (Safouan, 1976, p. 124), but fail to
recognize this *fact*: a desire for a body the same as, or different from,
one's own is not necessarily the same! Feeling, tasting, touching,
seeing, hearing a body which is the same or different is not without
its effects on desire. Isn't sex [*sexe*] always inscribed in the qualities

of a body in a non-secondary way? Are the genitals [*sexe*] an object which is separated–abstracted from the body in which it has its place? Is the imaginary from within which you listen, and in which you locate all your analysands – male and female – an incorporeal? Denying, disavowing from the outset that sex/the genitals too is/are constitutive of the body? That may correspond to *male fantasies* about the possible separation of the two, but it does not mean much to a woman, unless she is trapped in *your* imaginary. An imaginary exclusively dependent upon organs? Erogenous zones and their 'objects', sex(es) and language(s) [*langages*]?

Making psychoanalysis a theory and a practice of organs? Like medicine? At a more general level, both psychoanalysis and medicine would seem, without realizing it, to be caught up in a technocratic process which cares little for sexuate matter, for the site where organs are assembled into a living body.

Besides, the system of representations or signifiers supposed to account for the analytic experience is curiously impoverished when it comes to representatives of the body: blood, and circulation, air and respiration, consumption and the metabolism of food, etc. How does a psychoanalyst look at, conceive of or listen to the body? As a dead body? As something purely mechanical? As a machine for producing libido? What is immediately forgotten or foreclosed about the body, about sensible, corporeal sexuate matter when this mechanism is put in place?

And does not the fact that you have so much to say about the *debt* to the father, but very little, if anything, about the debt to the mother, mean that, for you, blood, life and the body have no value? Only organs, it would seem, have any value. You might, then, be asked whether the things that make the sexual relation impossible – fantasy, *objet-a* – might not be *symptoms* of an unpaid debt to the mother, false bodies, so to speak, semblances or pure objects which take the place of a repressed-censored relation with the body that gives life. Perhaps we are reminded of this unpaid debt – which can never be repaid in full, though it should be taken into account – by the impossibility of the sexual relation and the obligation to reproduce children, fantasies, theory, science, etc. And it is women who go on providing the material substratum: the body, and blood, and the life which nourish them, whilst you exercise the power of your organs.

Going back to historically dated anatomico-physiological arguments is obviously out of the question, but we do have to question the empire of a *morpho-logic*, or the imposition of formations which correspond to the requirements or desires of one sex as the norms of discourse and, in more general terms, of language [*langue*].

The empire of the phallus – the Phallus – is necessitated by the establishment of a society based upon patriarchal *power* in which the natural-maternal power to give birth comes to be seen as the phallic attribute of god–men, and establishes a new order that has to *appear* natural. Hence the need for a representation of 'nature', seen as good or bad depending on whether it is created by men or engendered by women. We can still read of the upheavals this brought about in the organization of the imaginary or the symbolic in the Greek myths and tragedies that date from the dawn of our logical era. From that point on, the values which subtend its articulation and deployment are isomorphic with the male imaginary.

And reducing the challenge to phallic domination to anatomico-physiological criteria betrays a wilful ignorance, to say the least, a refusal to interpret this domination as determining, through the order of language it governs and which sustains it, all your systems of representation, a resistance to questioning your perception of male–female difference, a difference, as you see it, within a single discourse which misrecognizes its sexual determinations.

This means that your would-be universal only meets the requirements of *your* sex. And as they are *yours*, you fail to see their particularity. You reject any inside or outside which resists, and would rather accuse the other of all kinds of idiocies than undergo what you call . . . symbolic castration: the possibility of an order that is different to yours.

The repression you bring to bear on any women's speech that does not obey your conception of the symbolic, your symbolic world, is therefore perfectly predictable, as are the arguments(?) you invoke and the tone in which you hand them down. To date, you have neither said nor written anything surprising on the subject; you are implacably programmed by a history which you refuse to question.

And when you make the 'simple point' that 'the question of what she wants is as much the question of the girl herself as it is that of the Other, whether this be Freud, ourselves or, again and in the first instance, the Mother' (Safouan, 1976, p. 20; 1982, p. 131), you never ask about the nature of the 'Other' you apply to girl and mother alike (with a capital M to insert her into your system?). You go on: 'There is no "you" unless it comes from the Other with a capital O', unless, that is, it comes from an ecstatic projection constituted as an omnipotent imaginary reality (a key 'grapnel' for your symbolic concatenation?), from whence 'I' comes back to me in inverted form.

But what if this schema did not correspond to the girl's desire? What if this relation with projection, inversion, the transcendental and the imaginary depended upon a male economy? On erection and ejaculation, and on the ec-stasy [*hors de soi*] they imply? Man appears to have attempted, not without disappropriation, to reappropriate her desire for himself by using his transcendental imaginary to construct a phallic morpho-logic. What you are trying to impose as a universal law is therefore your response to *your* requirements, reducing sexual difference to nothing in an endlessly repeated gesture.

Trying to find or find anew a possible imaginary for women through the movement that brings the lips into contact (cf. *Speculum*, especially the section '*L'Incontournable Volume*',[4] and *This Sex Which Is Not One*, especially the title essay and the sections entitled 'When our lips speak together' and 'The "mechanics" of fluids') does not imply a regressive retreat to the anatomical or to a concept of 'nature', nor is it a call to go back to genital norms – women have two lips several times over! It is more a question of breaking out of the autologtical and tautological circle of systems of representation and their discourse so as to allow women to speak their sex. The 'at least two' lips no longer corresponds to your morpho-logic; nor does it obey Lacan's model of the 'not all' to which the One is necessary. There is something of One, but something escapes it, resists it, is always lacking; there is something of One, but it has holes, rifts, silences which speak, murmur to and among themselves, etc. [*s'inter-disent, se mi-disent*]. Something of the real rebelling against all laws, but already produced under the empire of the law? Woman – a–woman – [*la femme*; '*l'afemme*'] has the privilege of dwelling at the sign of this lack or defect.

An Aristotelian *model*? Or already a Parmenidian model? The circle of the same is postulated or presupposed. In the 'at least two' lips, the process of becoming form – and circle – is not only never complete or completable; it takes place (no ek-sistance) thanks to this non-completion: the lips, the outlines of the body reflect one another, and there is born of this movement a self-perpetuating and self-developing formation of desire, an imaginary of the sexuate body whose form never detaches itself from the matter which generates it. Form and matter – and even the distinction between the terms is blurred – beget one another endlessly, and no form can be extrapolated from the body-support that gives birth to it.

And so the constitution of the sex of woman does not mean a 'lack', 'atrophy' or even 'envy' of the male sex (unless it is a socioculturally induced envy), nor does it mean a one-sided call for completion by the male sex in a penile or phallic mode. The difference between the sexes – when it takes place – implies the possibility, and it is always somewhat unpredictable, of increased or decreased *jouissance*, or even desire. For both women and men.

On the other hand, where women are concerned, the possibility of diminished desire is all too predictable, given the sexual mechanism you describe as a norm. And it is easy to understand why, according to you, women are so often frigid, and why you pay such attention to the extinction – of which they 'are not even aware'! (Safouan, 1976, p. 15; 1982, p. 128) – of their sexual life. Does that mean that you are prepared to question the formations of your own narcissism so as to change things? Are you resolved to interrogate your topo-logic so that the difference between the sexes can be reorganized in such a way that the narcissistic price for *jouissance* is not paid quite so one-sidedly, and so that women no longer have to renounce, even forget, their auto-erotism to become the instrument of yours?

Hence, as your master Lacan suggests, the need for a new look at the question of the status of the unconscious for women. For, 'if only masculine libido exists, it is only insofar as the dear woman is all, that is insofar as man sees her, and in that alone that the dear woman can have an unconscious'[5] He concludes with the premise that: 'It is to that extent I say that the imputation of the unconscious is an incredible act of charity.' But does this unconscious protect desire or take it away from women? Does it grant them libido, or take it away from them? In men's view, it 'imputes' it to them. This does not mean a structuring of their supposed 'drives', except, yet again, by annulling the difference between the sexes in a complementarity whose division is governed by men?

So you hear women talking about the desires – some of them

phallic – that you 'imputed' to them from the outset. Don't they have other desires? When a great number of women say that, after analysis, they feel 'shut in', 'closed up', 'withdrawn', that 'something inside them has become inaccessible', that they 'don't know how to get back in touch with it', what symptoms are they talking about? And it is very rare for them to react as you imagine they might: with paranoiac accusations against you, explosions of hatred, or a wish for vengeance. It is more usually a matter of depression or deep anxiety. Stemming from the disappearance of their power? From the 'imputation' of a *jouissance* which is not theirs? And from the ensuing narcissistic effects?

'Why listen to them? Why concentrate on the "manifest" without attending to the "latent"?', you object. Isn't it your intention to shut women up in your projections? In the discourse which subtends your listening? A latent substratum of your economy which you leave uninterpreted?

At a more manifest level, you have got them to adapt a little better to your society. Many of them recognize the debt they owe you: you have helped them to put up with conjugo-familial institutions in their various modalities, and to enter or remain within the circuits of work. There are fewer 'crises' in their relationship with your order. But oh the distress, when they admit what it cost them! When they are not ashamed to say so . . .

No doubt some of them have, more or less triumphantly, acceded to the phallic 'lot/division', and have become past mistresses at applying your laws, terrorizing and despising women who do not submit to them. Like the vestals of a cult in which they *believe*. But not without having *sacrificed* something of themselves. Your women militants demand the same oblation from their sisters. But you don't notice this orthodox militancy, and you have yet to begin to analyse it. After all, isn't it necessary to the maintenance of order?

One of its current battlecries is that the (jubilatory?) assumption of *bisexuality* is the path to salvation. Parrying women's demands to accede to their desires and their language [*langage*]? Perhaps if they try to become men, they will cease their 'complaints' and 'demands'? And then silence can be restored?

But isn't bisexuality both genetically inscribed in the body and a process of identifications? And given that the anatomico-physiological tends to be something of a bugbear for you (at least consciously), I assume that when you claim that Freud is 'more revolutionary' than certain women 'when he posits a fundamental bi-sexuality and a signifying differentiation' (Lemoine-Luccioni, 1976, p. 65; 1987, p. 53) you are referring to questions of identity. And therefore to a play of identifications – assuming that you do not believe in sexual essences. How are identifications differentiated in men and women? Do women identify with the other, or do they identify the other with themselves? In the mechanisms you describe, and judging by your interpretative schemata, they identify with the other. How could they fail to do so, if there is only *one* language [*langue*] and if it is structured by principles, and especially principles of identity, which are determined by only one sex? Men begin by identifying the other with the self, assimilating, incorporating and introjecting the other so as to constitute a matrix of identifications.

At the level of sexual representatives or representations, this distribution of identifications means that all there is is a *double polarity* within the economy of a *single sex*. Because anyone who identifies with the other surrenders the 'identity' of his or her sex, and anyone who identifies the other with the self reduces the other to his or her own. So where might bisexuality lie for women? When they have become other – masculine or phallic – what place is left for women, for their desire of *jouissance* as women? In what is imposed upon them in a secondary way by such identifications?

The call for bisexuality does not pose any serious threat – but it does threaten to reinforce the established order. It has the further advantage of begging or masking the question of relations with the same body or the same sex. Bisexuality – fantasmatic or identificatory – is a pretext which allows psychoanalysts to keep their homosexual desires latent. Does that mean that they have sublimated them? How?

And even today. Would you not rather look at and theorize what goes on between women rather than analyse your own homosexuality? Or articulate something about it at long last? In that case, doesn't your practice as an analyst, be it a matter of listening to analysands or of the workings of your societies, and the theory you derive from it, remain in the register of *acting out* [English in the original]. Why the *show* [English in the original]? Who is it for? According to your own explanations, which you still apply to relations between women, it is meant to signify something to your father, 'something which occurs beyond . . . not beyond language [*langage*], but beyond what the subject can articulate in that language.' What is it in your relationship with your father – and in psychoanalysis – that 'has become "stuck" and that necessitates this detour through acting out before it can be signified' (Safouan, 1976, p. 39)?

As for women, would it not be more likely that they are trying to demonstrate something to their mothers, to other women? The fact that the father sees this purely as something which has been staged for his benefit can presumably be interpreted as meaning that in his case the scopic drive predominates, as the *belief* that a woman's desire can only be addressed to him.

Hence the lack of any possible woman-to-woman language [*langage*], a lack which seems to him to be a norm? Hence the fact that in his language [*langue*] women cannot signify themselves/their desire to themselves/each other? Whatever you may think, women do not need to go through the looking glass to know that mother and daughter have a body of the same sex. All they have to do is touch one another, listen to one another, smell one another, see one another – without necessarily privileging the gaze, without a beautifying mask, without submitting to a libidinal economy which means that the body has to be covered with a veil if it is to be desirable! But these two women cannot speak to each other of their affects in the existing verbal code, and they cannot even imagine them in the ruling systems of representations. Love and desire between women and in women are still without signifiers that can be articulated in language [*langue*]. The result is paralysis, somatization, non-differentiation between one woman and another, enforced rejection or hatred, or at best 'pretence' [*faire comme*]. The girl's earliest pleasures will remain wordless; her earliest narcissizations will have no words or sentences to speak their name, even retroactively. When a girl begins to talk, she is already unable to speak of/to herself. Being exiled in man's speech, she is already unable to auto-affect. Man's language [*ce parler homme*] separates her from her mother and from other women, and she speaks it without speaking in it.

Isn't the exclusivity of man's talk, and man-to-man talk a guarantee of strict cultural endogamy? Of incest between father and son, between brothers, endlessly perpetuated in the realm of semblance? And isn't that the incest we should be interpreting now? For if mother–son incest is a threat to the cultural order, the father–son incest perpetuated by this culture is a threat to the order of the living.

No doubt your all too mechanical mode of listening will already have found some interpretative palliative to what I am trying to say to you. You will see it as a 'desire for vengeance', for 'revenge' against 'my father', as a need to demonstrate it openly (cf. Safouan, 1976; 1982), or, more generally, as a drive to 'show myself' to 'expose' myself to you men so as to be able to prove that I exist(?) as a male or female subject [*sujet ou sujette*] (cf. Lemoine-Luccioni, 1976; 1987). Unless of course you see it as the 'hate' that results from a badly dissolved transference – or a well dissolved transference(?) – depending on how you describe the end of the analysis. Or perhaps you will read it as my inability to accomplish the work of mourning. Why?

Let me laugh aloud for a while. You see, you understand everything in terms of your schemas, your code, your imaginary, your fantasies . . . which really are far too partial, in every sense of the word. For the most part, women's desires, words and *jouissance* elude them. You listen to and perceive only those elements in them that signify a mimesis, impotent in the face of the power of your order, a wish or a need to seduce you by pretending to be what you say they are for fear of your various reprisals, a silence to which is added, thanks to the effects of suggestion, statements which are your statements. So you don't hear-perceive *everything*. Or every *woman*.

You hand out certificates of 'femininity' in due (masculine or feminine?) form and rate as 'theorists' of female sexuality the men and women who, consciously or unconsciously, fall in line with your discourse, who support your power and who lend themselves, in accordance with your wishes, to the phallo–capitalist–fetishist market economy. As for the others, you submit what they say to your value judgements without even having listened to them or understood them, without giving yourself time to understand. You *exclude* them.

But you use their work, their desire and their *jouissance* to feed the machines that churn out your *écrits*, seminars and colloquia. Without mentioning your resources, except in the mode of disavowal. Without indicating what is at stake in your debates: the reasons for your, after all, quite recent but so verbose, interest in women's sexuality, for instance. This revival of interest goes hand in hand with arrogant and derisory verdicts on the struggles women are waging to find or refind access to the language [*langage*] of their *jouissance*.

All this has to be seen, can only be seen, as a *symptom*, as a symptom of rejection of and scorn for the desire of the *other*, a rejection and scorn closely related to your need to remain enslaved to your male masters and their law(s).

Let me tell you, gentlemen psychoanalysts, you are pitiful exploiters. You don't even have the daring, the inspiration, the joy, the energy, or the pride of your own phallocratic assertions and positions. You hide – perhaps in shame – behind scientific honesty(?), benevolent neutrality(?) and conformity to the image – guaranteed by whom? – of the good little duty psychoanalyst who serves and defends the correct theoretical line, and therefore the future of psychoanalysis.

You forget just how old you are, you know. You are more anachronistic than the oldest man in the west. If you want to understand what the analysands are saying, you would do better to read Greek myths and tragedies than your *écrits*, which are already too doctrinaire for anything of what you call the real to speak its name in them. You remember nothing of your birth, of your childhood or, therefore, of *your language* [*langue*].

And before you set yourself up as judges of the desire that animates a woman, bear in mind that it might be time – if we are to re-evaluate the ethics of psychoanalysis – to think about a new ethics of the passions.

A suggestion for your future seminars? Yes, make sure you keep them even more exclusive. Keep to yourselves. Certain women might disturb you with their 'cries', 'chatter', 'naive remarks', 'complaints' or 'demands'. And so long as you have not interpreted the state of *your* passions – *amongst yourselves* –, all that can come of their wish to enter or remain in your circles is their death.

And when it comes to laws, there is one that you forget with a passion: the law of *real* death.

NOTES

1 [O[ther], o[ther]; in Lacanian 'algebra' A[utre] signifies the Other in the symbolic, a[utre], the other in the imaginary, (trans.)].

2 In accordance with the conventions of *Critique*, the journal which

published 'The poverty of psychoanalysis' in 1977, examples had to be given; even so, 'you' is used in the plural. My decision to write this text was bound up with the suicide of a woman psychoanalyst who was a friend. The workings of the analytic world are responsible for her suicide, and others, particularly because it refuses to heed an ethical and theoretical interpellation on the part of those men and women for whom self-destruction is the only remaining solution. [The references are as follows. Eugénie Lemoine-Luccioni, *Partage des femmes*, Paris: Seuil 1976; trans. Marie-Anne Davenport and Marie-Christine Réguis, *The Dividing of Women or Woman's Lot*, London: Free Association Books, 1987. Moustapha Safouan, *La Sexualité féminine dans la doctrine freudienne*, Paris: Seuil, 1976. The first chapter is translated by Jacqueline Rose as 'Feminine sexuality in psychoanalytic doctrine', in Jacqueline Rose and Juliet Mitchell, (eds), *Jacques Lacan and the Ecole freudienne: feminine sexuality*, London: MacMillan, 1982 (trans.)].

3 Jacques Lacan, *Encore*, Paris: Seuil, 1975, p. 90.
4 [In this volume under the title 'Volume without contours' (ed.)].
5 Lacan. *Encore*, p. 90.

Translated by David Macey with Margaret Whitford

6

The Limits of the Transference

The cathartic operation: that is the major difficulty in the analytic work, a task bordering on the impossible if it is to be accomplished without either amputation or sacrifice.

When it is a matter of *analysis of women, between women*, this path has to be invented, created. In concealed fashion, they have always been implicated in the sacrificial, already deprived of themselves, already ec-centric when the subject – object separation is posited as it is by discourse. Our grammar remains foreign to this becoming of feminine *jouissance*, which loses its self-affection and the possibility of speaking its name therein.

Unable to create their own words, women remain and move in an immediacy without any transitional, transactional object. They take-give without mediation, commune without knowing it with and in a flesh they do not recognize: maternal flesh not reducible to a reproductive body, more or less shapeless amorous matter to which there could be no debt, no possible return.

The Oedipus complex states the law of the non-return of the daughter to the mother, except in the *doing like* [*faire comme*] of motherhood. It cuts her off from her beginnings, her conception, her genesis, her birth, her childhood.

According to the norm, all that remains to her for her journey is half of herself: that [*celle*] which is not her, but of which only that [*ça: id*] remains for her to love.

Divided in two by the Oedipus complex (and henceforth situated between two men, father and lover?), exiled in the masculine, paternal world. Wandering, a supplicant in relation to values she could not appropriate for herself.

By that criterion, she would be the only one to desire, but she would desire in lack or a dereliction that dispossesses the father himself of his possible plenitude, as the fulfilment of desire can only take place in an attraction that preserves the path of the becoming of the desire of both.

According to Freud, this becoming woman is never finished (which does not preclude the possibility of woman being arrested at some moment of her journey). From his point of view, her becoming is effectively interminable, cannot be effected. It lacks a beginning and an end, roots and efflorescence, all memory of the event of their incarnation, all anticipation of blooming. And so women are dispossessed of access to life and to death as affirmative responsibilities, leaving their identity as free, living subjects in the trust of the other.

Imagined and thought of as a sheath or envelope for man's genitals [*sexe*], woman's genitals [*sexe*] put her in a position of reduplicating closure. They lack the porosity that is in excess of confinement, a fluidity that might be, not a loss, but a source–resource of new energies. Could the depth of immersion be proportional to as yet-undiscovered depths?

This does not mean regression to the intra-uterine, but access to the not-yet, or never-formed, -defined, -identified, -spoken. Not yet or never-born? Pouring forth in a flow which disconcerts entropy, reopens the world and regenerates the organism in a difference that is neither complementarity nor inversion – figures always bound up with the quantitative, with calculation and the maintenance of the already-economized, assimilated, disassimilated, instead of with access to the qualitative, or to the source.

Two qualitative differences need to be discovered, to be related – one which takes place in sexual difference, and one that can be lived in sympathy between women. No doubt the one cannot exist without the other, but they do not correspond to the same affection. Folding back or obliterating one into the other may reduce both to the quantitative; the effect of forgetting or failing to recognize that there can be, that there are two great others, two Others – one female and one male? Each sex [*sexe*] should be considered in relation to its corresponding ideal, its transcendental. If each sex does not strive to realize its powers, an alliance with or an encounter between the energies of both remains impossible. One always encroaches on the other, without fulfilling its own destiny, without finding the blossoming of its becoming and its fertilization by the other.

Deprived of any autonomous ideality, isn't the woman–mother in danger of being reduced to a fiction? The empty gestures of an enforced everydayness, a single or plural image, a mechanism or a dream, a shade or even a ghost, she is never unified in her insistence or existence,[1] for want of the words to envelop her, cover her, assist her in passing from interior to exterior, situate her in an identity, like a shelter that would accompany her, clothe her in herself and protect her without need to cling or give her allegiance to the world of the other. To which she can then open up and yet remain separate(d) without being continually split apart. Rifts between the sexes take place inside a forgotten, repressed, denied, confused maternal: a universe at once the same and other that allows neither difference nor encounter nor alliance.

Unless there is a space for sublimation by and between women, doesn't the analytic scene become impossible?

Women having no soul, how can one or the other of the women analytic partners re-mark the limits of their bodies, their desire? Quite apart from the fact that, for them, there is no transactional or transitional object unless they create one which they can exchange and share between them.

Traditionally, this creation, this sharing, took place through food. Providing food was woman's lot. That scene having been forbidden in the so-called analytic scene, and that creation having no words to speak its name in the enactment of the gesture, it remains for us to invent a practice in which neither analysand nor analyst is dispossessed by an irremediable voracity, a scene that is not restricted to orality or subsequent stages, which makes room for – and not like a child psychoanalyst – the intra-uterine and access to respiration and to the gaze opening on to what is not yet an object: sensitive, sensual touching, the still contemplative opening of the eyes before any precise definition or capture of the object.

The limit of the transference would appear to be this distanceless proximity between women – between mother and daughter? – distanceless because no symbolic process allows us to account for it. Rather than recognizing this deficiency and trying to remedy it, those who should be articulating this difference in the analytic scene, restricted or generalized, often play mother, play the archaism and psychoticizing regression card – doubles and stand-ins for the maternal that cannot satisfy the same relation with the placenta, milk, the skin or the mucous membrane and which therefore aspire in an empty transparence or in the void.

By standing in for the mother, the man–analyst gives up his own sex and frustrates the woman analysand of hers, reducing to nothing – despite an oneiric charm – the carnal mother–daughter, woman–woman relationship. And the man–woman relationship too, except as aspiration towards the lost flesh, to lack, to nostalgia?

Whilst it is relatively commonplace to talk of relations of merging or fusion, we still have to arrive at a different interpretation of what is in play in these fusional relationships. The placentary abode and the adhesion of the placenta to the mother's womb obey an other economy and are liberated otherwise.

But there is another mode of confusion between subjects, or rather psyches: the consumption(?) of the sex [*sexe*], the body of another woman, turning her inside-out and closing the threshold where she is open.[2] Here, the woman is neither in the place nor in place of the mother. She is taken as woman, exhausted long before any reproduction or miming of her/its appearance. What is innermost in her, the *jouissance* of her retouching, are used so that the other may become, without becoming, what she is because of her birth and her history. This becoming therefore lacks roots and growth. It wraps itself in the *jouissance* of another woman or uses it as a runway [*sol*] for a flight that neglects to ensure its foundations, its returns to earth,[3] something of its identity, of its self-identity, of its fidelity to self in the course of a trajectory. The absence of any imaginary and symbolic ground [*sol*] accorded or recognized 'on the side of women' means that all this takes place in a potentially deadly immediacy preceding any master–slave dialectic.

A chiasmus takes place in the immediate, with no mirror. Left and right are inverted in a face-to-face encounter which leaves no room for the image of the other, appropriated and traversed towards some – traditionally paternal – infinite. Where movements taken from the mother–woman are forgotten?

All women can do is return to some tactile in-finite/un-finished. Touch, the substratum of all the senses, acts before any clear-cut positioning of subject and object. Its operation is always almost immediate, the site of a *jouissance* indefinable as such, but which calls out to be given boundaries, covered up, completed.

Being without subject or object, what 'do women want'? Absolute wanting [*vouloir*]. Being without identity, what 'does she want'? The wanting of the Other. Not that of the God–Father, but a wanting *more*. They want the mystery of the infinite of numeration, the infinitely great, because they cannot perceive, in the tactile, the infinitely small, or the infinitely close. They want something that overflows the numerical within the number, that insists in the form of the account. They want what has not yet taken place, what is appearing, becoming, taking shape in front of their eyes, or even what they perceive before any gaze. In the absence of a language [*langue*] that would allow them to partake in begetting [*engendre-ment*], they want the movement of generation [*génération*]. They want to take for themselves all that grows, all that is beginning to be, emerging from a chaos in which they seek the place where they are lost. They want that which has not yet been fixed-frozen in a finished architecture, what is yet to be born.

Women? Yes, as something borrowed from the desire of an other or Other still in darkness. Scarcely unveiled? Even that is an over-statement. Becoming is more important to them than the secret of any fetish. Always unsatisfied? If it means that, being arrested in their generation, they want the very movement of begetting. They want, without end, without a model, the presumed wanting of the one who walks in wanting [*dans le vouloir*] – a model without a model, an example whose paradigm they erase. They want to seize that which already exists so as to bring it back to an invisible source – their source? – a place from whence they might create, create themselves *ex nihilo*? Has not history forced this impossibility upon them: they must continue to live, cut off from their beginning, and from their end?

Woman must ceaselessly measure herself against her beginning and her sexuate determination, beget anew the maternal within her, give birth within herself to mother and daughter in a never-completed progression. She who possesses, in the darkness, the subterranean resource is mother; she who moves on the surface of the earth, in the light, is daughter. She becomes woman if she can unite within her the most secret energies that lie deepest in her body-womb, with life in the broad light of day. Then, an alliance no longer means being drawn into an abyss, but an encounter in the blossoming of a new generation.

There, something happens of a psychic order, and of a cosmic order. An encounter that would never have taken place between the two? A long story to be sorted out, to be unfolded from morning to night, from night to a new dawn. A story to do with time and the way we measure it, and which might have an impact on the numerical itself? Another economy of the whole, which requires a new language [*langage*].

The *lips*? The open, the in-finite/unfinished, not the indefinite retreat from the impossible to live, but opening, here, now, continually. *Retouching*. The most subtle return, which progresses without going back, without closing the circle, sentient without resentment.

How to make this perceptible to one who feeds on this touch in order to wrap, enclose, themselves in it, to one who turns this gift of space–time into a skin enclosing their refusal to respond or correspond in the open? How can women – especially amongst themselves – refrain from taking from this gift the means to palliate their dereliction through a more or less immediate and paradoxical mimetic identification? This operation turns the donor inside out before there is any gift–object and closes the path of the taker; a gesture which involves a sort of capitalization of the mucous membrane, an exteriorization of what is most inner. The daughter–woman tries to re-wrap herself in the desiring flesh of the other, clothes herself in it again and again, heedless of her own birth and of her own retouching. She makes for herself protective gestures, without knowing from whence she obtains what shelters her, helps her.

Feeling safe now, she can attempt to look back at the woman who is the start of her journey and at that other birth which covers her – that other is no longer. Or at least is no longer visible to her, now that she is clothed in what could be seen of the other. Of the Other–woman? Never perceived as such, except in the fact that she is thought to be inexhaustible?

In the absence of the woman–mother's identity, the speech [*parole*] of the 'daughters' is spoken as a gestual mimesis or flows into the mysterious desire of/for that Other woman. Verbal exchange therefore becomes impossible or useless. Everything takes place before speech intervenes.

Mimetic appropriation by women is still the most terrible thing of all because it is practised without any feminine ideality or model. The absence of a ideal maternal and female figure for women results in the fact that mimicry between women becomes the flaying of one woman by the other, the reduction of the skin and of the most mucous to forms [*figures*] into which they flow in order to exist, often quite unconsciously. They take the appearance of the other before there is any image, and may leave her their own, which they no longer want, for lack of a self-representation to venerate, contemplate, admire or even adore.

This abduction takes place before any positioning of love or hate. In the absence of a valid image [*figure*] of themselves in the other – or the Other – they take apart the face and appearance of the other–woman in order to feed and clothe themelves. They are deprived of the artistic, iconic, religious(?) mediation that might allow them to look at and admire themselves in some ideal her, which might support the eventuality of their face-to-face encounter, some work of beauty that would be neither one nor the other and that could facilitate the transition between the in-finite/unfinished that they are morphologically and the quest for the infinite. In the absence of that support [*relais*], they enclose the infinite in an endless freeplay or collapse it into formlessness, into the archaism of a primitive chaos.

That which constitutes a temporality, an inhabitable space–time has no place or is accomplished blindly, in a night in which the other has no face. The other woman is exhausted from within, not recognized in the contours of a carnal existence. And unless it becomes the speech [*parole*] of the flesh, a gift and message of the flesh, speech remains an outer skin that again and again exhausts, flays, that falls and covers without giving up its secret.

Two lips? *Retouching*: the unclosed containment of the body. The envelope of the skin is neither sutured nor open on to a 'canal' which takes or rejects, but opening on to the touch of at least two, or four, mucous membranes: the upper and lower lips.

If the skin is peeled off or folded back, there is no more retouching. The mucous membrane of one becomes that which surrounds the other. The skin inside out? The absence of any possible caress and the capture of the intimacy of the body, consumption of the flesh becoming a placentary envelope for the other. A woman tacitly becoming a daughter? Within this habitat, all regressions can be imagined, or lived prior to any imaginable fantasy. Unconscious exploitation of a primitive shelter and of what is given there – the necessities of life.

Within this nourishing home screenplays, oral, anal, phallic are re-run. . . . This fiction exacts a high price from the one from whom this excess is borrowed, as the first house is used, used up without any debt, any payment, without any record made of it. And therefore without consciousness, without memory, except the terror of abandonment?

So this primitive cave or womb is henceforth imagined to be a dangerous rift, a chaos or an 'empty vase'? This container does not correspond, in interpretation, to a procreative womb: a maternal-feminine place capable of conceiving and not just in the strict sense of the term, the intimacy of a receptacle as a potential for engendering, from the retouching of the lips, a female desire.

Without it, without this reversal, or unless female *jouissance* is located in its relation to the maternal, how can we articulate limits between women? The very openness of their bodies, of their flesh, of their genitals [*sexe*] makes the question of boundaries difficult. That requires a qualitative difference. Of course no woman has the morphology of another. That might allow us to get beyond competition within the quantitative? But the *more*, the struggle for superiority between two sames persists in the absence of the discovery and valorization of a sensible-transcendental[4] – a female transcendental against which each woman can measure herself rather than progressing only by taking the place of the mother, the other woman or the man. Which is assigned her as a task? And without any indication of the subjective operation at work in it.

Usually, the moment of the *like* (the other) is skipped, erased. For lack of identity? If it is explicit, the *like* becomes the minimal object: 'like you'. And I owe you the difference of the leap from past to future? Without price. Like you, and I owe you my becoming and its measure.

What is lacking is the double measure, the double stake, the double risk [*mise en jeu*] and the qualitative difference. Sexual difference mobilized, potentially, in a relationship with the divine? In reserve, there. If God is always imagined to be a father, how can women find in Him a model of identity, a completed image or figure of themselves which could free them from the competition for measurable superiority?

How are they constantly to make greatest and smallest meet? And, above all, move from one qualitative to another? A difficult energetistic question, especially when there is no object, no comparison between the two poles. They must become creations. Art *objects?* In that way two subjects can advene one to the other, and an alliance between the two becomes possible.

This is not so much a problem of mastery as the question of a creation allowing participation in the *jouissance* of the object or its cocreation: a useful work because it marks, without destruction, the limits of energy, of the flesh and of the body, of desire and its possibilities. The creation or elaboration of the *object* becomes an architectonic of the body, of a life and a death that does not kill the other.

This creation might be the only thing that could allow the resolution of the transference. Although accustomed to privation, women are intolerant of frustration,[5] of the intervention of any discontinuity other than the one they know, of any segmentation of space–time which is not simply the amputation of part of the world. Of themselves as part of the world? They are more tolerant of the experience of not existing or insisting than feeling themselves measured in space and time, of remaining a pure reserve than perceiving their limits, which do not constitute those of a body or an envelope, but the living edges of a flesh opening.

Keep the lips closed? Sentient without resentment, feeling the touch that reduplicates before any reduplication in consumption: foetal, oral, mimetic. . . . This is said in silence, exchanged only with difficulty. . . . The means to assert and preserve that amorous female gesture without denudation or closure are yet to be found, created.

Within the transference, a certain limit, a certain threshhold is never crossed and always transgressed — the porosity of the mucous membranes. Many events can take place, through encounters with hands, eyes, ears, scents too, but the mucous never retouches itself carnally in the transference.

And already-constructed theoretical language [*langage*] does not speak the mucous. It remains a remainder, producing delirium, dereliction, wounds, sometimes exhaustion, mucous deployed in the journey that is an analysis, and which risks death if it is not resituated in its place. In that case, all thought becomes skin stripped from the other, speculation without roots or crown, feet or head, which devours–consumes the intimacy–interiority, of the body that ensures the passage from lowest to highest.

And so it comes about that the projection of 'the good' is reversed into the 'not good', anchored in an orality which forgets that it is already secondary. If the source is invisible, the other can believe himself to be the source, reversing the site from which he receives himself, standing above the site from whence flows that which gives birth to him, gives him to eat and to drink.

How can they – especially women – refrain from taking from this gift the means to palliate their dereliction through a more or less immediate mimetic gesture, turning the (self)-giver inside out and not leaving the path open to the one who seeks nourishment? What economy(?) must they be taught for them to become without becoming closed, to exchange in the open something which is not nothing, which is not reduced to nothingness, without misrecognizing this question in its full implications.

Sometimes naively vitalist, don't they become murderous through indifference to the significance of death? Our tradition has not taught them to take responsibility for and watch over their own death.

But the transference is not only the projection or reprojection of a history; it is also an appropriation of the other – here, now, the food the analysand partakes of to bring his/her analytic process to a successful conclusion and live his/her life well. The analyst also functions as the *raw material* of the treatment. Being a guarantor or cover of/for knowledge [*connaissance*] does not spare him/her from making these extremes meet: remaining a reservoir of dynamism, of breath, of what the analysand is looking for to sustain his/her subsistence and to stay firmly anchored to knowledge [*savoir*]. The analyst must remain the guarantor of both these places, of both *bridges* – and they can always be remodelled – between the other and him/herself without colluding in consumption and without confining or shutting up the needs or desires of he/she who trusts in him/her.

The issue of the transference seems to revolve around who can best perceive the other, who can return the other, or return in the other, closest to his/her source, a gesture almost never perceived as bilateral. The third term in the transference becomes the limits not only of the body but also of the mucous, not only the walls but also the experience of the most extraordinary intimacy: a communication or communion which respects the life of the other whilst still tasting the strangeness of his/her desire. Impossible to exhaust? The outer limits of interpretation, beyond which the risk of aggression is at its most implacable.

And where one also discovers the perception of the possibility or necessity of calm. An interval between the two, a release from quantitative estimates, to allow the opening on to an encounter of a different, peaceful quality. A ground other than, the same as, that of the highest intensity? Access to this is essential if there is to be an other.

The peaceful is not equivalent to death, either violent or contained within *neutrality*. It is a state of tranquillity which allows both to be, without eternal strife and without a lethal fusion. The peaceful can be engendered as self-harmony before and beyond the closure of language [*langue*], a harmony which lets the other be, a sort of extra-transferential reserve which allows the analyst to ensure his/her own solitude and to direct the other in or towards his/hers.

In the difference between the sexes, this peace and this harmony would signify acceptance and fulfilment of one's own sex, without seeking superiority over the alien or the stranger that insists in the other. This dimension of sexual difference constitutes the horizon of the possible unfolding of an analysis as an opening or an enigma rather than the peremptory imposition of the authority of a word [*parole*], a language [*langue*], a text. It contrives a space or site of liberty between two bodies, two flesh, which protects the partners by giving them boundaries.

In order to offer this alternative, the analyst must constantly keep present the dimension of his or her transference; the other to whom he or she listens must remain close and distant within a reversible and open transferential relationship, that links all possible positions in space and time. Remembering the configuration of bodies and their synchronic or diachronic relations, the analyst perceives him/herself as what he or she is, has been, is becoming, so as to hear the other without confusion. This listening marks the limits of his or her possibilities; it acts as the horizon dividing him or her from the analysand; the horizon of life and death, a matrix–envelope to be constantly reconstituted in its most nourishing and protective dimension, the opening remaining for becoming and reception by/of the other.

This matrix, anterior and posterior to that of any constituted discourse, the matrix for the singular history of a subject, is essential in the transferential relationship between women; there, it is found to be an absolute necessity. This does not mean that it is not an essential element in any analysis. But without it, listening to another woman becomes the destruction of the one, of the other, or the assimilation of both to a word [*parole*] or discourse they have not produced and of which they become the object.

For the analyst, constantly reinterpreting his/her transference is a necessity, not only his/her countertransference, but the basis on which he or she listens and gives space–time, the basis on which he or she gives himself or herself as the space–time in which he or she listens. The space–time he or she gives remains non-perceptible to the majority, who never restore to the analyst his or her skin or intimacy: a space–time that is a gift, moving from inside to outside, like a body already become flesh, offering itself or putting itself forward as the site in which the analytic scene takes place.

But who understands that the analyst creates room at the same time as listening? That he or she gives the horizon, listening in a space made possible by his or her relationship with space–time. Not every analysand succeeds in constituting an irreducible horizon for himself or herself. Yet that should be the end of the analysis – approaching the one and the other in their respective horizons, no longer constituted by rejection, hate or mastery, but moving and remaining open to the other. A permanent construction, without closure, whose rhythm and scansion are amorous, musical.

The end of the analysis might speak its name thus: 'Let us invent together that which allows us to live in and go on building the world, beginning with this world that is each of us.'

NOTES

1 [In Irigaray, these terms have the connotations, respectively, of transcendence on the male side (sometimes written 'ek-sistance' or referred to as ecstasy [*extase/hors-de-soi*]) and immanence on the female side (*insistance*, sometimes *instance*). They are linked to the idea of the sensible transcendental (see note 4 below) which is *both at once*, both transcendence and immanence. See also 'Questions to Emmanuel Levinas', note 4, in section III (ed.)].

2 [*le seuil de son entrouverture*. In the context of the morphology of women's bodies, Irigaray almost always uses *entrouvert*, meaning neither wide open nor completely closed, but partly, or slightly open, rather

than *ouvert*, open. *Entrouvert* has been translated throughout by *open* (ed.)].

3 [On the *sol* and the returns to earth, see 'Any Theory of the "Subject" Has Always Been Appropriated by the "Masculine"' in *Speculum*. Irigaray contrasts the male subject's need to *return to earth* (to the mother) with the continuous *retouching* of the two lips of the woman which structures – or could structure – her imaginary differently (ed.)].

4 [The sensible transcendental is a term which refers to the overcoming of the split between material and ideal, body and spirit, immanence and transcendence, and their assignment to women and men respectively. *Each* sex should be able to represent both possibilities (ed.)].

5 [See *Ce Sexe qui n'en est pas un/This Sex Which Is Not One*, pp. 57/61. *Privation* belongs to the register of the real; *frustration* to the register of the imaginary; *castration* to the register of the symbolic (ed.)].

Translated by David Macey with Margaret Whitford

7

The Power of Discourse and the Subordination of the Feminine

Interview

Why do you begin your book with a critique of Freud?

Strictly speaking, *Speculum* has no beginning or end. The architectonics of the text, or texts, confounds the linearity of an outline, the teleology of discourse, within which there is no possible place for the 'feminine', except the traditional place of the repressed, the censured.

Furthermore, by 'beginning' with Freud and 'ending' with Plato we are already going at history 'backwards'. But it is a reversal 'within' which the question of the woman still cannot be articulated, so this reversal alone does not suffice. That is why, in the book's 'middle' texts – *Speculum*, once again – the reversal seemingly disappears. For what is important is to disconcert the staging of representation according to *exclusively* 'masculine' parameters, that is, according to a phallocratic order. It is not a matter of toppling that order so as to replace it – that amounts to the same thing in the end – but of disrupting and modifying it, starting from an 'outside' that is exempt, in part, from phallocratic law.

But to come back to your question. *Why this critique of Freud?*

Because in the process of elaborating a theory of sexuality, Freud brought to light something that had been operative all along though it remained implicit, hidden, unknown: *the sexual indifference that underlies the truth of any science, the logic of every discourse*. This is readily apparent in the way Freud defines female sexuality. In fact, this sexuality is never defined with respect to any sex but the masculine. Freud does not see *two sexes* whose differences are articulated in the act of intercourse, and, more generally speaking, in the imaginary and symbolic processes that regulate the workings of a society and a culture. The 'feminine' is always described in terms of deficiency or atrophy, as the other side of the sex that alone holds a monopoly on value: the male sex. Hence the all too well-known 'penis envy'. How can we accept the idea that woman's entire sexual development is governed by her lack of, and thus by her longing for, jealousy of, and demand for, the male organ? Does this mean that woman's sexual evolution can never be characterized with reference to the female sex itself? All Freud's statements describing feminine sexuality overlook the fact that the female sex might possibly have its own 'specificity'.

Must we go over this ground one more time? In the beginning, writes Freud, the little girl is nothing but a little boy; castration, for the girl, amounts to accepting the fact that she does not have a male organ; the girl turns away from her mother, 'hates' her, because she observes that her mother doesn't have the valorizing organ the daughter once thought she had; this rejection of the mother is accompanied by the rejection of all women, herself included, and for the same reason; the girl then turns towards her father to try to get what neither she nor any woman has: the phallus; the desire to have a child, for a woman, signifies the desire to possess at last the equivalent of the penis; the relationship among women is governed either by rivalry for the possession of the 'male organ' or, in homosexuality, by identification with the man; the interest that women may take in the affairs of society is dictated of course only by her longing to have powers equal to those of the male sex, and so on. Woman herself is never at issue in these statements: the feminine is defined as the necessary complement to the operation of male sexuality, and, more often, as a negative image that provides male sexuality with an unfailingly phallic self-representation.

Now Freud is describing an actual state of affairs. He does not invent female sexuality, nor male sexuality either for that matter. As a 'man of science', he merely accounts for them. The problem is that he fails to investigate the historical factors governing the data with which he is dealing. And, for example, that he takes female sexuality as he sees it and accepts it as a *norm*. That he interprets women's sufferings, their symptoms, their dissatisfactions, in terms of their individual histories, without questioning the relationship of their 'pathology' to a certain state of society, of culture. As a result, he generally ends up resubmitting women to the dominant discourse of the father, to the law of the father, while silencing their demands.

The fact that Freud himself is enmeshed in a power structure and an ideology of the patriarchal type leads, moreover, to some internal contradictions in his theory.

For example, woman, in order to correspond to man's desire, has to identify herself with his mother. This amounts to saying that the man becomes, as it were, his children's brother, since they have the same love object. How can the question of the Oedipus complex and its resolution be raised within such a configuration? And thus the question of sexual difference, which, according to Freud, is a corollary of the previous question?

Another 'symptom' of the fact that Freud's discourse belongs to an unanalysed tradition lies in his tendency to fall back upon anatomy as an irrefutable criterion of truth. But no science is ever perfected; science too has its history. And besides, scientific data may be interpreted in many different ways. However, no such considerations keep Freud from justifying male aggressive activity and female passivity in terms of anatomical-physiological imperatives, especially those of reproduction. We now know that the ovum is not as passive as Freud claims, and that it chooses a spermatozoon for itself to at least as great an extent as it is chosen. Try transposing this to the psychic and social register. Freud claims, too, that the penis derives its value from its status as reproductive organ. And yet the female genital organs, which participate just as much in reproduction and if anything are even more indispensable to it, nevertheless fail to derive the same narcissistic benefit from that status. The anatomical references Freud uses to justify the development of sexuality are almost all tied, moreover, to the issue of reproduction. What happens when the sexual function can be separated from the reproductive function (a hypothesis obviously given little consideration by Freud)?

But Freud needs this support from anatomy in order to justify a theoretical position especially in his description of woman's sexual development. 'What can we do?' he writes in this connection, transposing Napoleon's phrase: 'Anatomy is destiny'. From this point on, in the name of that anatomical destiny, women are seen as less favoured by nature from the point of view of libido; they are often frigid, nonaggressive, nonsadistic, nonpossessive, homosexual depending upon the degree to which their ovaries are hermaphroditic;

they are outsiders where cultural values are concerned unless they participate in them through some sort of 'mixed heredity', and so on. In short, they are deprived of the worth of their sex. The important thing, of course, is that no one should know who has deprived them, or why, and that 'nature' be held accountable.

Does this critique of Freud go so far as to challenge psychoanalytic theory and practice?

Certainly not in order to return to a precritical attitude towards psychoanalysis, nor to claim that psychoanalysis has already exhausted its effectiveness. It is rather a matter of making explicit some implications of psychoanalysis that are inoperative at the moment. Saying that if Freudian theory indeed contributes what is needed to upset the philosophic order of discourse, the theory remains paradoxically subject to that discourse where the definition of sexual difference is concerned.

For example, Freud undermines a certain way of conceptualizing the 'present', 'presence', by stressing deferred action, overdetermination, the repetition compulsion, the death drive, and so on, or by indicating, in his theory or his practice, the impact of so-called unconscious mechanisms on the language of the 'subject'. But, himself a prisoner of a certain economy of the logos, he defines sexual difference by giving *a priori* value to Sameness, shoring up his demonstration by falling back upon time-honoured devices such as analogy, comparison, symmetry, dichotomous oppositions, and so on. Heir to an 'ideology' that he does not call into question, Freud asserts that the 'masculine' is the sexual model, that no representation of desire can fail to take it as the standard, can fail to submit to it. In so doing, Freud makes manifest the presuppositions of the scene of representation: *the sexual indifference* that subtends it assures its coherence and its closure. Indirectly, then, he suggests how it might be analysed. But he never carries out the potential articulation between the organization of the unconscious and the difference between the sexes. – Which is a theoretical and practical deficiency that may in turn constrict the scene of the unconscious. Or might it rather serve as the *interpretive lever* for its unfolding?

Thus we might wonder whether certain properties attributed to the unconscious may not, in part, be ascribed to the female sex, which is censured by the logic of consciousness. Whether the feminine *has* an unconscious or whether it *is* the unconscious. And so forth. Leaving these questions unanswered means that psychoanalysing a woman is tantamount to adapting her to a society of a masculine type.

And of course it would be interesting to know what might become of psychoanalytic notions in a culture that did not repress the feminine. Since the recognition of a 'specific' female sexuality would challenge the monopoly on value held by the masculine sex alone, in the final analysis by the father, what meaning could the Oedipus complex have in a symbolic system other than patriarchy?

But that order is indeed the one that lays down the law today. To fail to recognize this would be as naive as to let it continue to rule without questioning the conditions that make its domination possible. So the fact that Freud – or psychoanalytic theory in general – takes sexuality as a theme, as a discursive object, has not led to an interpretation of the *sexualization of discourse* itself, certainly not to an interpretation of Freud's own discourse. His resolutely 'masculine' viewpoint on female sexuality attests to this as well as his very selective attention to the theoretical contributions of female analysts. Where sexual difference is in question, Freud does not fully analyse the presuppositions of the production of discourse. In other words, the questions that Freud's theory and practice address to the scene of representation do not include the question of the sexualized determination of that scene. Because it lacks that articulation, Freud's contribution remains, in part – and precisely where the difference between the sexes is concerned – caught up in metaphysical presuppositions.

All of which has led you to an interpretive rereading of the texts that define the history of philosophy?

Yes, for unless we limit ourselves naively – or perhaps strategically – to some kind of limited or marginal issue, it is indeed precisely philosophical discourse that we have to challenge, and *disrupt*, inasmuch as this discourse sets forth the law for all others, inasmuch as it constitutes the discourse on discourse.

Thus we have had to go back to it in order to try to find out what accounts for the power of its systematicity, the force of its cohesion, the resourcefulness of its strategies, the general applicability of its law and its value. That is, its *position of mastery*, and of potential reappropriation of the various productions of history.

Now, this domination of the philosophic logos stems in large part from its power to *reduce all others to the economy of the Same*. The teleologically constructive project it takes on is always also a project of diversion, deflection, reduction of the other in the Same. And, in its greatest generality perhaps, from its power to *eradicate the difference between the sexes* in systems that are self-representative of a 'masculine subject'.

Whence the necessity of 'reopening' the figures of philosophical discourse – idea, substance, subject, transcendental subjectivity, absolute knowledge – in order to pry out of them what they have borrowed that is feminine, from the feminine, to make them 'render up' and give back what they owe the feminine. This may be done in various ways, along various 'paths', moreover, at minimum several of these must be pursued.

One way is to interrogate *the conditions under which systematicity itself is possible*: what the coherence of the discursive utterance conceals of the conditions under which it is produced, whatever it may say about these conditions in discourse. For example the 'matter' from which the speaking subject draws nourishment in order to produce itself, to reproduce itself; the *scenography* that makes representation feasible, representation as defined in philosophy, that is, the architectonics of its theatre, its framing in space–time, its geometric organization, its props, its actors, their respective positions, their dialogues, indeed their tragic relations, without overlooking the *mirror*, most often hidden, that allows the logos, the subject, to reduplicate itself, to reflect itself by itself. All these are interventions on the scene; they ensure its coherence so long as they remain uninterpreted. Thus they have to be re-enacted, in each figure of discourse, in order to shake discourse away from its mooring in the value of 'presence'. For each philosopher, beginning with those whose names define some age in the history of philosophy, we have to point out how the break with material contiguity is made, how the system is put together, how the specular economy works.

This process of interpretive rereading has always been a *psychoanalytic undertaking* as well. That is why we need to pay attention to the way the unconscious works in each philosophy, and perhaps in philosophy in general. We need to listen (psycho)analytically to its procedures of repression, to the structuration of language that shores up its representations, separating the true from the false, the meaningful from the meaningless, and so forth. This does not mean that we have to give ourselves over to some kind of symbolic, point-by-point interpretation of philosophers' utterances. Moreover, even if we were to do so, we would still be leaving the mystery of 'the origin' intact. What is called for instead is an examination of the *operation of the 'grammar'* of each figure of discourse, its syntactic laws or requirements, its imaginary configurations, its metaphoric networks, and also, of course, what it does not articulate at the level of utterance: *its silences.*

But as we have already seen, even with the help of linguistics, psychoanalysis cannot solve the problem of the articulation of the female sex in discourse. Even though Freud's theory, through an effect of dress-rehearsal – at least as far as the relation between the sexes is concerned – shows clearly the function of the feminine in that scene. *What remains to be done, then, is to work at 'destroying' the discursive mechanism.* Which is not a simple undertaking. . . . For how can we introduce ourselves into such a tightly-woven systematicity?

There is, in an initial phase, perhaps only one 'path', the one historically assigned to the feminine: that of *mimicry.* One must assume the feminine role deliberately. Which means already to convert a form of subordination into an affirmation, and thus to begin to thwart it. Whereas a direct feminine challenge to this condition means demanding to speak as a (masculine), 'subject', that is, it means to postulate a relation to the intelligible that would maintain sexual indifference.

To play with mimesis is thus, for a woman, to try to recover the place of her exploitation by discourse, without allowing herself to be simply reduced to it. It means to resubmit herself – inasmuch as she is on the side of the 'perceptible', of 'matter' – to 'ideas', in particular to ideas about herself, that are elaborated in/by a masculine logic, but so as to make 'visible', by an effect of playful repetition, what was supposed to remain invisible: the cover-up of a possible operation of the feminine in language. It also means 'to unveil' the fact that, if women are such good mimics, it is because they are not simply resorbed in this function. *They also remain elsewhere*: another case of the persistence of 'matter', but also of 'sexual pleasure'.

Elsewhere of 'matter': if women can play with mimesis, it is because they are capable of bringing new nourishment to its operation. Because they have always nourished this operation? Is not the 'first' stake in mimesis that of re-producing (from) nature? Of giving it form in order to appropriate it for oneself? As guardians of 'nature', are not women the ones who maintain, thus who make possible, the resource of mimesis of men? For the logos?

It is here, of course, that the hypothesis of a reversal – within the phallic order – is always possible. Re-semblance cannot do without red blood. Mother–matter–nature must go on forever nourishing speculation. But this re-source is also rejected as the waste product of reflection, cast outside as what resists it: as madness. Besides the ambivalence that the nourishing phallic mother attracts to herself, this function leaves woman's sexual pleasure aside.

That *'elsewhere' of female pleasure* might rather be sought first in the place where it sustains ek-stasy in the transcendental. The place where it serves as security for a narcissism extrapolated into the 'God' of men. It can play this role only at the price of its ultimate withdrawal from prospection, of its 'virginity' unsuited for the representation of self. Feminine pleasure has to remain inarticulate in language, in its own language, if it is not to threaten the underpinnings of logical operations. And so what is most strictly forbidden to women today is that they should attempt to express their own pleasure.

That 'elsewhere' of feminine pleasure can be found only at the price of *crossing back through the mirror that subtends all speculation*. For this pleasure is not simply situated in a process of reflection or mimesis, nor on one side of this process or the other: neither on the near side, the empirical realm that is opaque to all language, nor on the far side, the self-sufficient infinite of the God of men. Instead, it refers all these categories and ruptures back to the necessities of the self-representation of phallic desire in discourse. A playful crossing, and an unsettling one, which would allow woman to rediscover the place of her 'self-affection'. Of her 'god', we might say. A god to which one can obviously not have recourse – unless its *duality* is granted – without leading the feminine right back into the phallocratic economy.

Does this retraversal of discourse in order to rediscover a 'feminine' place suppose a certain work on/of language?

It is surely not a matter of interpreting the operation of discourse while remaining within the same type of utterance as the one that guarantees discursive coherence. This is moreover the danger of every statement, every discussion, *about Speculum*. And, more generally speaking, of every discussion *about* the question of woman. For to speak *of* or *about* woman may always boil down to, or be understood as, a recuperation of the feminine within a logic that maintains it in repression, censorship, nonrecognition.

In other words, the issue is not one of elaborating a new theory of which woman would be the *subject* or the *object*, but of jamming the theoretical machinery itself, of suspending its pretension to the production of a truth and of a meaning that are excessively univocal. Which presupposes that women do not aspire simply to be men's equals in knowledge. That they do not claim to be rivalling men in constructing a logic of the feminine that would still take onto-theo-logic as its model, but that they are rather attempting to wrest this question away from the ecomony of the logos. They should not put it, then, in the form 'What is woman?' but rather, repeating/ interpreting the way in which, within discourse, the feminine finds itself defined as lack, deficiency, or as imitation and negative image of the subject, they should signify that with respect to this logic a *disruptive excess* is possible on the feminine side.

An excess that exceeds common sense only on condition that the feminine not renounce its 'style'. Which, of course, is not a style at all, according to the traditional way of looking at things.

This 'style', or 'writing', of women tends to put the torch to fetish words, proper terms, well-constructed forms. This 'style' does not privilege sight; instead, it takes each figure back to its source, which is among other things *tactile*. It comes back in touch with itself in that origin without ever constituting in it, constituting itself in it, as some sort of unity. *Simultaneity* is its 'proper' aspect – a proper(ty) that is never fixed in the possible identity-to-self of some form or other. It is always *fluid*, without neglecting the characteristics of fluids that are difficult to idealize: those rubbings between two in-finitely near neighbours that create a dynamics. Its 'style' resists and explodes every firmly established form, figure, idea or concept.

Which does not mean that it lacks style, as we might be led to believe by a discursivity that cannot conceive of it. But its 'style' cannot be upheld as a thesis, cannot be the object of a position.

And even the motifs of 'self-touching', of 'proximity', isolated as such or reduced to utterances, could effectively pass for an attempt to appropriate the feminine to discourse. We would still have to ascertain whether 'touching oneself', that (self-) touching, the desire for the proximate rather than for (the) proper(ty), and so on, might not imply a mode of exchange irreducible to any *centring*, any *centrism*, given the way the 'self-touching' of female 'self-affection' comes into play as a rebounding from one to the other without any possibility of interruption, and given that, in this interplay, proximity confounds any adequation, any appropriation.

But of course if these were only 'motifs' without any work on and/or with language, the discursive economy could remain intact. How, then, are we to try to redefine this language work that would leave space for the feminine? Let us say that every dichotomizing – and at the same time redoubling – break, including the one between enunciation and statement (*énoncé*), has to be disrupted. Nothing is ever to be *posited* that is not also reversed and caught up again in the *supplementarity of this reversal*. To put it another way: there would no longer be either a right side or a wrong side of discourse, or even of texts, but each passing from one to the other would make audible and comprehensible even what resists the recto-verso structure that shores up common sense. If this is to be practised for every meaning posited – for every word, *énoncé*, sentence, but also of course for every phoneme, every letter – we need to proceed in such a way that linear reading is no longer possible: that is, the retroactive impact of the end of each word, *énoncé*, or sentence upon its beginning must be taken into consideration in order to undo the power of its teleological effect, including its deferred action. That would hold good also for the opposition between structures of horizontality and verticality that are at work in language.

What allows us to proceed in this way is that we interpret, at each 'moment', the *specular make-up* of discourse, that is, the self-reflecting (stratifiable) organization of the subject in that discourse. An organization that maintains, among other things, the break between what is perceptible and what is intelligible, and thus maintains the submission, subordination, and exploitation of the 'feminine'.

This language work would thus attempt to thwart any manipulation of discourse that would also leave discourse intact. Not, necessarily, in the *énoncé*, but in its *autological presuppositions*. Its function would thus be to *cast phallocentrism, phallocratism*, loose from its moorings in order to return the masculine to its own language, leaving open the possibility of a different language. Which means that the masculine would no longer be 'everything'. That it could no longer, all by itself, define, circumvene, circumscribe, the properties of anything and everything. That the right to define every value – including the abusive privilege of appropriation – would no longer belong to it.

Isn't there a political issue implicit in this interpretation of the philosophic order and this language work?

Every operation on and in philosophical language, by virtue of the very nature of that discourse – which is essentially political – possesses implications that, no matter how mediate they may be, are nonetheless politically determined.

The first question to ask is therefore the following: how can women analyse their own exploitation, inscribe their own demands, within an order prescribed by the masculine? *Is a women's politics possible within that order?* What transformation in the political process itself does it require?

In these terms, when women's movements challenge the forms and nature of political life, the contemporary play of powers and power relations, they are in fact working towards a modification of women's status. On the other hand, when these same movements aim simply for a change in the distribution of power, leaving intact the power structure itself, then they are resubjecting themselves, deliberately or not, to a phallocratic order. This latter gesture must of course be denounced, and with determination, since it may constitute a more subtly concealed exploitation of women. Indeed, that gesture plays on a certain naiveté that suggests one need only be a woman in order to remain outside phallic power.

But these questions are complex, all the more so in that women are obviously not to be expected to renounce equality in the sphere of civil rights. How can the double demand – for both equality and difference – be articulated?

Certainly not by acceptance of a choice between 'class struggle' and 'sexual warfare', an alternative that aims once again to minimize the question of the exploitation of women through a definition of power of the masculine type. More precisely, it implies putting off to an indefinite later date a women's 'politics', a politics that would be modelled rather too simplistically on men's struggle.

It seems, in this connection, that the *relation between the system of economic oppression among social classes and the system that can be labeled patriarchal* has been subjected to very little dialectical analysis, and has been once again reduced to a hierarchical structure.

A case in point: 'the first class opposition that appears in history coincides with the development of the antagonism between man and woman in monogamous marriage and the first class oppression coincides with that of the female sex by the male'.[1] Or again:

> With the division of labour, in which all these contradictions are implicit, and which in its turn is based on the natural division of labour in the family and on the separation of society into individual families opposed to one another, is given simultaneously the distribution, and indeed the unequal (both quantitative and qualitative) distribution, of labour and its products, hence property: the nucleus, the first form of which lies in the family, where wife and children are the slaves of the husband. This latent slavery in the family, though still very crude, is the first property, but even at this early stage it corresponds perfectly to the definition of modern economists who call it the power of disposing of the labour–power of others.[2]

Of this first antagonism, this first oppression, this first form, this first property, this nucleus . . . we may indeed say that they never signify anything but a 'first moment' of history, even an elaboration – why not a mythical one? – of 'origins'. The fact remains that this earliest oppression is in effect even today, and the problem lies in determining how it is articulated with the other oppression, if it is necessary in the long run to dichotomize them in that way, to oppose them, to subordinate one to the other, according to processes that are still strangely inseparable from an idealist logic.

For the patriarchal order is indeed the one that functions as the *organization and monopolization of private property to the benefit of the head of the family.* It is his proper name, the name of the father, that determines ownership for the family, including the wife and children. And what is required of them – for the wife, monogamy; for the children, the precedence of the male line, and specifically of the eldest son who bears the name – is also required so as to ensure 'the concentration of considerable wealth in the hands of a single individual – a man' and to 'bequeath this wealth to the children of that man and of no other', which, of course, does not 'in any way interfere with open or concealed polygamy on the part of the man'.[3] How, then, can the analysis of women's exploitation be dissociated from the analysis of modes of appropriation?

This question arises today out of a different necessity. For male–female relations are beginning to be less concealed behind the father–mother functions. Or, more precisely, man–father/mother: because the man, by virtue of his effective participation in public exchanges, has never been reduced to a simple reproductive function. The woman, for her part, owing to her seclusion in the 'home', the place of private property, has long been nothing but a mother. Today, not only her entrance into the circuits of production, but also – even more so? – the widespread availability of contraception and abortion are returning her to that impossible role: being a woman. And if contraception and abortion are spoken of most often as possible ways of controlling, or even 'mastering', the birth rate, of being a mother 'by choice', the fact remains that they imply the possibility of *modifying women's social status*, and thus of modifying the modes of social relations between men and women.

But to what reality would woman correspond, independently of her reproductive function? It seems that two possible roles are available to her, roles that are occasionally or frequently contradictory. Woman could be *man's equal*. In this case she would enjoy, in a more or less near future, the same economic, social, political rights as men. She would be a potential man. But on the exchange market – especially, or exemplarily, the market of sexual exchange – woman would also have to preserve and maintain what is called *femininity*. The value of a woman would accrue to her from her maternal role, and, in addition, from her 'femininity'. But in fact that 'femininity' is a role, an image, a value, imposed upon women by male systems of representation. In this masquerade of femininity, the woman loses herself, and loses herself by playing on her femininity. The fact remains that this masquerade requires an *effort* on her part for which she is not compensated. Unless her pleasure comes simply from being chosen as an object of consumption or of desire by masculine 'subjects'. And, moreover, how can she do otherwise without being 'out of circulation'?

In our social order, women are 'products' used and exchanged by men. Their status is that of merchandise, 'commodities'. How can such objects of use and transaction claim the right to speak and to participate in exchange in general? Commodities, as we all know, do not take themselves to market on their own; and if they could talk. . . . So women have to remain an 'infrastructure' unrecognized as such by our society and our culture. The use, consumption, and circulation of their sexualized bodies underwrite the organization and the reproduction of the social order, in which they have never taken part as 'subjects'.

Women are thus in a situation of *specific exploitation* with respect to exchange operations: sexual exchanges, but also economic, social, and cultural exchange in general. A woman 'enters into' these exchanges only as the object of a transaction, unless she agrees to renounce the specificity of her sex, whose 'identity' is imposed on her according to models that remain foreign to her. Women's social inferiority is reinforced and complicated by the fact that woman does not have access to language, except through recourse to 'masculine' systems of representation which disappropriate her from her relation to herself and to other women. The 'feminine' is never to be identified except by and for the masculine, the reciprocal proposition not being 'true'.

But this situation of specific oppression is perhaps what can allow women today to elaborate a 'critique of the political economy', inasmuch as they are in a position external to the laws of exchange, even though they are included in them as 'commodities'. A critique of the political economy that could not, this time, dispense with the critique of the discourse in which it is carried out, and in particular of the metaphysical presuppositions of that discourse. And one that would doubtless interpret in a different way *the impact of the economy of discourse on the analysis of relations of production*.

For, without the exploitation of the body–matter of women, what would become of the symbolic process that governs society? What modification would this process, this society, undergo, if women, who have been only objects of consumption or exchange, necessarily aphasic, were to become 'speaking subjects' as well? Not, of course, in compliance with the masculine, or more precisely the phallocratic, 'model'.

That would not fail to challenge the discourse that lays down the law today, that legislates on everything, including sexual difference, to such an extent that the existence of another sex, of an other, that would be woman, still seems, in its terms, unimaginable.

NOTES

1 Frederick Engels, *The Origin of the Family, Private Property and the State*, trans. Alec West, rev. and ed. E. B. Leacock (New York, 1972), p. 129.
2 Karl Marx and Friedrich Engels, *The German Ideology*, parts 1 and 3, ed. R. Pascal (New York, 1939), pp. 21–2. (*Marxist Library*, Works of Marxism–Leninism, vol. 6.) Further references to this work are identified parenthetically by page number.
3 *The Origin of the Family*, p. 138.

Translated by Catherine Porter with Carolyn Burke

8

Questions

Now let me take up your second series of questions, about 'speaking (as) woman'.

> *Must we say: an* other *sex* = *an* other *writing*
> *an* other *sex* = *an* other *meaning? Why?*

Can we simply oppose writing to meaning, or present them as alternatives?

B:[1] *We are talking about supplementarity rather than alternatives. Writing and meaning: two things that intersect yet are not identical. Writing operates at the level of effects; if it is possible to speak (as) woman, writing is an effect of this. Meaning refers rather to the question of the unconscious, a feminine unconscious . . .*

Given this alternative, I haven't known how to respond . . .

The question lies rather in the equation (the 'equals' sign) and not between the two formulations.

I don't know whether writing is situated on the side of the 'effect' or the 'cause'. . . . That depends on the way this notion is interpreted. It seems to me that an *other* writing necessarily entails an *other* economy of meaning. On this basis, one may wonder whether all writing that does not question its own hierarchical relation to the difference between the sexes is not once more, as always, both productive of and produced within the economy of proper meaning. So long as it is 'defined', 'practised', 'monopolized' by a single sex, does not writing remain an instrument of production in an unchanged regimen of property?

But one might respond otherwise – not answer 'truly'. . . – by making a detour by way of Plato. In Plato, there are two *mimeses*. To simplify: there is *mimesis* as production, which would lie more in the realm of music, and there is the *mimesis* that would be already caught up in a process of *imitation, specularization, adequation*, and *reproduction*. It is the second form that is privileged throughout the history of philosophy and whose effects/symptoms, such as latency, suffering, paralysis of desire, are encountered in hysteria. The first form seems always to have been repressed, if only because it was constituted as an enclave within a 'dominant' discourse. Yet it is doubtless in the direction of, and on the basis of, that first *mimesis* that the possibility of a woman's writing may come about. We shall come back to this in the questions on hysteria.

What is the double syntax (masculine–feminine)?

That phrase refers to the fact that rather than establishing a hierarchy between conscious and unconscious and subordinating one to the other, rather than ranking them as 'above' and 'below', Freud might instead have articulated them and made them work as two different syntaxes.

To respond from another angle: might we not say that it is because it has produced and continues to 'hold' syntax that the masculine maintains mastery over discourse? Within this syntax, in this order of discourse, woman, even though she is hidden, most often hidden as woman and absent in the capacity of subject, manages to make 'sense' – sensation? – manages to create 'content'. This syntax of discourse, of discursive logic – more generally, too, the syntax of social organization, 'political' syntax – isn't this syntax always (how could it be otherwise? at least so long as there is no desire for the other) a means of masculine self-affection, or masculine self-production or reproduction, or self-generation or self-representation – himself as the self-same, as the only standard of sameness? And, as masculine auto-affection needs instruments – unlike woman, man needs instruments in order to touch himself: woman's hand, woman's sex and body, language – hasn't that syntax necessarily, according to an economic logic, exploited everything in order to caress itself? Whereas the 'other' syntax, the one that would make feminine 'self-affection' possible, is lacking, repressed, censured: the feminine is never affected except by and for the masculine. What we would want to put into play, then, is a syntax that would make woman's 'self-affection' possible. A 'self-affection' that would certainly not be reducible to the economy of sameness of the One, and for which the syntax and the meaning remain to be found. (See *This Sex Which Is Not One*: 'This sex which is not one', chapter 2, 'The "mechanics" of fluids', chapter 6, and 'When our lips speak together', chapter 11.)

In this connection, one may very well say that everyting advanced in psychoanalysis – especially since the masturbation of little girls is conceived according to the model of 'doing what the little boy does' – leaves completely aside whatever woman's 'self-affection' might be. For woman does not affect herself, does not practise 'self-affection' according to the masculine 'model'. What is 'unheard-of' – and this might be one explanation, but not the only one, for the fact that the affirmation of woman as the other should come so late and that her relation to language should be so problematical – is that woman can already be affected without 'instruments', that woman can touch herself 'within herself', in advance of any recourse to instruments. From this point of view, to forbid her to masturbate is rather amusing. For how can a woman be forbidden to touch herself? Her sex, 'in itself', touches itself all the time. On the other hand, no effort is spared to prevent this touching, to prevent her from touching herself: the valorization of the masculine sex alone, the reign of the phallus and its logic of meaning and its system of representations, these are just some of the ways woman's sex is cut off from itself and woman is deprived of her 'self-affection'.

Which explains, moreover, why women have no desire, why they do not know what they want: they are so irremediably cut off from their 'self-affection' that from the outset, and in particular from the time of the Oedipus complex, they are exiled from themselves, and lacking any possible continuity/contiguity with their first desires/ pleasures, they are imported into another economy, where they are completely unable to find themselves.

Or rather, they find themselves there, proverbially, *in masquerades*. Psychoanalysts say that masquerading corresponds to woman's desire. That seems wrong to me. I think the masquerade has to be understood as what women do in order to recuperate some element of desire, to participate in man's desire, but at the price of renouncing their own. In the masquerade, they submit to the dominant economy of desire in an attempt to remain 'on the market' in spite of everything. But they are there as objects for sexual enjoyment, not as those who enjoy.

What do I mean by masquerade? In particular, what Freud calls 'femininity'. The belief, for example, that it is necessary to *become* a woman, a 'normal' one at that, whereas a man is a man from the outset. He has only to effect his being-a-man, whereas a woman has to become a normal woman, that is, has to enter into the *masquerade of femininity*. In the last analysis, the female Oedipus complex is woman's entry into a system of values that is not hers, and in which she can 'appear' and circulate only when enveloped in the needs/ desires/fantasies of others, namely, men.

That having been said, what a feminine syntax might be is not simple nor easy to state, because in that 'syntax' there would no longer be either subject or object, 'oneness' would no longer be privileged, there would no longer be proper meanings, proper names, 'proper' attributes. . . .Instead, that 'syntax' would involve nearness, proximity, but in such an extreme form that it would preclude any distinction of identitites, any establishment of ownership, thus any form of appropriation.

Can you give some examples of that syntax?

I think the place where it could best be deciphered is in the gestural code of women's bodies. But, since their gestures are often paralysed, or part of the masquerade, in effect, they are often difficult to 'read'. Except for what resists or subsists 'beyond'. In suffering, but also in women's laughter. And again: in what they 'dare' – do or say – when they are among themselves.

That syntax may also be heard, if we don't plug our ears with meaning, in the language women use in psychoanalysis.

There are also more and more texts written by women in which another writing is beginning to assert itself, even if it is still often repressed by the dominant discourse. For my part, I tried to put that syntax into play in *Speculum*, but not simply, to the extent that a single gesture obliged me to go back through the realm of the masculine imaginary. Thus I could not, I cannot install myself just like that, serenely and directly, in that other syntactic functioning – and I do not see how any woman could.

What is the relation or the nonrelation between speaking (as) woman *and* speaking-among-women?

There may be a speaking-among-women that is still a speaking (as) man but that may also be the place where a speaking (as) woman may dare to express itself. It is certain that with women-among-themselves (and this is one of the stakes of liberation movements, when they are not organized along the lines of masculine power, and when they are not focused on demands for the seizure or the over-throw of 'power'), in these places of women-among-themselves, something of a speaking (as) woman is heard. This accounts for the desire or the necessity of sexual nonintegration: the dominant language is so powerful that women do not dare to speak (as) woman outside the context of nonintegration.

What is the relation between speaking (as) woman and speaking of woman?

Speaking (as) woman is not speaking of woman. It is not a matter of producing a discourse of which woman would be the object, or the subject.

That said, by *speaking (as) woman*, one may attempt to provide a place for the 'other' as feminine.

C: *Is it implicit in your discourse that the constitution of a woman's alterity implies the same thing for a man?*

If I understand your question correctly, yes. But is it up to me, I wonder, to speak of the 'other' man? It's curious, because it's a question that I am constantly being asked. I find it quite amusing . . . I am constantly being asked what that 'other' man will be. Why should I appropriate for myself what that 'other' man would have to say? What I want and what I'm waiting to see is what men will do and say if their sexuality releases its hold on the empire of phallo-cratism. But this is not for a woman to anticipate, or foresee, or prescribe . . .

What already to some extent answers the next question, concern-ing '*speaking (as) woman and speaking (as) woman about men*'. I think that speaking (as) woman has no more to say about men than about woman. It implies a different mode of articulation between masculine and feminine desire and language, but it does not signify speaking *about* men. Which would be once again a sort of reversal of the economy of discourse. Speaking (as) woman would, among other things, permit women to speak *to* men . . .

Speaking (as) woman and speaking (as) hysteric?

I should like to ask what it means 'to speak (as) hysteric'. Does the hysteric speak? Isn't hysteria a privileged place for preserving – but 'in latency', 'in sufferance' – that which does not speak? And, in particular (even according to Freud . . .), that which is not expressed in woman's relation to her mother, to herself, to other women? Those aspects of women's earliest desires that find themselves reduced to silence in terms of a culture that does not allow them to be expressed. A powerlessness to 'say', upon which the Oedipus complex then superimposes the requirement of silence.

Hysteria: *it speaks* in the mode of a paralysed gestural faculty, of an impossible and also a forbidden speech. . . . It speaks as *symptoms* of an 'it can't speak to or about itself'. . . . And the drama of hysteria is that it is inserted schizotically between that gestural system, that desire paralysed and enclosed within its body, and a language that it has learned in the family, in school, in society, which is in no way continuous with – nor, certainly, a metaphor for – the 'movements' of its desire. Both mutism and mimicry are then left to hysteria. Hysteria is silent and at the same time it mimes. And – how could it be otherwise – miming/reproducing a language that is not its own, masculine language, it caricatures and deforms that language: it 'lies', it 'deceives', as women have always been reputed to do.

The problem of 'speaking (as) woman' is precisely that of finding a possible continuity between that gestural expression or that speech of desire – which at present can only be identified in the form of symptoms and pathology – and a language, including a verbal language. There again, one may raise the question whether psychoanalysis has not superimposed on the hysterical symptom a code, a system of interpretation(s) which fails to correspond to the desire fixed in somatizations and in silence. In other words, does psychoanalysis offer any 'cure' to hysterics beyond a surfeit of suggestions intended to adapt them, if only a little better, to masculine society?

NOTES

1 The interlocutors are designated by capital letters – A, B, etc. – in the order of their participation. [Note of the Philosophy Department of Toulouse-le-Mirail].

Translated by Catherine Porter with Carolyn Burke

9

The Three *Genres*

The notion of *Genre*

The structure of discourse and its impact on meaning, the truth it translates and transmits, is still quite rarely analysed as an *instrument* in any of the sciences. We find debates about content which give little consideration to the *vehicle* of their message.

The sciences are constantly polishing new instruments, new machines (and very expensive ones, at that!) but the technique that is language [*langage*], the tool that is language [*langue*] are still rarely investigated in any research. Except for computer-programming purposes?

We were taught that man was the speaking animal. Today, man appears to be surrendering to the possibilities of the brains of machines for his present and his future – biological, affective, intellectual, social . . .

A curious epoch in which 'cold' hypertechnicity goes hand in hand with rustic magical passions, with a rather worrying irrationality. With medicine, and all its resources, being called in to help. And religion as such?

Shouldn't we be seeing, in this crisis of the dispossession of reason, signs of the mutation of an era in culture? An incentive to work towards the elaboration of a new discourse, especially in relations between microcosm and macrocosm? Between the universe and us, but also in us and between us, another world must be thought.

Hence my project of working on *genre* in discourse:

Genre as index and mark of the *subjectivity* and ethical responsibility of the speaker. *Genre* is not in fact merely something to do with physiology, biology or private life, with the mores of animals or the fertility of plants. It constitutes the irreducible differentiation *internal to the 'human race'* [*'genre humain'*]. *Genre* represents the site of the nonsubstitutable positioning of the *I* and the *you* and of their modalities of expression. Should the difference between the *I* and the *you* disappear, so do demand, thanks, appeals, questions . . .

It seems that, rather than becoming more human by developing the sexuate morphology of his discourse, man now wants to absent himself from language [*langage*], no longer saying *I*, *you* or *we*. Here, the sciences, technologies and certain regressions to religiosity appear to go hand in hand. In taking over from the *I* (here and now), from the subject and from a possible *you*, these truths seem to have the force of law.

Which brings me to my second question. Not saying *I* implies leaving speech, voice, to that which is supposed to be more worthy of articulating our truth. What is the status of this something that could speak better than us? In a *universal* and *neutral* manner? Does neutrality exist? Where? How?

When I question discourse – starting with the language [*langue*] I speak, which made me a subject – I observe, first of all, that the neuter is apparently something to do with *nature*. *Il pleut, il neige, il vente, il tonne* (it is raining; it is snowing; it is windy; it is thundering) . . . express forces [*puissances*] that resist human power [*pouvoir*], its formalization. This is not an inert matter which imposes itself upon or is distinct from man, this is an *animate* nature whose language [*langage*] is spoken more or less capriciously and is now expressed *in the neuter*: in its movements, its manifestations, its rhythms, but also when we grasp it through our sense–perceptions: it shines [*ça brille*], it's bright [*ça luit*], it smells good [*ça sent bon*], it's beautiful [*c'est beau*], it's thundering [*ça tonne*]. The sense which could invert things is basically *touch*, our body as *tactile tool* for apprehending and manipulating the world, ourselves, the other. This tool is a hand-tool, but also a speech-tool: translation, relay, creation. This work of man – and I say man because man, the people of men, has for centuries been the active worker manipulating and transforming the world with his hands, his tools and language – wants to behave like [*faire comme*] nature? Mimic it? Impose itself as a force [*puissance*] without any subjective mark of gender? So we would move from *il fait beau* (it is fine) or *il pleut* (which corresponds to a rhythm and not a formal dichotomous opposition) to *il faut* (it is necessary to), *c'est vrai* (it is true), *c'est ainsi* (it is so) *ou pas* (or not). This order of laws claims to be neutral, but it bears the marks of he who produces them. Between 'the weather today' [*le temps qu'il fait*] and 'the time of history' [*le temps de l'histoire*], there is the time of the creation of worlds, of the establishment of their economies, and of gods or a God speaking in nature.

Three '*il*', three so-called 'neuters' which are worth questioning, especially in their intervention between the two human *genres*: the language of nature, the word(s) of exclusively male god(s), the cultural order and its discourse through things. Through machines? Things of our era that speak a language that sometimes swamps us, erases us, and whose noise superimposes itself on the noise or silence of the natural order.

This can be put differently: most of the time, language [*langage*] serves to convey a meaning, a content. How did discourse permit this content, this signification, this culture? How can it replace them with others? These aspects of the message are not usually investigated.

Hence my decision to question the structure of discourse, the language-tool, so as to interpret its sexuation and to attempt to effect a change in its order. This work must be carried out at two levels of discourse:

1 that of the formalization, automatic or conscious, of its means, its powers;
2 that of style, of the subjective involvement of he or she who is speaking, of his/her relationship with the body, with the sexuate body.

It is in fact necessary to analyse the relationship within discourse between:

1 that which can be formalized: passively/actively; popularly/ scientifically, etc.;
2 that which, as style, resists formalization.

This is a matter of elaborating the problem of ethical responsibility in relation to formalization, but also of the expression or translation of identity in style. Is one dissociable from the other? Is not the sexuate the *brake* and the *reserve* in the face of a life-threatening formalization, a heedless development of sciences and technologies, and the subsequent atrophies or paralyses of the body? The issue is not simply a matter of justice for one sex, but of responsibility for the preservation, organization, consciousness and creation of life, of the world. Such a task demands that we consider the responsibility of the speaker and question any discourse which claims to be indifferent to the subject – in its dimensions of perception, sensitivity, understanding and sex –, which calls itself universal and neutral. What does the neutral conceal? Where in the economy of discourse does the sexuate lie hidden? How to discover it?

It is not enough to talk of content, especially historical content. To approach the sexuate dimension of discourse, change its rules, we must analyse quite rigorously the forms that permit that content. If the ethical, or simply cultural, transformation concerning sexual difference is not brought about, or is brought about badly, it is for want of an *active* mutation in the laws and order of discourse.

The unconscious translation of *genre* in discourse

I insist upon the fact that I am not going to define an ideal model of language [*langue*]. This means that I do not claim to be indicating in any *absolute* manner the most important elements of the language spoken by men and women. I can say what I have observed. Nor do I wish to establish a *fixed* and *immutable* schema for the production of discourse; I want to show that the generation of messages is not neutral, but sexuate. Sexual difference has always been used for procreation. For a long time, it has not been used for the *creation of culture*, except in a division of roles and tasks which does not permit both sexes to be subjects. We thus find ourselves faced with a certain *subjective pathology* on both sides of sexual difference. This pathology appears with varying degrees of clarity in social behaviour. It is covered up by different masks, and there is a great reluctance to analyse it, even to admit its existence, either because language [*langage*] is considered an ideal alien to the body which produces it or because it is asserted to be reducible to the superstructure of a restricted economy. There are other possible hypotheses, notably that of repression or censorship being exercised on a sexuate language [*langage*]. Even those who profess sexual liberation (in the therapeutic mode or in a more directly political mode) often deny the fact that language is sexuate. They, men or women, stick to content, to certain sexual representations, but overlook the fact that sexuation corresponds to a general structure of discourse.

The sexuation of discourse does not in fact correspond to a few words more or a few words less, even though the non-existence of terms in the *vocabulary* may be structurally significant. Nor does the *mark of gender* in language [*langue*] (masculine, feminine, neuter) exhaust the meaning of a sexuate generation of messages. It is often revelatory of social and historical phenomena. It shows how one sex has subordinated the other or the world. Thus, in French at least, the masculine gender always takes syntactic precedence: a crowd of 1,000 people made up of 999 women and 1 man will be described as *ils étaient* ('they were'); it will be said of a couple that *ils s'aiment* ('they love one another'); a woman telling the story of her love must employ the masculine form '*nous nous sommes aimés*' ('we loved each other'), etc. What is more, the neuter is expressed by the same pronoun as the masculine: *il tonne, il faut*, and not *elle faut, elle tonne*. These syntactic laws reveal the dominance of one sex over the other.

This sex has, besides, appropriated the most highly valued truths: *God* is now masculine in most, if not all, languages; so is *sun*; in countries where the *moon* is important, it is masculine in gender, etc. Man gives his *genre* to the universe, just as he wants to give his name to his children and his property. Anything which seems valuable to him must belong to his *genre*. The feminine is a secondary mark, always subordinated to the principal *genre*. The neuter is reserved for certain domains that vary from language to language. An analysis of its origins often reveals that it stems from an erased sexual difference. Thus, cosmic phenomena which were once the attributes of gods *and goddesses* are now expressed in the neuter form: *il tonne, il fait soleil, il pleut* etc. This necessity was once bound up with sexuate acts. Similarly, the '*ananke*' [*il faut* or *il est nécessaire*] of the Greek philosophers, or derived from the Greeks, probably conceals a sexual necessity associated with a destiny at once human and divine.[1] This necessity was later subordinated to the Roman juridical order. But laws were then decreed by men alone. Necessity [*il faut*] signifies a duty or an order established by one sex, one *genre*. It is only apparently neutral and, once more, it is expressed, in French at least, by the same *genre* as the masculine.

Our social organizations and the discourse that stems from them are therefore regulated by a neuter governed by the masculine *genre*. A place of respite from wars and polemics between men, this neuter does not resolve the problem of the hierarchy of masculine and feminine genres, of its injustices and of the pathogenic neutralization of languages [*langages*] and values that ensues.

For this long-standing taboo on a truly sexuate morphology of and in culture leads to repressions, compensations and pathologies. Hence the invention of various individual or collective therapies. Psychoanalysis is the most obvious example. Given the conventions of the analytic session, it is also the site where language disorders are seen most clearly, quite apart from the fact that language is the means used in treatment. It is in this non-social context that the difference between subjects at the level of the structure of the utterance is manifested at its simplest. If I start with traditional classifications, it becomes apparent that so-called hysterics and obsessionals do not produce a discourse in accordance with the same structures. Hysterics (or at least women hysterics) generate messages of the type: (I) ⟨You love me?⟩ (you) or (I) ⟨I love what you love⟩ (you). Obviously, they do not produce sentences in precisely this form. This sentence model is derived from the analysis of several samples, from their reduction to kernel sentences and so on.[2] The male obsessional, for his part, produces a discourse of the type: (I) ⟨I say to myself that perhaps I am loved⟩ (you) or (I) ⟨I wonder if I am loved⟩ (you). In the first case, the message, the object exchanged, the world view or perspective often belong to *you*; in the second, it often belongs to *I*. The objection that there are hysterical men and obsessional woman is not valid as a counter-interpretation. The model of the male hysteric is different to that of the female hysteric. The same applies to the obsessional structure.[3]

But sexual difference can also be observed within so-called homogeneous groups. Thus, female *schizophrenics* do not elaborate the same neocodes as male schizophrenics. Women tend mainly to structure a corporeal geography; men, new linguistic territories.

The sexuate structure of discourse is also found in cases other than those specifically identified as pathological. Students of different sexes do not, for instance, produce the same sentences on the basis of given inductor words. This is not simply a matter of the content of the messages, but also of their form. In the sentences I analysed, the words were, for example: marriage, celibacy, motherhood, fatherhood, femininity. The samples were collected by a team working on obstetrical psychoprophylaxis.[4] The findings obtained by the authors differed considerably from mine. It is true that they were concerned with a study of content and not an analysis of the structure of discourse. In my view, the sentences produced by men and women differ in their choice of subjects, verbs, tenses, modes, transformations of the predicate, etc. This can be interpreted as a different positioning of the subject generating the message in relation to language [*langage*], the object of discourse, the world, the other. Contrary to what is usually said or thought, women construct more objective sentences whose meaning or denotation is often supported by an extra-linguistic context. Men connote their messages much more. They assert their subjective mark in somewhat impassioned terms ('I claim the paternity of these sentences' was one man's response to the word *paternity*), whereas women, reputedly incapable of neutrality, reply in a much more impersonal manner, in a more 'scientific' style. These findings may be a source of surprise. They are, however, related to those obtained in the psychoanalytic situation. With men, the *I* is asserted in different ways; it is significantly more important than the *you* and *the world*. With women, the *I* often makes way for the *you, the world*, for the objectivity of words and things. From that point of view, women appear to be more capable of listening to, discovering or accommodating the other and the world, of remaining open to *objective* invention or creation, provided that they can also say *I*.[5]

I have just given two examples of the sexuation of discourse. I have approached the question of the sexual order of discourse in various ways: the discourses of the hysteric and the obsessional, the production of sentences by men and women students, Freud's theory *on* Dora, the text addressed by Schreber *to* his wife, the sexual language of fairy tales and legends, the sexuate determination of the discourse of science, philosophy, art, religion, etc.[6]

What becomes apparent when we analyse the expressions of the subject in language, representations, art, legends and myths is that *sex [sexe] is a primal and irreducible dimension of subjective structure.* We are sexuate and we produce sexuate forms. We know little about this production – and not merely reproduction – in difference, but, more so than ever, we need to safeguard ourselves against a technocratic imperialism that often cares little for the regeneration of living beings, for freedom and the future. This also means that we need it if we are to be capable of using our technical powers to construct, and not destroy, human values.

For me, working on language does not correspond to a matter of mere statistical surveys, nor to the registration of a de facto state. I use the scientific apparatus to bring out certain tendencies that we habitually misrecognize, forget. But can we speak and be conscious of the form, the forms, of our discourse? Not necessarily. Indeed, it seems impossible in the immediate. Hence the need for an investigation.

Its project is to reveal who is speaking, to whom, about what, with what means. In technical terms, this means that it is a matter of uncovering the dynamics of the utterance [*énonciation*] underlying the statements [*énoncés*] produced. Beneath what is being said, it is possible to discover the subject, the subject's economy, potential energy, relations with the other and the world. The subject may be masked, bogged down, buried, covered up, paralysed, or may be engendered, generated, may become, and grow through speech [*en parlant*].

Working on language in its sexuation therefore means bringing out who *I*, *you*, *he*, *she* are in the discourses of men and women. That allows us to interpret the misunderstandings and impasses to which their sexual relations, both in the strict sense and in the social, cultural sense, are often reduced. This type of work allows us to analyse the symptom, to name and understand the problem, to find the openings that allow us to modify the economy of the utterance [*énonciation*], of exchanges in general. A formalism undergone, unconsciously produced, can thus become a style.

The expression of *genre* in a style

This work may seem austere to some, even if it does have its intellectually amusing and stimulating side. I therefore want to state another reason why it seems to me indispensable. No narrative, and no commentary on a narrative, is enough to bring about a change in discourse. They may, moreover, establish a moralizing repression of sexual and affective freedom, unless they create a style, transcend the statement [*énoncé*] in the creation of new forms. I am thinking in this connection of all the contemporary autobiographical narratives which are not transposed into novels, poems, tales, legends, theories. The transformation of the autobiographical *I* into another cultural *I* seems to be necessary if we are to establish a new ethics of sexual difference. To avoid turning it into a traditional morality, abstract norms of feeling, formal frameworks or a truth resulting from the personal experience of an *x* or *y* who can shout louder than the rest, it is also important not to reduplicate this ethics by *explaining* what is being invented, discovered by way of gestures of creation, love and freedom. Two approaches are important for the establishment of different norms of life: the analysis of the formal structures of discourse, and the creation of a new style. Thus, in *Ethique de la différence sexuelle*, which presupposes a lot of cultural analyses,[7] there is no basic narrative and no possible commentaries by others, in the sense of an exhaustive deciphering of the text. What is said in this book is conveyed by a double style: a style of amorous relations, a style of thought, exposition, writing. Consciously or unconsciously, the two are connected; on the one hand, there is a more immediately corporeal and affective side and, on the other, a more socially elaborated side. But its language [*langage*] is already allied with other languages. And an alliance is an act which cannot easily be transposed. Nor can an alliance with language [*langue*].

Gestures made in accordance with a style do not constitute a formal model. Even if fashion does try to take it over, even if imitation does caricature it or use part of its content, a style remains irreducible. It cannot be reduced to a grid that can be transposed or imposed elsewhere. A style resists coding, summarizing, encrypting, pigeon-holing in differently programmed machines. It cannot be reduced to oppositions like sensible/intelligible, poetic/conceptual . . . or the masculine/feminine, as presented to us by all these dichotomies. A style will not let itself be reduced to bipolar alternatives: positive/negative, better/not so good, etc. It may permit them, especially in the form of (digestive? and) in one way or another contradictory commentaries, but it escapes them insofar as it creates and is neither resolved nor dissolved into dichotomies, however refined.

Hence the resistances. What is it all about? What exactly is she saying? What is its, already given, meaning? The answers to these questions are not forthcoming, especially out of context, which sometimes leads to the objection that the thought is esoteric. But any text is esoteric, not because it conceals a secret, but because it constitutes the secret, the not-yet-revealed or the never-exhaustively-revealable. The only reply that can be given to the question of the meaning of the text is: read, perceive, feel. . . . *Who are you?* would be a more pertinent question, provided that it does not collapse into a demand for an identity card or an autobiographical anecdote. The answer would be: *and who are you?* Can we meet? Talk? Love? Create something together? Thanks to which milieu? What between-us [*entre-nous*]?

We cannot do that without the horizon of sexual difference. No world can be produced or reproduced without sexual difference. Everything is sexuate: plants, animals, the gods, the elements of the universe.

Whether or not the force of matter alone (which? and what are we calling matter?) engenders organized beings remains an insistent question, especially in relation to the origins of our life. Although research has gone a very long way, in every sense and direction, in an attempt to prove it, it sometimes overlooks our most elementary realities and needs. But, to date, no one has been able to assert that they belong to a monosexuate or asexuate universe. Except in fiction? And in certain formal truths of science, abstracted from life and said to be neutral?

Man appears to have forgotten this destiny in its most universal, and most creative, dimensions. In the beginning, 'God' (or some animal, vegetable pair) created us naked, man and woman, in a garden that sufficed us for our shelter, our food. Working to make a living, and especially procreating in pain, signify *exile* from that garden. What have become our duties, *our only horizon*, may be no more than exile as we wait to return, the taboo on the flesh, the obligation to work, and to suffer, representing the reverse of, the fall from, our first birth. Man is now excavating his mythical archaeology, when he is not looking for himself on the most distant planets, being still bound here and now to a *fault* from which he cannot deliver himself, which he cannot manage to replace with a third element such as: love, grace, jubilation in the flesh, and therefore their sharing in the word.

An apocryphal gospel reports Christ saying to Salome that happiness will not return to earth until women cease procreating! That can be understood as the discovery of a love in which the child is no longer *necessary*. But the text, the texts, add that sexual difference will then be erased. One might as well say that it existed only for or through the child, and in hierarchy: there will be neither man nor woman, master nor slave.

If sexual difference is to be transcended, must it not first find its ethics? If we are to be as one, isn't it necessary for us first to be *two*? Lest we lapse into some empty, formal *one*, into the hierarchies we know or into a nostalgia for intra-uterine regression where the other is no more than a place, food, a conveyance. Hasn't man, on his travels, confused what is most archaic on earth with what is most celestial in heaven?

How has the sexual ethic been neglected to this extent? Why does it make so many detours: animal ecology, the sexuation of plants, the more or less pathological language of our cells, the sex of our chromosomes, of our brain, etc.? Sexuality appears to have become little more than an issue of power, and pain. . . . Man no longer even takes the time for any courtship display [*parade*]. He must work faster, ever faster. As for woman, her gestures as lover seem yet to be invented. She has become lost in the mother, or in a display of adornment [*parade*] which does not describe her space for either encounter or embrace. She may perhaps express her need-desire to be loved, but not her own love. Why? The woman with a value in her own right [*la femme valable*] has been reduced to giving birth to the son, to mothering and to the corresponding language [*langage*]. Man, who, thanks to his labour, has a monopoly on the symbolic, has not thought his body or his flesh. And, quite apart from the need to think himself, perhaps he would have some difficulty in saying what constitutes the singularity of the feminine sexual world: a different energy and morphology, a particular relationship with the mucous and the threshhold that goes from outside to inside the body, from the exterior to the interior of the skin (and the universe?) without a wound.

For women, it is therefore a matter of learning to discover and inhabit a different magnetism and the morphology of a sexuate body, especially in its singularities and mucous qualities. But this flesh (and aren't the mucous membranes the very stuff of flesh for many?) has remained ignored, often imagined as chaos, abyss or dregs. Raw material, or a cast-off from what has already been born, it has yet to find its forms, to flower in accordance with its roots. It has still not been born into its own growth, its subjectivity. The feminine has not yet deployed its *morphology*. Yoked to the maternal, reduced to the womb or to seductive adornment, the feminine has been used only for the conception, growth, birth and rebirth of the *forms* of the other.

But how to espouse that which has no *forms*, no edges, no limits? No style of nuptials and alliance to propose? In this absence of her self-assertion, man drowns, consumes or undertakes some nostalgic odyssey. Woman mothers her little one, her externalized one; she makes him grow and flourish in her place. As a wife, she masks herself, adorns herself. Yet when she has no intention of her own, adornment leads only to disappointments. Clothes that are only *for the other*, that are not an expression of my flesh, unveil a sort of void once they are taken off: woman's inability to love herself, to care for herself, to become an *other* partner, irreducible to what man expects, and therefore still desirable, attractive. Then she is beautiful, not only with the beauty of more or less artificial appearances, but with the radiance of an interiority, an intimacy. These words make us smile today, but in many traditions they are weighty. In other traditions, they designate an energy that can be conserved.

In ours, don't women suffer from not having known and lived *together* an initiation to their sexuality? In certain societies, men live through the rites of their transition to manhood together in groups. In one way or another, that persists in our cultures. For women, initiation, even when it is marked as a stage, remains solitary. The little girl becomes a woman and a mother alone, at best with her mother or a substitute. This burden of solitude still weighs upon women. Even when they are together, they rarely know how to live and speak this transition from one state to another. They do not go beyond criticizing existing situations, beyond rivalry, beyond their complaints and cares. They are rarely initiated together into their becoming women. They may, perhaps, talk about their pregnancies or their mothers. They almost never speak of their sexual needs and desires as women. If they do, they rarely go beyond describing their sufferings, the damage suffered. They exchange scraps of games that have already been played. They rarely invent new games, *their* games.

Language [*langage*] seems to have paralysed our gestures, including our verbal gestures. As adults, we no longer have any mobility. Once childhood is over, our moving trajectories are limited to poetry, art, prayer. Does not the still silent understanding of the feminine signify *movements* to be liberated? This is not a matter of women outbidding technology, even if they can, but of their discovering forgotten, misrecognized gestures, and also verbal gestures other than those of mothering, shedding a different light on corporeal generation in the strict sense.

The most forgotten symbol in the universe and in our cultures is the sexual symbol, *the living symbol*. In their failure to recognize this living symbol, men – men alone – exchange women, children, products of labour, tokens, money (often struck in the image of the feminine?). They exchange some*thing* instead of exchanging love, god(s), art, thought, language [*langage*]. Any assertion stating that God constitutes the most noble of human exchanges, its celestial cornerstone, the basis of language, is redundant if God is not really exchanged. And he has for centuries been the focus of a monopoly on truth(s), rites. But one apparently negative predicate still remains to him: that of invisibility. Invisible too, to a large extent, our sexual relation, our carnal act, especially through the mediation of woman. What birth takes place, is yet to come, between these two poles of invisibility? How can we discover and interpret its traces in discourse? How can we remodel existing languages [*langages*] so as to give rise to a sexuate culture? That is what is at issue in my researches.

NOTES

1 [Irigaray does not give the Greek term signifying 'necessity'; '*ananke*' is in fact feminine (ed.)].
2 Cf. 'Grammaire de l'énonciation de l'hystérique et de l'obsessionnel', in *Parler n'est jamais neutre*, Paris: Minuit, 1985.
3 Cf. 'L'Ordre sexuel du discours', in *Langages*, March 1987: *Le Sexe linguistique*.

4 Cf. *Bulletin de la Société nationale de Psychoprophylaxie obstétricale*, 1971, pp. 21–40.
5 Cf. *Langages*, March 1987.
6 Cf. the texts in *Sexes et parentés* and my other work. The studies of Dora and Schreber remain unpublished.
7 Cf. *Speculum, This Sex Which is Not One, Marine Lover, L'Oubli de l'air*, and most of the texts in *Parler n'est jamais neutre*.

Translated by David Macey

SECTION III

Ethics and Subjectivity: Towards the Future

Introduction to Section III

The opening piece in this section, 'Sexual difference' ('La Différence sexuelle'), was given first as a lecture at the Erasmus University in Rotterdam on 21 September 1982, and reprinted as the opening chapter of *Ethique de la différence sexuelle* (1984). It appeared in Seán Hand's translation in *French Feminist Thought: a reader*, Toril Moi (ed.), Oxford: Blackwell, 1987, which is the translation reprinted below.

We saw in section II that Irigaray's preoccupation with ethics goes back to the 1970s; it has emerged as one of her central concerns in the 1980s. The symbolization of sexual difference, of two *genres* or kinds, is presented as a possible force for renewal against the destructive tendencies which Irigaray sees in our society: in thought, in culture, in science, and so on. But, '[f]or the work of sexual difference to take place, a revolution in thought and ethics is needed'. This is a project which would require a massive upheaval in the ways in which we conceptualize the world, including a revolution in the modalities of space and time as they are at present conceived. Woman has always been for man his space, or rather his *place*, but has no place of her own. This deprives her of identity for-herself. We find in this essay the philosophical expression of ideas that were put forward in psychoanalytical terms in 'The limits of the transference' (section II above): the need for a separate identity, for a container which is not simply constructed out of the maternal body. Without limits, Irigaray wrote in that essay, there is a danger of murderous fusion or incorporation. Here, the limits are represented by 'a relationship with the divine, death, the social or cosmic order'. In *Ethique*, the concepts of *admiration* (here translated as *wonder*), the *angel* and the *mucous* are introduced. *Admiration* is linked to the non-substitutability of woman and man; it is the passion that should correspond to sexual difference, to what is evoked by the unknowable and non-substitutable other. The angels are mediators or messengers; their essential characteristic is mobility; they pass from highest to lowest, from the celestial to the terrestrial and back again. They link what has been split by patriarchy – the flesh and the spirit, nature and gods, the carnal and the divine, and are a way of conceptualizing a possible overcoming of the deadly and immobilizing division of the sexes in which women have been allocated body, flesh, nature, earth, carnality while men have been allocated spirit and transcendence. Thus, '[a] sexual or carnal ethics would demand that both angel and body be found together'. The *mucous*, as Irigaray explains in *Ethique de la différence sexuelle*, puts into words 'what is to be thought today', or sexual difference itself: 'the burning issue', as Seán Hand translates 'la question qui est à penser à notre époque' (literally 'the question which is to be thought in our time'). The mucous, or mucosity, undermines the possibility of thinking of the divine or transcendence as 'foreign to the flesh'; if brought into thought, it crosses the split which separates flesh from spirit and woman from man. The ethics of sexual difference is an ethics of love, of the passions, in which fertility is not just the reproduction of children, but the fertility of a symbolic relationship, a value which cannot be realized in a monosexual culture. (On Irigaray's ethics and the divine, see Elizabeth Grosz's book, *Sexual Subversions*, (1989), particularly chapter 5).

The themes of 'Sexual difference' are developed at greater length in the subsequent lectures in *Ethique de la différence sexuelle*, which should soon be available in an English translation. However, they can be seen from another aspect in the following text. 'Questions to Emmanuel Levinas' ('Questions à Emmanuel Levinas') was translated into English before its first French publication. It appears in *Re-Reading Levinas*, Robert Bernasconi and Simon Critchley, (eds), (1991) and appeared in its final form in French in the journal *Critique*, 522 (November 1990).

Irigaray had previously responded to Levinas's work in an essay which appears at the end of *Ethique de la différence sexuelle* under the title 'Fécondité de la caresse' (translated by Carolyn Burke as 'The fecundity of the caress' in *Face to Face with Levinas*, Richard A.

Cohen, (ed.), (1985), pp. 231–56). Although she is sympathetic to Levinas's ethical stance, Irigaray feels, as she explains in 'Questions to Emmanuel Levinas', that his work has not gone far enough, and at certain moments, falls radically short of ethics, since it leaves the feminine other 'without her own specific face'. To put it very briefly, the feminine is always defined as man's other, the 'other of the same'. What Irigaray is concerned with is the possible alterity of 'woman-for-herself', instead of woman simply as the 'other of the same'. Thus in 'Questions to Emmanuel Levinas', she suggests that Levinas's 'caress' reduces the body of the other (woman) for the purposes of his own becoming – he transforms the flesh of the other into his own temporality. As in 'Sexual difference', Irigaray is setting out the conditions for the 'amorous exchange' in which the woman would be a desiring subject too. The central condition would be a maternal genealogy, so that the daughter could situate herself in her identity with respect to her mother. The maternal should have a spiritual and divine dimension, and not be relegated to the merely carnal, leaving the divine to the genealogy of the father. As Irigaray makes clear in her essay *Divine Women* (1986), the divine is related to the question of women's generic identity in the symbolic order: 'Women lack a mirror for becoming women.' The divine can be seen as a kind of mirror or ideal which women need in order to mediate relationships between themselves, and particularly to symbolize their own 'death'. One of Irigaray's main points is that woman is used by the male imaginary to deflect or mediate the death drives of *men* (see 'The blind spot of an old dream of symmetry' and 'Plato's *Hystera*', both in *Speculum*, and 'Veiled lips', in *Marine Lover*). They are, like Antigone, the 'guardians of death', but there are no social/symbolic forms which mediate *their* death; again, like Antigone, they are imprisoned, buried alive in the culture, sacrifices that ensure the maintenance of patriarchy. The divine, and the maternal genealogy, are conditions for ending women's status as sacrificial objects.

'Women-Amongst-Themselves: Creating a Woman-to-Woman Sociality' (Créer un Entre-Femmes) is a shortened version of an interview which Irigaray gave in 1985 in Bologna. The interviewer was Franca Chiaromonte, a journalist working for *Rinascita*, the Italian Communist Party journal of culture. Extracts from this interview were published in *Rinascita* on 28 September 1985 under the title

'Sorella donna, libera nos'. The version reprinted here is translated from the French text which appeared in *Paris-Féministe*, 31–2, (September 1986), pp. 37–41. The title 'Créer un entre-femmes' was added by the editors of *Paris-Féministe* and is not Irigaray's own title. The complete interview has still not appeared.

Among its other themes, the interview discusses the possibility of a sensible transcendental (i.e. a transcendental which is not 'foreign to the flesh'), the ethics of sexual difference, the necessity for collective and public recognition of women's difference and for symbolic forms which correspond to women's specificity, the need for an *identity*. It reaffirms Irigaray's ecofeminist suspicion that modern technology merely reproduces monosexuate values and is not an automatic instrument of liberation for women, despite its undoubted advantages. Perhaps the most interesting aspect of this interview for English-speaking readers is its discussion of *affidamento*. *Affidamento* (entrustment) was the attempt on the part of Italian feminists to create symbolic mediations for relationships between women, particularly relationships which recognized *differences* between women. The common situation of shared oppression was felt to be a barrier to women's empowerment; it led to marginality and prevented women from having any real effect on the wider society. *Affidamento* was an attempt to create symbolic links, and therefore social networks, which recognized differences of power and status among women. (For further discussions in English, see Mirna Cicioni, ' "Love and respect, together": the theory and practice of *affidamento* in Italian feminism' (1989, pp. 71–83); Teresa de Lauretis, 'The essence of the triangle or, taking the risk of essentialism seriously: feminist theory in Italy, the US and Britain', (1989, pp. 3–37); The Milan Women's Bookstore Collective, *Sexual Difference: A Theory of Social–Symbolic Practice*, (1990); Sandra Kemp and Paolo Bono, (eds), *Italian Feminist Thought*, (1991).) In this interview, Irigaray warns against the dangers in relationships between women, and makes a number of suggestions for dealing with them. In particular she locates the problem as 'the transition from contiguity to another figure'. In *Speculum* and *This Sex Which Is Not One*, contiguity was the figure for mother and daughter: the two lips represented (among other things) the two women continually in touch with each other. But even then, Irigaray was warning that contiguity in patriarchy could mean fusion and confusion of identity between women, and thus the impossibility of relationships between them (since they were not separate enough for the 'between' to exist), and the impossibility therefore of a maternal genealogy. (See also 'Volume without contours' in section I above, which discusses in more philosophical terms the problem of contiguity, and the one plus one to the *n*, which falls short of identity.) Irigaray hints at the necessity for an ideal or divine horizon to mediate and prepare the way for a new social order.

Irigaray makes similar points in her work on the law. After the ethical perspective, we turn to the question of women's civil rights, which for Irigaray is a question that should be thought within the perspective of sexual difference rather than that of equality. 'The necessity for sexuate rights' ('La Nécessité des droits sexués') introduces the collection *Sexes et parentés* (1987). It puts forward the idea that each *genre* or sexual kind should have rights and responsibilities which correspond to its specificity. Irigaray takes up the Hegelian account (discussed in *Speculum* in 'The eternal irony of the community') of the question of women's role in the maintenance of society. For Hegel, men operate within the domain of the universal and the ethical (as citizens) but also have their *particular* needs attended to within the family. Women do not have this dual possibility; their particularity is subordinated to the needs of the family and the state. (This is another formulation of the ethical question. While men can be spirit (universal), the family represents 'nature'. So long as women are confined to the family, their access to the universal is derivative, via the husband or son, rather than direct.) For Irigaray, Hegel 'does not succeed in thinking the family other than as *one* substance'; he does not consider the possibility of the woman who is not subordinate to the family. As a result, the maternal genealogy is condemned by the patriarchal state (as Irigaray, following Hegel, interprets Sophocles' *Antigone*), with the backing of patriarchal and monotheistic religion. Women's rights, when acquired, are likely to be of short duration, given the weight of the patriarchal organization of society, unless the whole civil (and family) law is rethought to take into account the needs of two *genres*, rather than focusing exclusively on reproduction and the transmission of patrimony from one generation to the next. One effect of this rethinking might be to modify the process of history as a sacrificial development

– tension/discharge (e.g. war)/return to homeostasis – which Irigaray sees as a particularly patriarchal characteristic. On this point it would be helpful to read René Girard, *Violence and the sacred* (1977) and Irigaray's critique of Girard in 'Women, the sacred and money' (1986). Other essays in *Sexes et parentés* are also relevant here; see particularly 'Le Genre féminin' and 'L'Universel comme médiation'.

The interview which follows, 'How to define sexuate rights?' ('Comment définir des droits sexués?') was first published in Italy in 1988 in *Il Diritto delle donne, trimestriale d'informazione giuridica, regione Emilia-Romagna*, under the title 'Il Sesso della legge'. The interviewer was Maria Cristina Lasagni. It appears under the title 'Pourquoi définir des droits sexués?' in *Je, Tu, Nous* (1990). The published French version was not available at the time this book was being prepared, so the translation was made from the unpublished French typescript which may differ slightly from the final version.

Like other texts, this interview bears witness to Irigaray's fear that the world is heading for increasing destruction. Although she shares this fear with others, her recommendations are different: what is needed above all is the recognition, enshrined in law, custom and citizenship, of woman's identity as a genre distinct from the male genre. Further reflections on the importance of the civil domain – as distinct from equal rights – can be found in Irigaray's book *Le Temps de la différence* (1989). Her main point is that what she calls 'the people of men' has appropriated women's bodies, children's bodies, nature, space, symbolism, the divine and representation in general. To define rights for women, therefore, is to try and imagine what it might be like for women to share in culture *as women* and to become full citizens in their own right. She sketches out a provisional agenda – a kind of draft Declaration of the Rights of Woman – to indicate the kind of concrete changes that might be necessary. As she herself points out, this theme has been present in her work since *Speculum*, and the chapter on 'Plato's *Hystera*' makes the link between social forms and Platonic metaphysics. Any philosophy that splits the Sensible from the Intelligible, material from ideal, will tend towards the installation or maintenance of patriarchy, the privilege accorded to paternal genealogy and the obliteration of the maternal genealogy. We can see also in this interview (as in 'The necessity for sexuate rights') Irigaray's link with ecofeminism. For Irigaray, nature, like women, belongs to the material world which has to be transcended in the pursuit of the ideal. The consequences of this transcendence have been harmful to both the natural world and to women. Irigaray rejects any kind of transcendence which depends for its ascension on an unacknowledged maternal or natural base. It is time, she says, to acknowledge the debt. On this theme, see also 'Une Chance de vivre' in *Sexes et parentés*.

The final text, 'He Risks who Risks Life Itself' is in fact untitled in the original. It is the final chapter of *L'Oubli de l'air chez Martin Heidegger* (1983), but was also used as part of Irigaray's lecture at the conference on Derrida's 'Les Fins de l'homme' ('The ends of man') which was published in *Les Fins de l'homme*, Jean-Luc Nancy and Philippe Lacoue-Labarthe, (eds), Paris: Galilée, 1981, and in Irigaray's *La Croyance même* (1983). The latter is reprinted in *Sexes et parentés* (1987). These versions are all slightly different; the translation below is based on the one in *L'Oubli de l'air*.

From hints elsewhere in her work, we know that Irigaray reserves a special role to the words of the poet or lover: their function is to speak words that change or 'touch' the hearer. The passage both speaks of the role of the poet, and also shows Irigaray at her most utopian in her incarnation as a poetic visionary. We can perhaps interpret this passage as an intervention in the imaginary, an attempt to appeal directly to the psychic forces and resources for change. I am not entirely sure myself how to interpret it in detail, and perhaps in any case, its power to evoke is more important than its propositional content. As Irigaray writes in 'The three genres' (section II above), her work cannot be reduced to commentaries. However, I can offer some suggestions about possible lines of approach, since there are clear links between this poetic passage and other parts of Irigaray's work.

In previous chapters in *L'Oubli de l'air*, Irigaray has been writing of the way in which Heidegger's 'house of language' continues to use the material of the maternal-feminine body for its construction, thus immobilizing women in their becoming. Immobility is linked to death, mobility to life; the underside of this appropriation (the appropriation of nature or *phusis*) is death and hatred. So Heidegger too is caught up in the pathology of a culture he denounces and from which 'only a god can save us' (quoted by Irigaray in *Ethique de la différence sexuelle*, p. 123). One of the horizons evoked by this text is the *parousia*, the second coming, or the advent of the divine which, writes Irigaray in *Ethique*, should not be a distant event, but possible *here and now*. This horizon – the horizon of sexual difference – would open up the possibility of an undreamed-of fertility: a kind of re-creation of the world. *Parousia* should not simply be a utopian future, but the construction by men and women in the present of a bridge between past and future: *'we would be* the bridges' (*Ethique* p. 124). This horizon is also described in *Ethique* as the third era: the age of the Spirit and the Bride, beyond the Old Testament (the reign of the Father) and the New Testament (the reign of the Son). This is another way of talking about the need for a symbolic redistribution, so that women too, like men, might be *both* spirit and flesh (as we shall see in 'Questions to Emmanuel Levinas'). Another way of approaching this text is to see it as yet another version of one of Irigaray's frequent figures: that of a world 'without exchange, without terms', that she had already described in the final pages of 'Commodities among themselves' and 'When our lips speak together' (both in *This Sex Which Is Not One*), or that of the 'amorous exchange' in 'Questions to Emmanuel Levinas'. In this exchange, there would be 'no geometry, no accounts'. It would be beyond the calculable and the measurable, beyond the *quantitative*: like 'the first instants of love' or like *admiration*, perhaps. And this text too, like so many others, is written under the sign of love: that which does not calculate, does not ask what it risks, gives without guarantee, does not seek to protect itself. The possibility of stepping outside the circle of the 'proper' is presented here as risking life itself – in order perhaps to have it more abundantly?

Margaret Whitford

10

Sexual Difference

Sexual difference is one of the important questions of our age, if not in fact the burning issue. According to Heidegger, each age is preoccupied with one thing, and one alone. Sexual difference is probably that issue in our own age which could be our salvation on an intellectual level.

But wherever I turn, whether to philosophy, science or religion, I find that this underlying and increasingly insistent question remains silenced. It is as if opening up this question would allow us to put a check on the many forms of destruction in the universe, like some kind of nihilism which affirms nothing more than the reversal or proliferation of existing values – whether we call these the consumer society, the circular nature of discourse, the more or less cancerous diseases of our age, the unreliable nature of words, the end of philosophy, religious despair or the regressive return to religion, scientistic imperialism or a technique that does not take the human subject into account, and so on.

Sexual difference would represent the advent of new fertile regions as yet unwitnessed, at all events in the west. By fertility I am not referring simply to the flesh or reproduction. No doubt for couples it would concern the question of children and procreation, but it would also involve the production of a new age of thought, art, poetry and language; the creation of a new *poetics*.

Both in theory and in practice, the arrival or discovery of such an event is resisted. In theory, philosophy wishes to become literature or rhetoric, by breaking with ontology or returning to ontological origins. It presumably does this in order to use the same ground and the same basic framework as the 'very first philosophy', working at its disintegration, but without showing that there is anything else at stake that might assure new foundations and new works.

In politics, some openings have been presented to women, but these have resulted from partial and local concessions on the part of those in power, rather than from the establishment of new values. Such new values are all too seldom thought out and proclaimed by women themselves, who often remain simply critical. But by not building foundations different to those on which the world of men rests, will not all the concessions gained by the women's struggle be lost again? As for psychoanalytic theory and therapy, which are the scenes of sexuality as such, they have hardly brought about a revolution. With a few exceptions, sexual practice today is often divided into the two parallel worlds of men and women. An untraditional encounter between the fertility of both sexes scarcely exists, and makes its demands in public only through certain forms of silence or polemic.

For the work of sexual difference to take place, a revolution in thought and ethics is needed. We must re-interpret the whole relationship between the subject and discourse, the subject and the world, the subject and the cosmic, the microcosmic and the macrocosmic. And the first thing to say is that, even when aspiring to a universal or neutral state, this subject has always been written in the masculine form, as man, despite the fact that, at least in France, 'man' is a sexed and not a neutral noun.

It is man who has been the subject of discourse, whether in the field of theory, morality or politics. And the gender of God, the guardian of every subject and discourse, is always *paternal and masculine* in the west. For women, there remain the so-called minor artforms; cooking, knitting, sewing and embroidery; and in exceptional cases, poetry, painting and music. Whatever their importance, these arts today do not lay down the law, at least not overtly.

We are, of course, presently bearing witness to a certain reversal of values: manual labour and art are both being revalorized. But the relationship of these arts to sexual difference is never really thought through, and properly sorted out, although on occasion it is all related to the class-struggle.

In order to live and think through this difference, we must reconsider the whole question of *space* and *time*.

In the beginning was space and the creation of space, as stated in every theogony. The gods or God first of all creates *space*. And time is there, more or less at the service of space. During the first few days the gods or God organize a world by separating the elements. This world is then peopled, and a rhythmical pattern is established among its inhabitants. God then becomes time itself, lavishing or exteriorizing itself in space or place.

Philosophy confirms this genealogy of the task of the gods or God. Time becomes *interior* to the subject, and space *exterior* (this is developed by Kant in the *Critique of Pure Reason*). The subject, the master of time, becomes the axis, managing the affairs of the world. Beyond him lies the eternal instant of God, who brings about the passage between time and space.

Could it be that this order becomes inverted in sexual difference, such that femininity is experienced as a space that often carries connotations of the depths of night (God being space and light), while masculinity is conceived of in terms of time?

The transition to a new age in turn necessitates a new perception and a new conception of *time and space*, our *occupation of place*, and the different *envelopes known as identity*.[1] It assumes and entails an evolution or transformation of forms, of the relationship of *matter* to *form* and of the interval *between* the two. This trilogy gives us our notion of place. Each age assigns limits to this trinity, be they *matter*, *form*, *interval* or *power*, *act*, *intermediate – interval*.

Desire occupies or designates the place of the *interval*. A permanent definition of desire would put an end to desire. Desire requires a sense of attraction: a change in the interval or the relations of nearness or distance between subject and object.

The transition to a new age coincides with a change in the economy of desire, necessitating a different relationship between man and god(s), man and man, man and the world, man and woman. Our own age, which is often felt to be the one in which the problem of desire has been brought to the fore, frequently theorizes about this desire on the basis of certain observations about a moment of tension, situated in historical time, whereas desire ought to be thought of as a dynamic force whose changing form can be traced in the past and occasionally the present, but never predicted. Our age will only realize the dynamic potential in desire if the latter is referred back to the economy of the *interval*, that is if it is located in the attractions, tensions, and acts between *form* and *matter*, or characterized as the *residue* of any creation or work, which lies *between* what is already identified and what has still to be identified, etc.

In order to imagine such an economy of desire, we must re-interpret what Freud implies in the term *sublimation*. Note that he does not speak of the sublimation of *genitality* (except, perhaps, through reproduction, which, if it were a successful form of sublimation, would lead him to be less pessimistic about the parental education of children). Nor does he speak of the sublimation of *female partial drives*. Instead he speaks of their repression (little girls speak sooner and more skilfully than little boys, since they have a better relationship with society, etc.: are these really qualities or aptitudes which disappear, leaving no trace of the source of such energy, except that of becoming a woman, an object of attraction?).[2]

In this non-sublimation, which lies within her and acts through her, woman always tends *towards* something else without ever turning to herself as the site of a positive element. In terms of contemporary physics, we could say that she remains on the side of the electron, with all that this implies for her, for man, and for an encounter between the two. If there is no double desire, the positive and negative poles divide themselves among the two sexes instead of creating a chiasmus or double loop in which each can move out towards the other and back to itself.

If these positive and negative elements are not present in both, the same pole will always attract, while the other remains in motion but possesses no 'proper' place. There is no attraction and support that excludes disintegration or rejection, no double pole of attraction and decomposition that would replace the separation that articulates all encounters and gives rise to speech, promises and alliances.

In order to keep one's distance, does one have to know how to take? or speak? It comes down in the end to the same thing. Perhaps the ability to take requires a permanent space or container; a soul, maybe, or a mind? Mourning nothing is the hardest of all. Mourning the self in the other is vitually impossible. I search for myself among those elements which have been assimilated. But I ought to reconstitute myself on the basis of disassimilation, and be reborn from traces of culture, works already produced by the other. I should search for the things they contain and do not contain, and examine what has and has not given rise to them, what are and are not their conditions.

Woman ought to rediscover herself, among other things, through the images of herself already deposited in history and the conditions of production of the work of man, rather than through the work itself or its genealogy.

If, traditionally, in the role of mother, woman represents a sense of *place* for man, such a limit means that she becomes a *thing*, undergoing certain optional changes from one historical period to another. She finds herself defined as a thing. Moreover, the mother woman is also used as a kind of envelope by man in order to help him set limits to things. The *relationship between the envelope and the things* represents one of the aporias, if not the aporia, of Aristotelianism and the philosophical systems which are derived from it.

In our own terminologies, which have evolved from this kind of thought, but nevertheless remain impregnated with a form of psychology that is ignorant of its origins, one might state, for example, that the mother woman is a *castrator*. This means that her status as envelope and as thing(s) has not been interpreted, and so she remains inseparable from the work or act of man, notably in so far as he defines her, and creates his own identity through her or, correlatively, through this determination of her being. If in spite of all this, woman continues to exist, she continually undoes his work, distinguishing herself from either envelope or thing, and creating an endless interval, game, agitation, or non-limit which destroys the perspectives and limits of this world. But, for fear of leaving her a subject–life of her own, which would entail his sometimes being her locus and her thing, in a dynamic inter-subjective process, man remains within a master–slave dialectic. He is ultimately the slave of a God on whom he bestows the qualities of an absolute master. He is secretly a slave to the power of the mother woman, which he subdues or destroys.

The mother woman remains the *place separated from its 'own' place*, a place deprived of a place of its own. She is or ceaselessly becomes the place of the other who cannot separate himself from it. Without her knowledge or volition, then, she threatens by what she lacks: a 'proper' place. She would have to envelop herself, and do so at least twice: both as a woman and as a mother. This would entail a complete change in our conception of time and space.

In the meantime, this ethical question is played out in the realms of *nudity* and *perversity*. Woman is to be nude, since she cannot be located, cannot remain in her place. She attempts to envelop herself in clothes, make-up and jewellery. She cannot use the envelope that she *is*, and so must create artificial ones.

Freud's statement that her stage is oral is significant but still exiles her from her most archaic and constituant site. No doubt the word 'oral' is particularly useful in describing a woman: morphologically, she has two mouths and two pairs of lips. But she can only act on this morphology and create something from it if she retains her relationship to the *spatial* and the *foetal*. She needs these dimensions in order to create a space for herself (as well as to maintain a position from which to welcome the other), but she is traditionally deprived of them by man who uses them to fabricate a sense of nostalgia for this first and ultimate dwelling-place. This is an obscure sort of commemoration, and it may have taken centuries to enable man to interpret the meaning of his work: the endless construction of substitutes for his prenatal home. From the depths of the earth to the vast expanse of heaven, time and time again he robs femininity of the tissue or texture of her spatiality. In exchange, though it never is one, he buys her a house, shuts her up in it, and places limits on her that are the counterpart of the place without limits where he unwittingly leaves her. He envelops her within these walls while he envelops himself and his things in her flesh. The nature of these envelopes is different in each case: on the one hand, they are invisibly alive, and yet have barely perceptible limits; and on the other hand, they offer a visible limit or shelter that risks imprisoning or murdering the other unless a door is left open.

It is therefore essential to look again at the whole question of our conception of place, both in order to pass on to another age of difference (since each intellectual age corresponds to a new meditation of difference), and in order to construct an ethics of the passions. It is necessary to change the relationship between form, matter, interval and limit. This last phenomenon has never been formulated in such a way as to permit a rapport between two loving subjects of different sexes.

Once there was the enveloping body and the enveloped body. The latter is the more mobile in terms of *transports* (maternity not really appearing to be 'transporting'). The subject who offers or permits desire transports and so envelops, or incorporates, the other. It is moreover dangerous if there is no third term. Not only because it is a necessary limitation. This third term can show up within the container as the latter's relationship with his or her own limits: a relationship with the divine, death, the social or cosmic order. If such a third term does not exist within and for the container, the latter may become *all-powerful*.

Therefore, if one deprives women, who are one of the poles of sexual difference, of a third term, then this makes them dangerously all-powerful in relation to men. This arises notably through the suppression of intervals (or enter-vals), the entry and exit which the envelop provides for both parties (on the same side, lest the envelope be perforated or assimilated into the digestive system), such that they are both free to move around, or remain immobile without the risk of imprisonment.

To arrive at the constitution of an ethics of sexual difference, we must at least return to what is for Descartes the first passion: *wonder*.[3] This passion is not opposed to, or in conflict with, anything else, and exists always as though for the first time. Man and woman, woman and man are therefore always meeting as though for the first time since they cannot stand in for one another. I shall never take the place of a man, never will a man take mine. Whatever identifications are possible, one will never exactly fill the place of the other – the one is irreducible to the other:

> When our first encounter with some object surprises us and we find it novel, or very different from what we formerly knew or from what we supposed it ought to be, this causes us to wonder and to be astonished at it. Since all this may happen before we know whether or not the object is beneficial to us, I regard wonder as the first of all the passions. It has no opposite, for, if the object before us has no characteristics that surprise us, we are not moved by it at all and we consider it without passion.[4]

Who or what the other is, I never know. But this unknowable other is that which differs sexually from me. This feeling of wonder, surprise and astonishment in the face of the unknowable ought to be returned to its proper place: the realm of sexual difference. The passions have either been repressed, stifled and subdued, or else reserved for God. Sometimes a sense of wonder is bestowed upon a work of art. But it is never found in the *gap between man and woman*. This space was filled instead with attraction, greed, possession, consummation, disgust, etc., and not with that wonder which sees something as though always for the first time, and never seizes the other as its object. Wonder cannot seize, possess or subdue such an object. The latter, perhaps, remains subjective and free?

This has never happened between the sexes. Wonder might allow them to retain an autonomy based on their difference, and give them a space of freedom or attraction, a possibility of separation or alliance.

All this would happen even before becoming engaged, during their first encounter, which would confirm their difference. The *interval* would never be crossed. There would be no consummation. Such an idea is a delusion. One sex is never entirely consummated or consumed by another. There is always a *residue*.

Up until now this residue has been offered up to or reserved for God. Sometimes a part of it became incarnated in a *child* or was thought of as being *neuter*. This neuter (like the child or God?) represents the possibility of an encounter that was endlessly deferred, even when it concerned an effect arising after the event. It always remained at an insurmountable distance, like a sort of respectful or deadly no-man's land. Nothing was celebrated, no alliance was ever forged. An immediate encounter was either cancelled or projected towards a future that never materializes.

Of course, the neuter might signify an alchemical form of the sublimation of 'genitality' and the very possibility of procreation or of creation of and between different kinds. But it must still welcome the advent of difference, still think of itself as waiting on this side of difference, rather than as existing already on the other side of difference, most notably as an ethics. The phrase *there is* usually upholds the present but postpones any celebrations. There is not and will never be any sense of that wonder conjured up by a *wedding*, an ecstasy that none the less remains *agency*. God may eventually put a strain on this present-tense *there is*, but it does not form the basis for the triumph of sexual fertility. Only certain Oriental traditions speak of an aesthetic, religious and energizing fertility of the sexual act, in which the two sexes give one another the seed of life and eternity, and between them create a new generation.

As for our own history, we must re-examine it thoroughly to understand why this sexual difference has not had a chance to flourish, either on an empirical or transcendental level, that is, why it has failed to acquire an ethics, aesthetics, logic or religion of its own that would reflect both its microcosmic and macrocosmic source or fate.

This certainly concerns the split between body and soul, sexuality and spirituality, the lack of a passage for the spirit or for God, between inside and outside, as well as the way in which these elements have been distributed among the two sexes in the sexual act. Everything is constructed in such a way as to keep these realities apart, if not opposed to one another. They must not mix, marry or forge an alliance. Their wedding must always be put back to a future life, or depreciated, and considered and felt to be ignoble in comparison with the marriage between mind and God which takes place in a transcendental realm that has cut all ties with the world of sensations.

The consequences of such a non-fulfilment of the sexual act remain, and there are many of them. To take only the most beautiful example, which has yet to be seen on the level of space and time, let us consider the *angels*. These messengers are never immobile nor do they ever dwell in one single place. As mediators of what has not yet taken place, or what is heralded, angels circulate between God, who is the perfectly immobile act, man, who is enclosed within the horizons of his world of work, and woman, whose job it is to look after nature and procreation. These angels therefore open up the closed nature of the world, identity, action and history.

The angel is whatever endlessly *passes through the envelope or envelopes* from one end to the other, postponing every deadline, revising every decision, undoing the very idea of repetition. They destroy the monstrous elements that might prohibit the possibility of a new age, and herald a new birth, a new dawn.

They are not unconnected with sex. There is of course Gabriel, the angel of the annunciation. But other angels announce the consummation of marriage, notably all the angels of the Apocalypse, and many from the Old Testament. It is as if the angel were the figurative version of a sexual being not yet incarnate. A light, divine gesture from flesh that has not yet blossomed into action. Always fallen or still awaiting the Second Coming. The fate of a love still divided between the here and the elsewhere. The work of love which, ever since that first lost garden of paradise, has perhaps been the original sinner. The fate of all flesh which is attributable, moreover, to God![5]

These swift messengers, who transgress all limits by their speed, describe the journey between the envelope of God and that of the world, be it microcosmic or macrocosmic. These angels proclaim that such a journey can be carried out by the body of man, and above all the body of woman. They represent another incarnation, another *parousia* of the body. They cannot be reduced to philosophy, theology or morality, and appear as the messengers of the ethics evoked by art – sculpture, painting or music – though they can only be discussed in terms of the gesture that represents them.

They speak as messengers, but gesture seems to be their 'nature'. Movement, posture, the coming-and-going between the two. They move – or disturb? – the paralysis or *apatheia* of the body, or soul, or world. They set trances or convulsions to music, and lend them harmony.

Their touch – when they touch – resembles that of gods. They are imperious in grace while remaining imperceptible.

The question that arises here, among others, is whether or not they can be brought together in the same place. The traditional reply is no. This question, both similar to and different from that of the co-location of bodies, rejoins the problem of sexual ethics. Mucosity ought no doubt to be thought of as linked to the angel, while the inertia of a body deprived of the mucous and the act associated with it is linked to the fallen body or corpse.

A sexual or carnal ethics would demand that both angel and body be found together. This is a world that must be constructed or reconstructed. A genesis of love between the sexes has yet to come about, in either the smallest or largest sense, or in the most intimate or political guise. It is a world to be created or recreated so that man and woman may once more or finally live together, meet and sometimes inhabit the same place.

The link uniting or reuniting masculine and feminine must be both horizontal and vertical, terrestrial and celestial. As Heidegger, among others, has written, this link must forge an alliance between the divine and the mortal, in which a sexual encounter would be a celebration, and not a disguised or polemic form of the master–slave relationship. In this way it would no longer be a meeting within the shadow or orbit of a God the Father who alone lays down the law, or the immutable mouthpiece of a single sex.

Of course, the most extreme progression and regression goes by the name of God. I can only strive towards the absolute or regress *ad infinitum* through the guaranteed existence of a God. This is what tradition has taught us, and its imperatives have not yet been overcome, since their destruction would bring about fairly pathological situations and terrible dereliction, barring quite exceptional lovers. And even then . . . Unhappiness is sometimes all the more inescapable precisely because it marks a glimpse of the divine, or the gods, or an opening unto something beyond, as well as the *limit* which the other may or may not penetrate.

How can one mark this limit of a place, and of place in general, if not through sexual difference? In order to bring about its ethics, however, we must constitute a place that could be inhabited by each sex, body or flesh. This supposes a memory of the past and a hope for the future, bridging the present, and confounding the mirror–symmetry that annihilates the difference of identity.

We need both space and time. And perhaps we are living in an age when *time must re-deploy space*. Could this be the dawning of a new world? Immanence and transcendence are being recast, notably by that *threshold* which has never been examined in itself: the female sex. It is a threshold unto *mucosity*. Beyond the classic opposites of love and hate, liquid and ice lies this perpetually *half-open* threshold, consisting of *lips* that are strangers to dichotomy. Pressed against one another, but without any possibility of suture, at least of a real kind, they do not absorb the world either into themselves or through themselves, provided they are not abused and reduced to a mere consummating or consuming structure. Instead their shape welcomes without assimilating or reducing or devouring. A sort of door unto voluptuousness, then? Not that, either: their useful function is to designate *a place*: the very place of uselessness, at least on a habitual plane. Strictly speaking, they serve neither conception nor *jouissance*. Is this, then, the mystery of female identity, of its self-contemplation, of that strange word of silence: both the threshold and reception of exchange, the sealed-up secret of wisdom, belief and faith in every truth?

(Superimposed, moreover, these lips adopt a cross-like shape that is the prototype of the crossroads, thus representing both *inter* and *enter*, for the lips of the mouth and the lips of the female sex do not point in the same direction. To a certain extent they are not arranged as one might expect: those 'down below' are vertical.)

Approached in this light, where the edges of the body join in an embrace that transcends all limits and which nevertheless does not risk falling into the abyss thanks to the fertility of this porous space, in the most extreme moments of sensation, which still lie in the future, each self-discovery takes place in that area which cannot be spoken of, but that forms the fluid basis of life and language.

For this we need 'God', or a love so scrupulous that it is divine. Perhaps we have not yet witnessed such a love, which delays its transcendence in the here and now, except in certain experiences of God. Such a desire does not act sufficiently upon the porous nature of the body, and leaves out the communion that takes place through the most intimate mucous membranes. This exchange communicates something so subtle that we must show great perseverance to prevent it falling into oblivion, intermittency, deterioration, sickness or death.

This communion is often left to the child, who is the symbol of an alliance. But are there not other signs of alliance prior to the child, a space where lovers give one another life or death? Regeneration or degeneration: both are possible when the intensity of desire and the filiation of each partner are involved.

And if the divine is present as the mystery at the heart of the copula, the *is* and *being* of sexual difference, can the forge of desire overcome the avatars of genealogical fate? How does it manage? How strong is it? It nevertheless remains incarnate. Between the idealistic fluidity of an unborn body that is untrue to its birth, and genetic determinism, how can we measure a love that turns us from mortals into immortals? Certain figures here, such as those in which gods become men, or in which God was made man, or those of the twice-born indicate the course of love.

Something of the consummation of sexual difference has still not been articulated or transmitted. Is there not still something held in reserve within the silence of female history: an energy, morphology, growth or blossoming still to come from the female realm? Such a flowering keeps the future open. The world remains uncertain in the fact of this strange advent.

NOTES

(The editorial notes to 'Sexual difference' are by Toril Moi.)

1 [Irigaray's text has *enveloppe/envelopper* in this and subsequent passages. We have decided to translate 'envelope' and 'envelop', although this translation risks losing something of the concrete sense of enfolding, wrapping, covering, englobing, etc., associated with the French words. While the philosophical idea under discussion is that of the relationship between the container and the contained, there may also be an allusion to certain psychoanalytic theories of an early 'skin-ego', conceptualized as a 'psychic envelope' (Bion, Winnicott, Anzieu) (ed.)].

2 See my *Spéculum de l'autre femme.* (trans. *Speculum of the Other Woman.*)

3 [The original French expression is *admiration.* (ed.)].

4 René Descartes, *The Passions of the Soul*, article 53 in *The Philosophical Writings of Descartes*, I, trans. J. Cottingham, R. Stoothoff, D. Murdoch, Cambridge: Cambridge University Press, 1985, p. 350.

5 See my 'Epistle to the last Christians', in *Amante marine* (trans. *Marine Lover*).

Translated by Seán Hand

11

Questions to Emmanuel Levinas

On the divinity of love

(1) Is there otherness outside of sexual difference? The feminine, as it is characterized by Levinas, is not other than himself. Defined by 'modesty', 'a mode of being which consists in shunning the light' (see *Time and the Other*),[1] the feminine appears as the underside or reverse side of man's aspiration towards the light, as its negative. The feminine is apprehended not in relation to itself, but from the point of view of man, and through a purely erotic strategy, a strategy moreover which is dictated by masculine pleasure [*jouissance*], even if man does not recognize to what limited degree his own erotic intentions and gestures are ethical. It is the culture of men-amongst-themselves, and in particular the monopoly of divine power by male gods, which is responsible for female sexuality, in so far as it is visible at all, being kept from the light and left without representation in terms of the divine. During the period when there were female goddesses, the woman's sexual organs always appear in the representation of the bodies of women, particularly goddesses, and not merely in the form of the triangle indicating the womb, but also in the form of the labia, an inscription which will later be erased. The cult of goddesses who are exclusively mothers, and mothers of sons, is a late episode in the history of women. In the symbolism of social exchanges, it is accompanied by the representation of the woman's sexual organs as the figure of the triangle representing the womb and standing as a symbol of the maternal function. This epoch also emphasizes the transition to a writing useful to trade and for this reason becoming phonogrammatic. One of the places where this transition can be pinpointed, is located at the junction of

Mesopotamian with Sumerian culture, a place where the songs celebrating sacred unions or marriages (in this connection, cf. S. N. Kramer's work) give birth to the *Song of Solomon*, which tells of the complexity of the nuptials between the two lovers [*l'amante et l'amant*], the two beloveds [*l'aimée et l'aimé*], who are born of different mothers and so do not belong to the same traditions, to the same genealogies or to the same gods.

Of this love and this grief in the *Song of Solomon*, of the sensual delight [*volupté*] of the lovers who wed each other with all their senses, with their whole body, inviting to their encounters the most succulent fruits of the earth, but who are already compelled to shun each other, to flee each other, to separate, nothing remains in the pleasure [*volupté*]² of which Levinas speaks. For Levinas, the feminine merely represents that which sustains desire, that which rekindles pleasure. The caress, that 'fundamental disorder' (TA 82/ TO 89) does not touch the other. What Levinas is seeking is neither the qualities of the other's flesh nor of his own, he seeks:

> a play with something elusive, a play absolutely without aim or plan [there is no union intended, therefore – Irigaray] not with that which may become ours and ourself, but with something other, always inaccessible, always in the future. The caress is the anticipation of this pure becoming, without content. It is made up of this intensified hunger, of promises ever richer, opening new perspectives onto the ungraspable. It is nourished by innumerable hungers. This intentionality of pleasure, directed purely and simply towards the future itself, and not an anticipation of any future event, has always been misrecognized by philosophical analysis. (TA 82–3/TO 89)

To caress, for Levinas, consists, therefore, not in approaching the other in its most vital dimension, the touch, but in the reduction of that vital dimension of the other's body to the elaboration of a future for himself. To caress could thus constitute the hidden intention of philosophical temporality. But in this 'play', the only function of the feminine other is to satisfy the hungers of the philosopher, to re-nourish the intentionality of his pleasure in the direction of a future without a 'future event', a future where no day is named for the encounter with the other in an embodied love. This description of the caress (of which I have already spoken at length in 'Fecondité de la caresse' in *Ethique de la difference sexuelle*)³ is a good example of the way in which the temporality of the male subject, of Emmanuel Levinas at any rate, makes use of the support of the feminine in the intentionality of pleasure for its own becoming. In this transformation of the flesh of the other into his own temporality, it is clear that the masculine subject loses the feminine as other.

To become other to himself, to return to self via the other, Levinas needs the son. The son is his being as same/other, in a simultaneous engenderment that he seems to forget somewhat.

The function of the other sex as an alterity irreducible to myself eludes Levinas for at least two reasons:

He knows nothing of communion in pleasure. Levinas does not ever seem to have experienced the transcendence of the other which becomes im-mediate ecstasy [*extase instante*]⁴ in me and with him – or her. For Levinas, the distance is always maintained with the other in the experience of love. The other is 'close' to him in 'duality'. This autistic, egological, solitary love does not correspond to the shared outpouring, to the loss of boundaries which takes place for both lovers when they cross the boundary of the skin into the mucous membranes of the body, leaving the circle which encloses my solitude to meet in a shared space, a shared breath, abandoning the relatively dry and precise outlines of each body's solid exterior to enter a fluid universe where the perception of being two persons [*de la dualité*] becomes indistinct, and above all, acceding to another energy, neither that of the one nor that of the other, but an energy produced together and as a result of the irreducible difference of sex. Pleasure between the same sex does not result in that im-mediate ecstasy between the other and myself. It may be more or less intense, quantitatively and qualitatively different, it does not produce in us that ecstasy which is our child, prior to any child [*enfant avant tout enfant*]. In this relation, we are at least three, each of which is irreducible to any of the others: you, me and our work [*oeuvre*], that ecstasy of ourself in us [*de nous en nous*], that transcendence of the flesh of one to that of the other become ourself in us [*devenue nous en nous*], at any rate 'in me' as a woman, prior to any child.⁵

Is it the fact that Levinas is a man that makes him unaware of this creation of pleasure prior to any son? Of pleasure's neither mine nor thine, pleasure transcendent and immanent to one and to the other, and which gives birth to a third, a mediator between us thanks to which we return to ourselves, other than we were.

Is what I am describing here only my pleasure as a woman? My pleasure with the lover of my flesh? In an act in which neither can be substituted for the other. We cannot be interchangeable, in so far as he is a man and I am a woman, and in so far as he is he and I am I. And because we are not interchangeable, pleasure is no longer proximity nor duality, neither loss nor regression, nor more or less infantile perversity, nor failure of communion or of communication etc. Pleasure is engendering in us and between us, an engendering associated with the world and the universe, with which the work [*oeuvre*] of the flesh is never unconnected. Either pleasure is a mere expenditure of fire, of water, of seed, of body and of spirit . . . or else it is a unique and definitive creation. In this sense, it is time. It is ineffaceable, unrepeatable, even by the child.

The second reason for which Levinas does not perceive the feminine as other is that he substitutes the son for the feminine. However, the child belongs to another time. The child should be for himself not for the parent. When one intends to create a child, giving the child to himself appears as an ethical necessity. The son should not be the place where the father confers being or existence on himself, the place where he finds the resources to return to himself in relation to this same as and other than himself constituted by the son. From my point of view, this gesture fails to achieve the relation to the other, and doubly so: it does not recognize the feminine other and the self as other in relation to her; it does not leave the child to his own generation. It seems to me pertinent to add that it does not recognize God in love.

(2) Who is the other, the Other [*l'autre, autrui*] etc.? How can the other be defined? Levinas speaks of 'the Other' [*autrui*], of 'respect for the Other' [*respect d'autrui*], of the 'face of the Other' [*visage d'autrui*] etc. But how to define this Other which seems so self-evident to him, and which I see as a postulate, the projection or the remnant of a system, a hermeneutic locus of crystallization of meaning, etc. . . . . Who is the other, if the other of sexual difference is not recognized or known? Does it not mean in that case a sort of mask or lure? Or an effect of the consumption of an other [*Autre*]? But how is transcendence defined?

Furthermore, this non-definition of the other, when the other is not considered to have anything to do with sexual difference, gives rise to an infinite series of substitutions, an operation which seems to me non-ethical. No one can be radically substituted for the other, without depriving the other of identity. Even a substitution which is authorized by proxy is questionable, given the irreducibility of each.

What Levinas does not see is that the locus of paternity, to which he accords the privilege of ethical alterity, has already assumed the place of the genealogy of the feminine, has already covered over the relationships between mothers and daughters, in which formerly transmission of the divine word was located.

Everything can slide in this historical and genealogical deracination. There is no longer any irreducible difference of the other. From this it results that ethics becomes indistinguishable from a kind of formalism or a disordered drift, whatever the nature of its passion [*pathos*].

Although temporarily useful and worthy of respect up to a certain point, this ethics no longer knows its faults. For such an ethics, the only faults are those which it openly produces. It turns on itself, in itself, failing to recognize its hidden faults; the fault remains invisible, nor is it recognized within the couple and the family, the nucleus of the socio-religious organization in which ethics is articulated.

The other sex, then, would represent the possible locus of the definition of the fault, of imperfection, of the unheard, of the unfulfilled, etc. But this fault cannot be named except by my other or its substitute. More precisely, there are at least two interpretations of the fault: that which corresponds to the failed fulfilment [*défaut de l'accomplissement*] of my sex, to the failure to become the ideal of my genre, and that which is defined in relation to the ideal of the other genre. These faults are not the same. For centuries, one has been cruelly masked by the other. This puts society permanently in the position of being ethically at fault, a position which often has the backing of religion.

(3) How to articulate the question of the cosmic economy with, on the one hand, that of sexual difference, and on the other, that of the gods, or more generally, the divine, the other? The question of the face of the natural universe does not seem to me to figure much in the work of Levinas. Without interrogating him here on the issue of

what the creation or the culture of the world might mean for him, I would like to pause at this question: who is the other if it is not rooted and situated in the natural universe? Is otherness defined uniquely in terms of the social body? Are its identity and its status sociological or ethnological? From such a conception of the other, I would distinguish that of an other with its roots also in the natural universe, in the body, and which, starting from this irreducible incarnation, continually elaborates a human universe, a human identity. We are not only culturally determined, we remain natural, and nature is the basis from which we can continue to create culture.

(4) Levinas uses a certain number of words without always defining or redefining them. Other [*autre*] is one of these. That gives a very insistent hermeneutical, metaphysical or theological tone to his writings, even though the same writings sometimes have recourse to phenomenological methods from which metaphysical entities have been detached. This means that Levinas's discourse has two levels. The phenomenological approach, in particular through the caress, to the carnal relation, to the alterity of the feminine, to the unseen of the flesh, would belong to the descriptive methods, indicating that we are no longer in the order of metaphysics. The assertion that the other is always situated within the realm of the father, of the father-son, man–God relation, and that it is there and only there that ethics may be established, seems to me to belong to the imperatives of the metaphysical tradition. So the phenomenology of the caress in Levinas falls back within the boundaries staked out by the philosophical constitution of the masculine subject. It does not lead either to the other, or to God, or to a new spiritual or rational level. It is submerged in animality, perversity, childhood (which/whose?), of which the feminine other is the condition of representation. After having been so far – or so close – in the approach to the other sex, in my view to the other, to the mystery of the other, Levinas clings on once more to this rock of patriarchy in the very place of carnal love.

Although he takes pleasure in caressing, he abandons the feminine other, leaves her to sink, in particular into the darkness of a pseudo-animality, in order to return to his responsibilities in the world of men-amongst-themselves. For him, the feminine does not stand for an other to be respected in her human freedom and human identity. The feminine other is left without her own specific face. On this point, his philosophy falls radically short of ethics. To go beyond the face of metaphysics would mean precisely to leave the woman her face, and even to assist her to discover it and to keep it. Levinas scarcely unveils the disfigurements brought about by onto-theology. His phenomenology of the caress is still implicated in it.

(5) The philosophy of Levinas does not resolve the question (shelved by Heidegger) of the relations between philosophy and theology: being as thought and being as other. Levinas, usually intentionally, fails to distinguish between the foundations of philosophy and the foundations of theology. Thus, unlike Heidegger, he writes that Being is the other or he points to the other as Being. According to Heidegger, Being corresponds to an operation of thought, to a logical and grammatical economy. No other is ever Being. We consider the other within the dimension of Being, or outside this dimension. But Being [*être*] does not correspond to any being [*étant*], neither the Other nor God. Being [*être*] is used to refer to a disposition which leads me to approach any being [*étant*] in a certain way. In this sense, the philosophy of Heidegger cannot simply be seen as an 'ethics of the "fruits of the earth"' [*nourritures terrestres*][6] nor of the enjoyment [*jouissance*] of objects, such as the other in sexual love (cf. TA 45–6/ TO 62–4). The philosophy of Heidegger is more ethical than that expression conveys, than his philosophy itself says explicitly. To consider the other within the horizon of Being should mean to respect the other. It is true that the definition of Being in terms of mortal destiny rather than in terms of living existence raises a question about the nature of respect. And in addition, this philosophy is more or less silent on man's sexual dimension [*la dimension de l'homme comme sexué*], an irreducible dimension of human existence. Perhaps Heidegger's thought was preparing the way for thinking the sexually identified subject [*sujet comme sexué*], in particular as a possible future for thought. The dissociation between philosophy and (patriarchal) theology can also be understood as an opening for a new epoch of Being.

To assimilate philosophy and theology as Levinas often does, is it not equivalent to assimilating philosophy and the thought of a people at a particular moment in their history, assimilating philosophy and ethnology or sociology? Is this still philosophy? And further, is it possible to assimilate philosophy and theology until one has interpreted what is at stake in monotheism? In my opinion, it is not. Is monotheism wisdom or a patriarchal and masculine passion? The obligation to believe or to give one's allegiance, the injunction not to touch, form an integral part of a monotheism which conceals its passional nature. But monotheistic religions cannot claim to be ethical unless they submit themselves to a radical interrogation relative to the sexual attribution [*caractère sexué*] of their paradigms, whether these be God, the ways in which God is referred to (in particular the masculine gender used by language, when he is not represented pictorially), God's commandments, etc.

(6) In this connection, I would like to return to the question of substitution, and point out once again that a place of irreducible non-substitutability exists within sexual difference. If an example is needed, let me suggest this question: are the peoples of monotheism ready to assert that their God is a woman? How will they realign their entire socio-religious economy if this substitution is made? What upheaval in the symbolic order will be a necessary pre-requisite to achieve such a substitution?

(7) In 'Fecundity of the caress', I used the term 'woman lover' [*l'amante*] and not only, as Levinas does, the word 'beloved' [*aimée*]. In this way, I wanted to signify that the woman can be a subject in love [*un sujet amoureux*] and is not reducible to a more or less immediate object of desire. Man and woman, woman and man can love each other in reciprocity as subjects, and not only in that transitive fashion whereby the man loves the woman, one accomplishing the act of love to which the other submits, already in the past tense,[7] in the passive. This description of pleasure given by Levinas is unacceptable to the extent that it presents man as the sole subject exercising his desire and his appetite upon the woman who is deprived of subjectivity except to seduce him. So the woman's pleasure is alienated to that of the man, according to the most traditional of scenarios of temptation and fall. In my opinion, if there is a fall, it is located in the reduction of the feminine to the passive, to the past tense and to the object of man's pleasure, in the identification of the woman with the beloved [*aimée*].

This economy of love does indeed lead to despair. . . . But this is because of the obliteration of the woman as subject desiring *along with* man as subject. Such a situation exists in certain traditions. So it is not merely a woman's utopia or imagination. It is possible to live and simultaneously create sexual love. Here would lie the way out from the fall, for in this case, love can become spiritual and divine.

But what chance has it to exist in the genealogical economy of patriarchy? Without relationships between both natural and spiritual mothers and daughters, that are relationships between subjects, without cultural recognition of the divinity of this genealogy, how can a woman remain the lover [*l'amante*] of a man who belongs to the line of a Father God? And does not the latter need a Mother God? The two genealogies must be divinized in each of the two sexes and for the two sexes: mother and father, woman and man, for it to be possible for female and male lovers [*amante et amant*] to love each other.

The most precious thing that I wanted to say in 'Fecundity of the caress' has unfortunately not been possible to translate into English. For in fact English – in which, so I have been told many times, there is no hierarchy of sex or gender[8] – has no specific word for woman as lover [*amante*]. How is sexual non-hierarchy in the act of love expressed in this language?

(8) When it is not traditional metaphysics, what governs the ethical order in Levinas is fundamentally a law deriving from God. His work displays a hesitation or oscillation between these two principles or measures, linked perhaps to an evolution in the process of his thought. But how are God's commandments brought to bear in the relationship between lovers? If this relationship is not divinized, does that not pervert any divinity, any ethics, any society which does not recognize God in carnality? And who is the other if the divine is excluded from the carnal act? If these gestures of ultimate relations between living humans are not a privileged approach to God, who is he? Who are those who testify to such a God? Who are, where are the others? And why, and how long ago did God withdraw from the act of carnal love?

(9) In so far as I am acquainted with him, Levinas has little taste for mysticism. What is the link between this lack of interest and his conception of sexual difference? In other words, is mysticism not linked to the flesh in its sexual dimension [*comme sexuée*]? But

outside of mysticism, who is God? What is God? What is the point of flesh without mysticism? To commit sacrileges, since the subjectivity of the other is not respected if the woman is reduced to animality, perversity or a kind of pseudo-childhood? To exploit the woman as reproducer, depriving her of her desire as a virgin–daughter or as a woman? To expend like an animal – or worse? – an excess of energy that men have? No longer even art. It is forbidden or impossible. So the caress sinks into despair, the fall, for Levinas too.

He certainly aspires to something else and to the Other [*Autrui*]. But the other, woman, he does not notice her existence. And what other or Other [*Autre*] is possible outside of this realization? Except for that or those which are substituted by authority.

(10) That brings me to my last question. What radical difference distinguishes the God who makes his presence known in the law from the one who gives himself, through his presence, as nourishment, including nourishment of the senses? How does it come about that the God of the writing of the law cannot be looked upon? What relation in particular is established between non-figurative writing and this God? For God, in this period of theophany, does not share, he dictates [*il impose*]. He separates himself, when he gives Moses the inscription of the law, an inscription which is not immediately legible. He no longer provides anything to be eaten or grasped by the senses. He imposes forms on a nation of men as he might have given forms to a man's body. But the man's body remains a visible creation, while the law, in a sense, does not. The law creates invisibility, so that God (in his glory?) cannot be looked upon. What happens to seeing, to flesh, in this disappearance of God? Where can one's eye alight if the divine is no longer to be seen? And if it does not continue to dwell in the flesh of the other in order to illuminate it, to offer up to the look the other's flesh as divine, as the locus of a divine to be shared? For this exchange, do not figurative writing and art represent necessary articulations? In particular to harmonize listening and seeing.

Why, at this period of the covenant, does God suspend the link between the two most spiritual of the senses, thereby depriving men of the carnal representation of the covenant? Is this not a gesture that breaks with the more feminine cultures? The *Song of Solomon* harks back to the break and evokes the painful separation between she who wants to be initiated in her mother's chamber, he who awakes her beneath the tree, the apple-tree where her mother is said to have conceived her, and that which takes them into a banqueting house, the chamber or the armies of the king. The two lovers are separated. The nations of women and of men are also divided; they no longer occupy the same places, they are no longer faithful to the same genealogy, or the same tradition. But the *Song of Solomon* bears the trace of the woman as lover [*l'amante*] for it says, and repeats: 'do not awaken (my) love until *she* please'.[9] She, the lover, remains a subject in the act of love.

NOTES

[I should like to thank Robert Bernasconi and Simon Critchley for their helpful comments on the translation. (ed.)].

1 [*Le Temps et l'autre*], Montpellier: Fata morgana, 1979, p. 79. Trans. Richard Cohen, *Time and the Other*. Pittsburgh: Duquesne University Press, 1987, p. 87, hereafter TA and TO respectively. Richard Cohen translates this phrase as 'a mode of being that consists in slipping away from the light'. *Se dérober* can be translated both as 'shun' and as 'slip away', it does not exclude either meaning (ed.)].

2 ['Pleasure' translates *volupté* except where otherwise stated. Other translators prefer to use 'voluptuousness' or 'voluptuosity' (ed.)].

3 [In *Ethique de la différence sexuelle* (1984), pp. 173–99; 'The fecundity of the caress' (1985) (ed.)].

4 [*Extase instante* is a term which, like sensible transcendental, indicates the bringing together of what has traditionally been split, transcendence and immanence, ideal and material. See 'The limits of the transference' (section II above), note 1 (ed.)].

5 [Syntax imitates content here. Although the meaning seems to be fairly clear from the rest of the paragraph – a union/communion of two sexes, in a crossing of boundaries or exchange, in itself produces a third, a work, an ecstasy, a 'child' which is not yet necessarily a physical child – the grammar of this sentence makes it difficult to disentangle. *Devenue* [become] agrees with *transcendance* [transcendence], *chair* [flesh], *celle de l'autre* [that of the other] and possibly also *l'autre* [the other], so that it is difficult to know exactly what has become *nous en nous* [ourself in us]. The fusion of syntax perhaps poetically echoes the fusion of bodies (ed.)].

6   [*Les Nourritures terrestres* is the title of a well-known book by André
    Gide, first published in 1897. Its English title is *The Fruits of the Earth*.
    (Cohen translates this phrase as 'morality of "earthly nourishments"'.)
    (ed.)].
7   [*Aimée*, 'beloved', is a past participle in French as well (ed.)].
8   [In French, because of grammatical gender, the masculine subsumes the
    feminine, so that for example, to refer to a group of men and women,
    the masculine plural, *ils*, is used, even if there is only one man and a
    hundred women. (See 'The three genres', above.) The feminine plural,
    elles, is only used where the reference is exclusively female. There is no
    neutral plural corresponding to *they*. I think this is what Irigaray means
    by her reference to absence of hierarchy in English. (In the singular, of
    course, there is the now much-contested generic 'he'.) (ed.)].
9   [*The Song of Solomon*], 2^7, 3^5 and 8^4. In French: 'ne réveillez pas
    l'amour avant qu'elle ne le veuille'. In the King James Bible, the
    translation is quite different; it reads: 'nor awake my love, till he please'.
    The New English Bible gives: 'Do not rouse her, do not disturb my love
    until she is ready [or: while she is resting].' This paragraph needs to be
    related back to the first question: the two lovers are 'born of different
    mothers' – on the one side, the feminine cultures represented by the
    mother's chamber and the apple tree, on the other side, the patriarchal
    culture linked to the king (ed.)].

Translated by Margaret Whitford

12

Women-Amongst-Themselves: Creating a Woman-to-Woman Sociality

You write: 'Nothing is more spiritual than female sexuality' (Ethique de la différence sexuelle, p. 57). Such a statement might suggest that the female is endowed with a higher value, but that would be in contradiction with an ethics (and, primarily, a logic) of difference, which, if it is to be an ethics, precludes imagining or theorizing the superiority of one sex over the other.

Insofar as I can divorce the sentence from its context – which is always very difficult – it means that female sexuality, which does not copy models of the type: tension, discharge and return to homeostasis, seems to me to correspond to the generation of a *sensible* transcendental. Female *jouissance* would be of the order of the constant and gradual creation of a dimension ranging from the most corporeal to the most spiritual, a dimension which is never complete and never reversible. Before, or in a different way to, any procreation of a child, woman generates through her *jouissance*, not, as they say or fear, a 'hole', but a passage or a bridge between what is most earthly and what is most celestial (there are figurative examples of this: the rainbow of the goddess Isis, for example). Women's dissatisfaction, their so-called hysterical symptomatology, no doubt stems from this perpetual deferment of a *jouissance* which is theirs, where they might find themselves, or find themselves anew, as subjects, where they would no longer wander and beg, for lack of a continuity, of a possible temporalization responsible with respect to their eroticism, their love. Does that make them superior to men? Why think in quantitative terms? They are *different*. And so *jouissance* (and not only children) is produced *inside them*, takes place more in their interior, in their innermost heart, whatever the complexity of its spatial trajectories. For men, things are different. If women were not so deprived of sensory [*sensible*] or imaginary landmarks, I think they would suffer much less from loss or abandonment and be less eager to 'play at being men'. As for the ethics of sexual difference, what I observe is that men have never elaborated it. Why? Why has sexuality always been made secondary, devalorized, at least in our cultures? Men have had speech, the written word, all the instruments of expression, for centuries. Few, if any, of the sexual models on offer are ethical, particularly not that of pornography, nor that of psycho-analysis. Why the deficiency? How are we to explain it? Men had socio-cultural power. No one else could have forbidden them to valorize sexuality. Why did they rate so many values higher than that one? Why are they still today discussing the 'genotypes'–'phenotypes' distinction so much, or the intentionality of living beings, without asking themselves the ethical question of the cultural role of women?

'No love of the other without love of the same' you write (p. 102). Could we say that this is an a priori principle for an ethics of sexual difference?

In my view, there are no *a priori* principles. That goes against my method to the extent that that type of principle cuts us off from the sensible. Whilst I try to use art, speech, to transform the sensible, I never cut myself off from it with theoretical *a prioris*. They correspond to a history of the conceptual, of the transcendental, which has not allowed women to assert or deploy their identity. The need for love of the same is an established historical fact. Our societies are built upon men-among-themselves [*l'entre-hommes*]. According to this order, women remain dispersed and exiled atoms because, for them, love of the same comes first: they are conceived within a woman, born of and fed by a woman. The origins of our societies are economic and religious: the two went together. What do we see when these social groups are established? Collective initiation rites for men. These rites are perpetuated in socially and politically organized gatherings that are almost always mono-sexuate. Women's rites reverted to being individual centuries ago, and have remained so. They are initiations into puberty, marriage or maternity which, moreover, often have no rites. The little girl becomes a woman, a wife and a mother alone, or at best with her mother or a substitute. It is probably the economic conditions bound up with industry that have allowed us to come together again, provisionally (women's jobs will be replaced by machines more quickly than men's). But together in what sense? Without rites and myths to teach us to love other women [*nos semblables*], to live with them, mutual destruction is a permanent possibility. We need values we can share if we are to coexist and create together. And it is important for us to exist and love one another as women if we are to love the other – man. Society and morality act as though woman, without being a full social or political person in her own right, had to love a social person: man. How is such love humanly possible without subjective status? Now, a subjective status is constituted in relation to self and to like, the two being connected.

Love for the same in the feminine – that is, love of self and love of like – has almost no symbolic forms and often remains bogged down in fusion or rivalry, as we can read in your Ethique.

There are indeed almost no symbolic forms of love of the same in the feminine. Which is in keeping with our social order. Two or more women who meet therefore look for the secret of their identity in one another. If they merge into one another or become rivals, it is often because the mystery of their personal status remains imperceptible to them. Except in motherhood, relations with children and nurturing functions? But that is not necessarily a human identity. Machines will probably be able to do both in the near future, and animals are not incapable of those functions. The problem of women-amongst-themselves [*l'entre-femmes*], however, of part of the order of life, has not yet been resolved. Nor their *human* identity, perhaps. In my view, its precondition is that both sexes should belong, in their difference, to a human identity. If we look at the past (and at the impasses, the shortcomings of the present), it seems that the economy of the same between women has always been bound up with respect for, and the fertility of the natural order. The goddesses, and not just the mother goddesses, all valorizations of the female, all female rites, remain bound up with cosmic rhythms. Monosexuate male societies tend, rather, to be founded upon their sacrifice or their reduplication within a culture which eventually forgets them or destroys them. In order to constitute a sociality of women-amongst-themselves, it is therefore important to remember our relationship with the micro- and macrocosm. Entering society presupposes a shared stake and a shared horizon. And that is what we lack because of our history.

However that may be, it seems to me that the third party (as defined above) must, for us, remain more specifically bound up with the natural universe, its culture and its art. If a new covenant is to be sealed between us, it seems to me indispensable that we take this into account *together*, rationally and wisely. That will prevent us from lapsing back into a language [*langage*] and a social organization which exile us and exclude us, not least by our internal exclusion within society. Is this a backward-looking position? I think that it reflects, rather, a link between past, present and future. It requires us to invent another style of collective relations, another relationship to space and time, relationships which reject the body–mind split and contrive constant growth without any sacrificial break, a permanent becoming with alternations and not breaks, an active and responsible transition from what is most vegetative in our identity to what is most divine. This amounts to attempting to constitute a new subjective and socio-cultural order despite, and sometimes against, the current reign of technocracy and its often abstract, cold . . . and weak rationality. Respect for the order of the universe, the question of our relation to the divine are not irrelevant and can help us in this task of seeking a personal and collective identity. These dimensions are resources, reserves, supports and frameworks for preserving and potentializing an energy which is not based on the conscious or unconscious sacrifice of the other, of others.[1]

Affidamento also seems to me to be a mode of energetistic support and potentialization which does not constantly try to destroy female values, but to assert them and deploy them. This style of relations between women, at once new and traditional, has the merit of having been established at a time when discouragement and desertion from struggles for our liberation were almost universal. It takes account of a certain number of psychological impasses that occur in women's groups: the unspoken, the implicit, the flare up of passions, persecution through silent consumption, demands or claims always expressed elsewhere or to others, the seizure of power by some women and the reduction of all women to 'like everyone' or 'like me' (on this point, cf. *Ethique*, pp. 100–108 and 66–9).

In Italy, we have for some years been thinking about and practising a relationship of affidamento: *a bond between one woman and the other based upon a recognition of the qualities which distinguish one woman*

*from the other. The idea is gradually to turn it into a generalized form of
sociality between women. This proposal, which has aroused the interest of
many women, has aroused fear in equal proportions: fear of losing the
self-confidence given by the group. What are the origins of this fear in
women? How can we continue searching for a social distinction of the
feminine without leaving behind those women who fear that they will be
obliterated by other women?*

In an attempt to bring the light of my experience and research to
bear on this approach, I will make some suggestions, and I hope that
they will be constructive and not the opposite. In *affidamento* (insofar
as I have any clear understanding of what is involved), there is
always the possibility of uncontrollably hierarchical relations, and
their reversal ('senior' becomes 'junior' in various senses), if there is
no perspective that is irreducible to the *quantitative*, to the *two*. That
is why I suggest a reference to the cosmic and to respect for the
micro-/macrocosm relationship if we are to contrive for ourselves a
possibility of bodily autonomy, and autonomy with respect to already-
existing language [*langage*]. In my view, this reference has major
political implications insofar as: (1) it represents a *horizon* where
women – one plus one to the *n* – can gather or await one another
without destructively competing or wiping each other out; (2) it
remains a *guarantee* against the hold of, or lapses back into, the
monocratic or monovalent discourses of phallocrats, 'mothers' or
technicans; (3) it is the *token* of another culture which preserves for
us a possible and inhabitable future, a culture whose historical face is
as yet unknown to us but whose elementary necessities we can
glimpse or analyse; (4) it can act as a *guarantee of freedom* for women
who are afraid of being dominated or obliterated by other woman.

Given the importance and difficulty of the task, there is indeed a
great risk that women will encroach on one another's territory, even
involuntarily. Each woman and all women must therefore have a
refuge other than individual or collective regression. I would like to
ask my Italian sisters of the *affidamento* one more question: how do
we move from the one + one to the group (s), from counting one +
one to a larger unity? For example, what reception will the little cells
now in existence give to a public intervention on the part of *one*
woman? What type of relationship will be created between the *one*
woman who creates a cultural work and women who are bound

together by *affidamento?* It is a difficult question, as it involves the transition from contiguity to another figure. There is a qualitative threshold at which it is not only a matter of accepting the differences between us (a considerable achievement in itself), but of constituting another relationship. In this struggle, I would say that each and every one of us is faced with what I have called our double threshold (mother and woman) and *our* sexuate relationship with language [*langage*], ideation, idealization and becoming divine. Women are often suspicious of these dimensions for themselves, and amongst women. And yet they are indispensable if a human social order is to be realized. This does not mean that women's mode of figuration or symbolization is the same as that of men.

'Sexual difference represents one of the questions or the question which must be thought in our era', we read at the beginning of the Ethique *(p. 13). Does the sexuation of the symbolic and social order spontaneously result in the encounter between the two sexes? Or do we have to think up a strategy for women too? And what position can a woman take up today, in relation to the other sex?*

To a certain extent, the answer lies in the form of the question. The sexuation of the symbolic order cannot be accomplished all at once, via technology or magic. It will correspond to an intellectual, ethical, aesthetic and political effort on the part of both sexes. Is a women's strategy necessary too? Of course. There are two sides, two poles, to the difference between the sexes. Besides, it is funny that you should ask that question of a woman, the only woman to date to have written an *Ethique de la différence sexuelle* [*Ethics of Sexual Difference*] and to have asserted that it corresponds to what has to be thought today. Why a woman? Perhaps because women – at least I as a woman – are physically and mentally somewhat alien to the techno-cratic 'paradise' and its almost fatal hold over its workers. This is not simply a question of protecting children, but of bodily style, of the dynamics of energy. Their economy is less isomorphic with the instruments of technology.

That is not to say that women are incapable of entering techno-cratic society. On the contrary! They can enter it more easily than an economy which demands, for example, more muscular strength, more warlike courage. The world of technology offers them jobs as operatives or as machine minders, and it is accepted that women are very good at them, perhaps better than men, because they are more patient, more obedient, and because they have a talent for more delicate, more precise gestures. A certain number of women are demanding to enter this technological empire without realizing that its effect on them is like a transposition of the family into the State. The world of technocracy is becoming a sort of vast domain where anyone prepared to believe it feels sheltered, protected, assigned easy work which involves even less responsibility than mothering, cooking or washing. But we have to stop and think. When they demand access to these workplaces, are women capable of thinking through and modifying conditions within them?. The hierarchy of the technological universe is still on the whole very traditional. It brings about a sexuate levelling at a certain level, neutralizes sexual differences, but makes careful use of them when it comes to distributing work, and recruiting and paying workers. Sorting out our relations with the other sex implies that we are capable of thinking and distancing ourselves from the current situation and history, without any public – and especially aggressive, reactive – spontaneism.[2] The latter often destroys the possibility of constituting a shelter or a territory of one's own. How are we to construct this female shelter, this territory in difference? I make many suggestions in the *Ethique*, notably by speaking of love as an intermediary, of the need for admiration, of the generation of place and interval in eroticism, of the fertility of the gestures of the bodily encounter – the caress, for example – and by analysing, by discovering and inventing love of self, love of the same, love of the Other and of the other in their spiritual, carnal and affective dimensions. For us, it is a matter of being able to preserve, sustain and cultivate potential physical and imaginary forces so as to give ourselves, create for ourselves, forms, a world, that allow us to respect ourselves, the other, and fertility in social and cultural difference. Which means the non-reduction of women to the work of social reproduction either as mothers, wives, nurses and housekeepers to both children and men, or as technical assistants to or collaborators with the present world.

NOTES

1   [See *Divine Women* (1986) (ed.)].

2 [*Spontaneism*: this is a political term, referring to the acting-out of emotions in a public context in an unpremeditated and politically inappropriate way (ed.)].

Translated by David Macey

13

The Necessity for Sexuate Rights

In terms of the law, one of the sectors that is today undergoing a mutation concerns relations between the male and female genres, especially in the family, and their relationship with reproduction. The laws relating to the obligation to have children, the right to contraception and abortion, choice of surnames for women and children within marriage, the freedom of members of a couple to choose where they live, the pertinence of wages for housework, the length of maternity leave, the protection of women's work, etc. are laws undergoing a mutation in our cultures. They lie at the intersection between natural, civil, penal and religious rights. The totality of these domains is rarely thought in its signification, its distribution.

Hegel attempted the project of interpreting the total workings of a society, of a culture. He wanted to describe and think the workings of the spirit of man as individual and citizen. The weakest link in his system seems to be at the level of his interpretation of spirit and right within the family. Hegel, who always tries to break down every non-differentiated unity, does not succeed in thinking the family other than as *one* substance in which individuals lose their rights as particulars. Except the right to life? It is not that simple . . .

Origins of the family . . .

The chapter of *The Phenomenology of Mind* in which Hegel speaks of the family comes at the begining of his analysis of man's relationship with spirit in culture. This chapter deals first of all with the question of the ethical order and its relationship with morality. In this chapter, Hegel says something very important in terms of the rights of genres.

This decisive thing seems to have been forgotten in its implications for the spirit of the people, of peoples.

What is it about? In these analyses devoted to the family in its relationship with the State, Hegel explains that the *daughter* who remains faithful to the law relating to her *mother* must be excluded from the city, from society. She cannot be put to death by violence, but she must be put in prison, deprived of liberty, air, light, love, marriage, children. . . . We may as well say that she is condemned to a slow and solitary death. The figure of this daughter is represented by Antigone. This analysis of Hegel's is based upon the content of Sophocles' tragedies.

What is the nature of the laws respected by Antigone? They are religious laws concerning the burial of her brother, killed in a war between men. These laws relate to cultural obligations towards the blood of the *mother*, blood shared by brothers and sisters in the family, and pertaining to which there are duties which the transition to a patriarchal culture will forbid. This tragic episode in the life, and the war, between the genres, represents a transition to patriarchy. This forbids the daughter to respect the ties of blood *with her mother*. From a spiritual point of view, they have a religious character, they go together with the fertility of the earth in its flowers and fruits, protect love in its corporeal dimension, watch over female fertility inside or outside marriage (depending on whether we are talking about the realm of Aphrodite or Demeter), correspond to periods of peace.

When patriarchy is established, the daughter is separated from her mother and, more generally, from her family. She is transplanted into the genealogy of her husband, must live in his house, must bear his name, and so must her children etc. The first time this occurs, the separation is recounted as the abduction of a woman by a man–lover. A war between men is organized to recover the kidnapped woman and to bring her back to her original group.

Our current morality is still dependent upon these very ancient events. This means that love between mother and daughter, rendered impossible by the patriarchal regime (and Freud, as it happens, tells us the same thing), is transformed for the woman into the obligatory cult of her husband's children, and her husband as male child. Indeed, despite the incest taboo, it seems that man has not sub-limated the natural immediacy of his relationship with his mother, but has transferred it on to his wife as mother substitute. Couples and generations have therefore been out of step ever since male and female genealogies were collapsed into a single genealogy: that of the *husband*.

Whatever the rules of morality, this collapsing of one genealogy into the other is an ethical fault which perverts the spirit of the people, of peoples, and which prevents the constitution of an ethics of the couple.

The double meaning of the word nature

The sexual liberations of recent times have not established a new *ethics* of sexuality. They do, however, tell us that this question really is a question, especially because of the liberation of energies that find no positive outlet. They flow back into natural immediacy: the obligation to have children, violence only just contained in sado-masochistic scenarios, regression to animality (without the court-ship?) in the erotic act, fear and destruction between the sexes . . .

There is obviously no question of going back to a more repressive, moralizing conception of sexuality. On the contrary, it is necessary to elaborate an art of the sexual, a sexuate culture, and not merely to make bodies available for the reduction of neuropsychical tensions and for reproduction.

Historically, the obligation, for women, to give birth to children within their husband's genealogy corresponds to the beginnings of *non-respect for nature*, to the establishment of a notion or concept of nature that is substituted for the fertility of the earth, abandons its religious character, its link with the divinity of women and with the mother–daughter relationship. Paradoxically, the cult of the mother often goes hand in hand, in our cultures, with scorn for or neglect of nature. It is true that patriarchal genealogies refer to *the mother of the son*, to the detriment of the mother of the daughter. The cult of the mother of the son ties our tradition to the horizon of mother–son incest, and the taboo on it. In their fascination with that incest, our societies forget that the genealogy of woman has already been col-lapsed into that of man.

In this reduction of one genealogy to the other, it becomes impossible or at least difficult to arrive at a definition of two genres, two sexes, unless we think about it a little. Man is positioned in relation to his father for his name and possessions, in relation to his mother in terms of natural immediacy. The wife has to submit to her husband and to reproduction. This means that genre, insofar as it is sexual, is never sublimated. *Genre is confused with species.* Genre becomes the human race [*le genre humain*], human nature, etc., as defined within patriarchal culture. This genre corresponds to a people of men which rejects, consciously or unconsciously, the possibility of an other genre: the female. There is nothing but *le genre humain*, in which sex only has real value if it pertains to the reproduction of the species. From that point of view, genre would always be subordinate to kinship. Man and woman would not have reached intellectual maturity in the thought and the culture of their sexual difference. They would be children, then more or less sexuate adolescents, and then reproductive adults. In this perspective, the family is there to serve possessions, the material patrimony and the reproduction of children. It is not a cell in which individual differences are respected and cultivated.

As for life, it has to be said that rights are unevenly distributed, and that they become mainly duties, especially for women: the duty to have children, sexual duties. No legislation protects women vis-à-vis their lives. This anomaly is often attributed to the authority of religious morality in questions of mores and reproduction. This influence, a survival of ancient gynocratic traditions, is now marked by patriarchal imperatives: giving possessions to the husband, and children to the State . . .

We have to reinterpret the notion of nature that underlies such imperatives. Often, it is not a question of life, but of an idea of life and of a viable life style. But value, values, are thought by the people of men; they are neither appropriate to women nor inscribed in law so as to defend their lives, their possessions.[1] Some partial modifications of the rights of women have been won in recent times. But they are subject to regressions. They were won by partial and local pressures, whereas we have to rethink the whole of the law in such a way that it is just to two genres different in their needs, their desires and their properties.

Sex as ethical dimension

Some men and women now say that the answer to these questions is *love*. But it takes two to love, and a relationship that is not subject to one genre, not subordinated to reproduction. It necessitates the inscription of the rights of every man and woman in civil law. The inscription of the rights of the couple in civil law would have the effect of converting individual morality into a collective ethic, of transforming relations between genres within the family, or its substitute, into rights and duties concerning culture in general. Religion could then recover its meaning as a relationship with the divine for both genres; it would be liberated from the tutelage of one genre and from protecting the possessions of one genre rather than the other. Which is not very divine! What is more, the inscription of the rights of each genre in agencies representing society and culture would have the effect of not divorcing civil law from natural law, of establishing a concrete private right taking into account the demands of the life of every man and woman. What does the right to private property mean when pollution from noise, smells, the violence conveyed by telecommunications, etc., destroy sense *perceptions* indispensable to life and to mind in each man and woman? All it means is a somewhat abstract demand based upon money, and without much concern for the bodies, love and understanding of those who inhabit a perimeter of space for which they often pay quite dearly.

These living conditions do not contribute to the development of human peoples. Oppressed in their sensitivity, disturbed by a mode of existence which is often far from peaceful, stimulated by what is at stake in micro- or macroeconomic competition, they are ex-centric to themselves, dragged into war as though into something which could restore a little order, open up new horizons. That was often true. It can no longer remain true unless we establish an ethics of the couple as an intermediate space between individuals, peoples, states. Wars occur when the latter stray too far away from their natural possibilities, and when the ensuing accumulation of abstract energy can no longer be mastered by subjects and is not reducible to one or more concrete responsibilities. Panic then finds a concrete sacrificial object to reduce the inflation of abstraction.

In the exercise of a sexuate social and cultural ethics, History could experience a more continuous development, one less subject to periodic expansions and reductions without any real control over those moments.

NOTES

1 ['Possessions' translates *biens* and refers here to spiritual as well as material possessions (ed.)].

Translated by David Macey

14

How To Define Sexuate Rights?

Why are you now concerning yourself with law, when you used to approach problems in such a different way?

As a philosopher, I take an interest in all sectors of reality and of knowledge so as to think them. In terms of the history of culture, it was only very recently that philosophy and the sciences became separated. That results from the growing sophistication of methods, which then become inaccessible to thought. The hypertechnological tendencies within the contemporary sciences result in the creation of ever more complex formulae which correspond, it is believed, to an increasingly true truth. That truth therefore escapes the reflection of wisdom, including that of scientists themselves. That results in nothing good for our culture and its development.[1]

So I have always been concerned with the issue of law from the point of view of the difference between the sexes. In *Speculum*, for example, I talk about it very explicitly on pp. 119–23 and 214–26, but the whole of the text on Plato also deals with it. Two chapters in *This Sex Which Is Not One* ('Women on the market' and 'Commodities among themselves') deal with the problems of economic and social rights. Nowadays, perhaps I approach the problem more concretely, or perhaps I am understood differently. In my view, there is no break between my earlier and later texts, particularly not over this question.

Why do I approach juridical problems more concretely? Because, since 1970, I have often worked with women or groups of women belonging to liberation movements, and I have noted certain difficulties and impasses which cannot be resolved unless we establish an equitable jurisdiction for both sexes. When such social structures are not established, men and women alike become lost in escalating demands, legal or extra-legal, whereas the elementary rights of each man and woman are not protected and world disorder grows. So attempts are made to re-establish a pseudo-order, attempts to make good the disorders of another country on the part of nations incapable of dealing with their own problems. Supplying aid is preferable to letting a country die. But is this really a matter of aid? Or of apparently generous excuses for remaining masters? It is not clear. And the laws most useful in the here and now, those which concern us, are always deferred, as though the world had opted for disorder, as though all that mattered, when our civilizations are being almost inundated, was finding a solution that could save man's identity without listening to the civilization that women bear. Any excuse for not taking account of their truth is good enough. Men are even reverting to archaic stages of culture, publicly imposing in different ways their more or less domesticated animals as their last totem. Rather than pursuing its cultural evolution, the world is falling back on minimal definitions of the human: no more religion adapted to the times, no more perfectly mastered language [*langue*] as a tool for social exchanges or an instrument for acquiring or creating knowledges, legislation inadequate for settling national, religious, or private conflicts, especially where the protection of life is concerned. So, no more god(s), no more language [*langue*], no more familiar cultural landscape. . . . Then what can a social group be founded upon? I know that some men imagine that the great day of the good-for-everyone universal has dawned. But what universal? What new imperialism is hiding behind this? And who pays the price for it? There is no universal valid for all women and all men outside the natural economy. Any other universal is a partial construct and, therefore, authoritarian and unjust. The first universal to be established would be that of a legislation valid for both sexes as a basic element in human culture. That does not mean forced sexual choices. But we are living beings, which means sexuate beings, and our identity cannot be constructed without a vertical and horizontal horizon that respects that difference.

In the absence of such an order, many people are looking for a non-human source of yardsticks. Man defines himself in terms of his house or his neighbour's house, his car or some other means of locomotion, the number of kilometres he has covered, the number of matches he has played, his favourite animals, his one gods, in whose name he kills others and despises women, etc. Man is not concerned with improving the quality of man. 'No time . . .', 'Nostalgia . . .', 'Oh, how archaic . . .' 'All that's out of date', etc. All these unthinking reactions passively expressed by irresponsible citizens seem to me to be the result of a lack of rights and duties adapted to today's civil persons [*personnes civiles*]. As a result, there are many forms of authoritarianism, violence and scarcity.

You speak of a sexuate law, of a law in which the female genre is inscribed. That implies a very different idea to the traditional concept of 'parity'. So it is a question not of 'equal laws for all', but of the idea of laws which take account of the fact that women are not equal to men. Can you explain the concept of sexuate law?

I think that in certain areas, we have to struggle for equality of rights so as to bring out differences. At least I did think that. I now think that what appears to be the path of rational method is a utopia or a delusion. Why? Women and men are not equal. And the equality strategy, when it exists, should always aim at the recognition of difference. For instance, equal numbers of women and men could take part in all social activities, so as to make them evolve. At one level, that solution is obviously perfectly desirable. But it is not enough. And its inadequacy leads to regressions and scepticism about the existence of difference between men and women, which are perpetuated by women themselves. Why is this strategy of equality inadequate? Firstly because the contemporary social order, including the order defining the professions, is not neutral from the point of view of the difference between the sexes. Working conditions and production techniques are neither equally invented by both sexes nor equally adapted in terms of sexual difference. The goals of work, its modalities, are not defined equally by or for women and men. Equality will therefore be achieved over the wage issue, at best. Of course the right to equal pay for equal work is legitimate, and it is also legitimate for women to be able to get out of the house and acquire an economic autonomy. Some men and some women think that this is enough to guarantee respect for their human identity. Personally, I say it isn't. These new economic conditions are an incentive to rethink the whole social organization; otherwise, we sanction the fact that, in order to acquire a minimal freedom, women must submit to the imperatives of a culture which is not theirs. So they should collaborate on building weapons of war, or instruments of pollution, or should adapt to men's working rhythms and lend themselves to the development of artificial languages which still do not correspond to their natural language. Which depersonalizes them more and more, and so on. That does not correspond to equality of rights. In order to stand some chance of living free, women are in fact forced to submit to men's means of production and to increase their capital or socio-cultural patrimony. Despite everything, they enter into the circuits of labour, but they alienate their female identity in them. And the incentives offered to women to go back to the home are highly unlikely to fall on deaf ears, not necessarily only amongst the most reactionary women, as some are quick to point out, but also amongst women who want to try to become women. What I mean is that there is still almost no type of work which allows a woman to earn a living like any male citizen without alienating her identity in issues and working conditions which are adapted to men alone. The non-consideration of this problem leads to a lot of confusion and to disagreements between people who are collaborating on the liberation of women. A lot of time is wasted on mistakes, a lot of misunderstandings are perpetuated, either cynically or unwittingly, by the micro or macro powers that be. Women themselves are caught in a cleft stick between the minimum of social rights they can obtain: getting out of the house, acquiring economic autonomy, having some social visibility, etc., and the psychological or physical price they have to pay for that minimum, whether they know it clearly or not. All this confusion could be resolved by the recognition that there are different rights for each sex and that equality of social status can only be established when these rights have been codified by the civil powers. That operation must therefore be a priority target.

Can you give some examples to explain the way in which the present law has been created and has evolved to suit men? What would laws based upon sexual difference look like?

It seems to me that it is possible to give a provisional answer to both questions at the same time in the sense that what has to be defined as rights for women is what the people of men, of men-amongst-themselves, has appropriated as its property, including that which concerns women's bodies, children's bodies, as well as natural space, dwelling places, the economy of signs and images, social and religious representationality.

I therefore approach things in terms of what we now have to assert as rights for women:

1   The right to human dignity, and therefore:

- An end to the commercial use of their bodies or their images.
- Valid self-representations of women, in gestures, in words and images, in all public places.
- An end to the exploitation of a functional part of their selves by the civil and religious powers: motherhood.

2   The right to human identity, that is:

- legal recognition of *virginity*[2] as a component in female identity that is not reducible to money, cannot be converted into cash in any way by family, state or patriarchal religion. This component in female identity allows girls to be given a civil status and a right to preserve their virginity (for their own relationship with the divine too) for as long as they like, and to lay charges against anyone inside or outside the family who interferes with it. Whilst it is true that it is less common for girls to be exchanged between men in our cultures, their virginity is still on sale in many places, and nothing has replaced the identity status of girls as bodies that can be traded by men. Girls need a positive identity to relate to as individual civil and social persons. This autonomous identity of girls is also necessary if women are to consent freely to love relations and if marriage is to be instituted as a non-alienation of women to male power.
- The right to *motherhood* as a component in female identity. If the body is a legal issue, and it is, the female body must be identified in civil terms as virgin and potentially mother. This means that the mother will enjoy a civil right to choose to be pregnant and to decide the number of her pregnancies. She, or her authorized representative (male or female), will register the child's birth.

3   Mutual mother-child duties will be defined in the code. This is to ensure that the mother can protect her children and can

receive assistance from them in accordance with the law. That will allow her to bring charges in the name of civil society in the events of rape, violence or abduction, where children, and especially girls, are concerned. The respective rights of mother and father will be the object of a separate provision.

4 Women will have a civil right to defend their lives, the lives of their children, their dwelling places, their traditions and their religion against any unilateral decision based on male law.

5 At the purely financial level:

- The unmarried will not be penalized by either direct or indirect taxation.
- If the state wishes to grant family allowances, they will be the same for each child.
- Women pay the same taxes as men for the media and for television, and half of all coverage will be adapted to them.

6 Systems of exchange, for example linguistic exchange, will be reshaped so as to ensure women and men a right to equivalent exchange.

7 Women will have equal representation in all places where civil or religious decisions are taken, as religion too is a civil power.

There are women who have theorized their exteriority to, their estrangement from, the law, their lack of interest in these subjects. What do you think about this?

This position seems to me to be a poor analysis of the present conditions for recognition of female identity. But I can quite understand that women – being supported by citizen-men, and not being full citizens in their own right – forget this essential dimension of social organization. I can understand them all the more easily in that, at the time when female law did exist, it was not usually written down and was exercised without the weight of the institutions that have proliferated under patriarchal regimes. But that female law did exist. The historical time in which women managed the social order cannot be reduced to chaos, as it is claimed. Female law was characterized, amongst other things, by:

* the handing down of property and names from mother to daughter with sisters and the youngest male child playing a privileged role in their transmission;
* the importance of the divinity and of the religious in lines of descent;
* the use of motherland [*matrie*] to refer to the land of one's birth;
* respect for place and for local divinities;
* respect for the food produced by nature: first fruits, and then cereals;
* a temporality that respected the rhythm of life, the cycle of light, of the seasons and the years;
* a lofty morality based upon love and peace;
* a communality between all members of the human race;
* arbitration by women in matters of alliance and the resolution of conflicts;
* symbolic systems bound up with art.

It is possible to find trace elements of this female law in the work of Johann Jacob Bachofen, but also in Mircea Eliade's descriptions of the aboriginal cultures that still exist today in India. These references are far from being exclusive. They, and their bibliographies, can be guides to research. In this brief account, I choose them partly with men in mind.

To ensure that these laws, which seem to me to be correlative with female subjectivity, are respected today, we have to work through written law. Otherwise, written law will continue to be exercised to the detriment of girls who are alienated in it from birth onwards, and by their genealogies. What is more, it seems to me desirable that women should create a social order in which their subjectivity can unfold along with its symbols, its images, its realities and dreams, and so on.

I would like to end this conversation by asking what advice you would give to women (and men too) who take an interest in law.

- Ensure the preservation of nature insofar as it is the locus that allows every man and woman to live freely and to live by their labour, without speculationary or alienating mediations.
- Define elementary rights concerning the life of all individuals: women and men, girls and boys, mothers and fathers, male and female citizens, male and female workers, etc., starting with women and men, or at least keeping that difference as a horizon, should strategy dictate other priorities.
- Restrict the rights of groups and societies governed by one or more persons; as democracy does not exist in the sense in which it is evoked, its very principle must be called into question, particularly in the light of the age and the way in which democracy has been defined and established by men alone.
- Redefine and revalorize a reliable law concerning housing, or even private property. Women, men and children need somewhere to live without being frustrated in that legitimate necessity, desire, investment, by the pollution of the environment (cars, planes, noisy machines, etc.), insecurity resulting from poor buildings or from building permits for land that was not originally zoned for building depriving older inhabitants of light, air and peace and forcing them into semi-nomadism because of their lack of legal protection in matters of real estate.
- Restrict the power of money, and especially of the monetary surplus value which accompanies the caprices of the desires of the wealthy or the less wealthy (as with modern property speculation on human dereliction that fosters the belief that a smaller piece of inhabitable ground costs more because it is wanted by buyers with a yen for a new nest, when the promoters know perfectly well that is nonsense), and go back to exchanges which are valid in terms of price and choice of means of production (which means going back to more natural means of production without speed-ups or over-production where the land, the sun, the ocean, and human bodies, are concerned).
- Query the origins of the prevailing law, with particular reference to the time when women really were social persons, a time which has wrongly been described as prehistory. This will lead us to ask what has to be modified in current jurisdiction and to question the notion that 'civil' and 'religious' are comparable or that they guarantee free choices.

NOTES

1 See my 'Sujet de la science, sujet sexué', in *Sens et place des connaissances dans la société*, vol. iii, Paris: Editions du CNRS, 1988.
2 [In *Je, tu, nous*, Irigaray defines virginity as follows: 'For me, to become virgins would mean women's attainment of the spiritual' (p. 142). (ed.)]

Translated by David Macey

15

He Risks Who Risks Life Itself

He risks who risks life itself. In excess of it, scarcely, by a breath; a breath which, if it is held, saves through song. Prophet of pure forces that call for and refuse shelter. Does not all that already exists paralyse respiration? Imperceptibly inhabiting the air. Holding it back from lavishing itself freely. Immobilizing, in countless tangles, what would still like to traverse this preoccupied atmosphere.

And who goes not into the abyss can only repeat and restate paths already opened up that erase the traces of gods who have fled. Alone, always alone, the poet runs the risk of venturing outside the world and of folding back its openness to touch the bottom of the bottomless. Saying yes to what calls him beyond the horizon. In this abandonment, one breath, at most, is left to him. First and last energy that is forgotten when he is not short of it. Present everywhere, but invisible, granting life to all and to everything, on pain of death.

A risk taken at every moment by the poet, that seeker after a still sacred ether. Now so covered up or so deeply buried that he can trust in no heaven, no earth. Learn his way from no mouth. Find no meaning in any sign. No place is inhabitable by one who is summoned to reopen a ferial site. He must therefore leave the world, whilst remaining mortal. And go onward towards some distant shore that does not announce its name. For some non-assured life. A flowering for which he lacks the ground. Tearing himself away from the land of his birth to plunge his roots into a land still virgin. And therefore unknown. Unpredictable. Free, for risk.

Disenchanted even with that captivating magic that relates men to one another. Exiling himself from all the will appropriate to an existing community. Descending into the hell of history to seek traces of life. Seeds still held captive by a sub-stratum to be reopened. To be freed. Let into the air in the future of what has not yet appeared. Bringing into play the danger of a new flowering devoid of protection. Unsheltered. Outside any abode. Unveiled? Advancing into danger without any answer already granted to his trust. No betrothal, no abandonment here. It is still too early for such alternations. In terms of the final reckoning, everything still hangs in the balance. Going forward with no heed for dimensions or directions already there. The attraction of an adventurous growth alone impels movement. Confident – no doubt.

Doubts only he who already knows the right direction. Unstable sometimes, he for whom paths are already traced. But one who makes his way in accordance with his gravity, before the determination of any centre, does not hesitate. And withdraws again from inscription within a perimeter. Removing himself from any environment to risk, once more, the unpredictable outcome in a gamble with his historial partner. The game is never won. Will not be subordinated to an end in which one or the other could abolish the intermediate site of their mutual perception. Which holds the balance of their relationship in difference.

An equilibrium always and forever in the balance between the heart of the venture and what is ventured in its entirety. Between that which gives itself up to a new flowering and the whole of the already-established. Between what is projected into the non-situatable and he who already belongs to the world. Between he who already inhabits and he who leaves his abode, and all forms of property, to enter into a boundless openness. Access to unfenced encounters wherein those who risk most come one towards the other and depart anew, without restraint. Discharging themselves of the in-finite/ unfinished without dissolving into the void. An unaccustomed destiny.

Not the dream of a boundlessness that is reached through the reversion of measures. That still calculates with a target. A departure which does not go counter to anything save the perception that nothing counters. Which forces no closure, but which obeys the gravity of pure forces appealing to a whole with no possible end. Air infinitely free of obstacles. Not even that of a horizon.

The immensity discovered in the first instants of love? In which the other still escapes representation. There and not there. Immediate perception in an openness barred by no consciousness. Native bonds, foreign to any reflection. Being together before any face to face encounter in which evaluation is inaugurated. An obscure attraction in which they belong together to one another in an environment which absorbs them prior to any relationship. Resting in depths which bear them. Spilling into one another in the environment they are becoming. Having abandoned calculations that go no further than a more or less veiled confrontation. A separation of earth, heaven, space in which he who listens to or obeys only pure attraction no longer has a place. Acceptance of an open sea that cannot be mastered, of a multiplicity irreducible to the one. No geometry, no accounts here. What opens up does not stop in any direction. No waymarkers in this total risk.

From which there escapes the very content of desire. Unpredictable, uncoerceable. Free of domination – in itself or in the other. Of any precondition governing production. Except of the attraction of advancing towards the unaccustomed. A call in a will that wills nothing, but abandons all resistance. Responds without knowledge or intention which give account of obedience to anything. Only the force that does not stint itself, gives itself unconditionally, allows itself to be raw material. Still innocent of appropriate(d) techniques.

It is lived, lavished without safeguards. Before the subject–object distribution – that effect of the means useful to an imperialist will on the part of man. The establishment of a market where nothing is delivered without being introduced into a system of exchanges that blurs or erases tangible reality in a speculative spirituality. No one encountering or apprehending anything without coming before the court of a general calculation, whose reign is all the more imperative in that numbers do not appear there. So it is with love.

Without shelter, and barred, when it surrenders to the value estimates that organize the world through and through. Already yesterday. Love becomes mere material subordinate to the goal of production, specific or absolute. Wherein man loses that obscure desire that makes him man. Engulfed in an infinite difference between the attraction that is his deepest inspiration and self-willing in self-imposition.

Between the two, no transition: the abyss of a nihilating that nothing can save. Which opens on to nothing. A memorial to man's separation. From all – against all. The constitution of a closure where he isolates himself, impervious to the innocent perception of calculation. A technologist, henceforth exiled from his innermost impulse. Confined in the unconditional of a deliberate self-imposition. Of a will that wills itself? Only a few would risk themselves outside this confinement. Wanting more? Or consenting, rather to want no more. Renouncing their own interests, the acquisition of a more for themselves. And claiming the authority of no exploits. These bold ones do not seem such when they venture into danger. What they risk is fleeting and imperceptible – scarcely a breath.

Are they in search of supplementary protection? No. That would still mean cutting themselves off from the open. They breathe with no cares. Confident, because devoid of anxiety about their security. Discarding the framework of their own will. Relying solely upon the attraction they perceive, that impels them outside all frontiers. Consenting to advance where they feel themselves borne – to the source from whence they receive themselves. Unreservedly accomplishing the fullness of that attraction and redeploying it in the plenitude of a gift.

No dwelling will have been fashioned, no shelter built, on this journey there and back. For those who risk themselves in this way, this consent and its rendering take place without any supplementary production. They do not find themselves once more within a closure preserving them from danger. Or separated. Passionately consenting, they give and receive themselves/one another in the open.

Access to this strange adventure is afforded by the renunciation of any path already suggested. All that offered itself as a possible future must be left, unfolded, like a limited horizon; the veil imperceptibly protecting the *en face*. Before leaving, all ends must at least be subject to retroversion. Any objective must be disconcerted. They who dare all go forth blindly, without projects. No longer spellbound by the fear of being without shelter. Unreservedly abandoning themselves to the unbounded open, holding nothing back. A flowering environment in which those who are free of all fear would be embraced. Showing their faces completely, frankly, merging their strengths, acting on one another in the integrity of a perception that does not resist the centre of its pure gravity. Unreservedly saying 'yes' to the whole of all that comes to pass.

To death, as the other face of life? Yes. And to the other as other? Yes?

Or is it a matter of remaining inside the circle of the proper? Whilst accepting the reverse, of course. Making the negative a positive, no doubt. But always in accordance with the same gesture. Extending its sphere of application. Bringing into it that which determines its horizon, now folded back into a broader horizon. An imperceptible film whose outside is endlessly given inside. Unveiling-reveiling confinement in a site. The reversibility of aversion into consent to all. Willing to be moved by all that touches. No refusal, no withdrawal. Protected by risk itself. Insensibly, invisibly sheltered in its being. In its own heart? Not yet open to the other, save to the other of the same?

Alien to that supernumerary existence made for he who lets go; receives himself, lavishes himself on the other, ex-centric. Acceding to an interminable space and time. Dimensions that go beyond the sideral, but also beyond the imaginary of any consciousness. Objective and subjective lose their limits. Each one and all 'things' resting in one another, spilling into one another, without limits. The re-collection of a state so ancient that few can recall it. Recrossing the frontiers of their own lives. Flowing back, risking their breath. Surrendering to the other the very *rhythm* of their breathing. Ready to miss the beat so as to discover a new range to it. Expiring in the other so as to be reborn more inspired. Imperilling language [*langue*], the perimeter of the other, so that it may find its voice once more. Its song. Leaving the already-consecrated temple to find traces of the ferial bond with the wholly other. Now speechless [*n'ayant plus la parole*] – risking saying [*le dire*] itself. Without worries, for without calculation. Foreign to exchanges and business. Outside the market. Trembling at the coming of what is promised. Of that other breath that is born unto them when all already-known resonances have died away. Beyond everything that has already been attained. A sonority unheard by onlookers who do not venture into the in-finite/unfinished abode of the invisible. The only guide there being the call to the other. Whose breath subtly impregnates the air, like a vibration perceived by those lost in love. Their senses awake, they boldly go forward by ways where others see only shadows and hell. They go foward and, sometimes, a song comes to their lips. From their mouths come sounds which mean nothing – only the inspiration that will strike the other with the feelings and thoughts that pour out of them. A response, inaudible to most, to what they sense in the wind.

And so, those who renounce their own will go towards one another. Calling on one another beneath all saying [*dire*] already said, all words already uttered, all speech [*parole*] already exchanged, all rhythms already hammered out. They draw one another into the mystery of a word [*verbe*] seeking to be made flesh. Trusting inordinately in that which makes the body and the flesh of all diction: air, breath, song. Giving, receiving themselves/one another in the as yet unfelt/beyond reason [*l'encore insensé*]. So as to be reborn of it, invested with the telling [*dire*] of a forgotten inspiration. Buried beneath all logic. Surplus to any existing language [*langue*]. The abeyance of all signification, unveiling the trade that underlies it, and venturing beyond. Before the separation took place, or estimates of greater or lesser value. In this opacity, this night of the world, they discover traces of the gods who have fled, at the very moment when they have given up ensuring their salvation. Their radiance comes of their consenting that nothing shall ensure their keeping. Not even being – that perimeter of man's narrative. Nor God – that guarantee of the meaning or non-meaning of the whole?

These prophets feel that, if something divine can still come to us, it will do so when we abandon all calculation. All language [*langue*] and all meaning already produced. In risk. Only risk, of which no one knows where it will lead. Of which future it is the harbinger. Of what past, the secret commemoration. No project here. Only this refusal to refuse themselves to what is perceived. Whatever distress and hardship may come of it.

These predecessors have no future – they come from it. Within them, it is already present. But who hears it? Obscurely, their song waters the world. Of today, of yesterday, of tomorrow. The necessity of a destiny which is never heard clearly, never appears in broad daylight. Unless it is already disfigured.

Yet the breath of he who sings, mingling his inspiration with the divine breath, remains out of reach. Cannot be situated. Faceless. He who perceives it sets off. Obeys the attraction. Goes to encounter nothing – only the more than all that is.

Translated by David Macey

Bibliography

Works by Luce Irigaray

The bibliography below refers to Irigaray's major writings, with details of English translations. A fuller bibliography of writing in French can be found in my book, *Luce Irigaray: philosophy in the feminine*.

Le Langage des déments (1973). Collection 'Approaches to semiotics', The Hague: Mouton.

Speculum. De l'autre femme (1974). Paris: Minuit. Trans. (1985), *Speculum of the other Woman*. Trans. Gillian C. Gill. Ithaca: Cornell University Press.

Ce Sexe qui n'en est pas un (1977). Paris: Minuit. Trans. (1985), *This Sex Which Is Not One*. Trans. Catherine Porter with Carolyn Burke. Ithaca: Cornell University Press.

Et l'une ne bouge pas sans l'autre (1979). Paris: Minuit. Trans. (1981), 'And the one doesn't stir without the other'. Trans. Hélène Vivienne Wenzel. *Signs*, 7 (1), pp. 60–7.

Amante marine. De Friedrich Nietzsche (1980) Paris: Minuit. Extracts from this have been translated by Sara Speidel (1983), under the title 'Veiled lips', *Mississippi Review* 11 (3), pp. 98–119. Complete trans. (1991), *Marine Lover of Friedrich Nietzsche*. Trans. Gillian C. Gill. New York: Columbia University Press.

Le Corps-à-corps avec la mère (1981). Montreal: Editions de la pleine lune.

Passions élémentaires (1982). Paris: Minuit. A translation of this book is being prepared for The Athlone Press, London.

L'Oubli de l'air chez Martin Heidegger (1983). Paris: Minuit.

La Croyance même (1983). Paris: Galilée. Reprinted in *Sexes et parentés*.

Ethique de la différence sexuelle (1984). Paris: Minuit. A translation of this book is being prepared for Cornell University Press. Extracts have already appeared in translation as follows: (1) 'Sexual Difference'. Trans. Seán

Hand (1987). In *French Feminist Thought*, Toril Moi, (ed.), Oxford: Basil Blackwell. (2) 'Sorcerer Love: a reading of plato's *Symposium*, Diotima's speech'. Trans. Eléanor Kuykendall (1989). *Hypatia*, 3 (3), pp. 32–44. (3) 'The fecundity of the caress'. Trans. Carolyn Burke (1985). In *Face to Face with Levinas*, Richard A. Cohen, (ed.), Albany: SUNY Press, pp. 231–56.

Parler n'est jamais neutre (1985). Paris: Minuit. One essay from this has been translated: 'Is the subject of science sexed?' It appears in three places: (1) Trans. Edith Oberle (1985). *Cultural Critique*, 1 (Fall). (2) Trans. Carol Mastrangelo Bové (1987). *Hypatia*, 2 (Fall), pp. 65–87. (3) Trans. Carol Mastrangelo Bové (1989). In *Feminism and Science*, Nancy Tuana, (ed.), Bloomington: Indiana University Press, pp. 58–68.

Sexes et parentés (1987). Paris: Minuit. Three extracts from this have been translated as follows. (1) *Divine Women*. Trans. Stephen Muecke (1986). Sydney: Local Consumption Occasional papers no. 8. (2) 'Women, the sacred, and money'. Trans. Diana Knight and Margaret Whitford (1986), *Paragraph*, 8 (October), pp. 6–18. (3) 'The gesture in psychoanalysis'. Trans. Elizabeth Guild (1989). In Teresa Brennan (ed.), *Between Feminism and Psychoanalysis*. London: Routledge, pp. 127–38.

Le Sexe Linguistique (1987). Special issue of *Langages*, 85 (March), Luce Irigaray, (ed.).

Le Temps de la différence: pour une révolution pacifique (1989). Paris: Librairie générale française (livre de poche).

Je, tu, nous: pour une culture de la différence (1990). Paris: Grasset. Two extracts from this have been translated as follows: (1) 'The culture of difference'. Trans. Alison Martin (1990). In *Pli* (formerly *The Warwick Journal of Philosophy*), 3 (1), pp. 44–52 (special issue on feminist philosophy). (2) 'Interview'. Trans. Margaret Whitford (1991). In Alice Jardine and Anne Menke, (eds), *Shifting Scenes: interviews on women, writing and politics in post '68 France*. New York: Columbia University Press.

Sexes et genres à travers les langues: éléments de communication sexuée (1990). Luce Irigaray (ed.), Paris: Grasset.

J'aime à toi: Esquisse d'une félicité dans l'histoire (1992). Paris: Grasset. One extract from this has been translated as follows: 'Love Between Us', trans. Jeffrey Lomonaco (1991) in *Who Comes After the Subject?*, ed. Eduardo Cadava, Peter Connor and Jean-Luc Nancy, New York and London: Routledge, pp. 167–77.

Other English translations available

'Women's exile' (1977). Trans. Couze Venn. Interview in *Ideology and*

Consciousness no. 1, pp. 62–76. Reprinted (1990) in Deborah Cameron, (ed.), *The Feminist Critique of Language: a reader*. London: Routledge, pp. 80–96.

'Luce Irigaray' (1983), interview with Lucienne Serrano and Elaine Hoffman Baruch in Janet Todd, (ed.), *Women Writers Talking*. New York and London: Holmes and Meier, pp. 230–45. Reprinted (1988) in Elaine Hoffman Baruch and Lucienne Serrano, (eds), *Women Analyze Women*. London: Harvester Wheatsheaf, pp. 147–64.

'An interview with Luce Irigaray' (1983), interview with Kiki Amsberg and Aafke Steenhuis. Trans. Robert van Krieken. In *Hecate*, 9 (1–2), pp. 192–202.

'Language, Persephone and sacrifice' (1985–6), interview with Luce Irigaray. Conducted and trans. Heather Jon Maroney, *Borderlines*, 4 (Winter), pp. 30–2.

'Equal to whom?' (1989). Trans. Robert L. Mazzola. *differences*, 1 (2), pp. 59–76.

'Interview' (1991) in *French Philosophers in Conversation: Derrida, Irigaray, Levinas, Le Doeuff, Schneider, Serres*, interviews with Raoul Mortley, London: Routledge, pp. 63–78.

Writings on Irigaray and other works referred to in the introductions and notes

There is now an enormous number of articles and chapters on Irigaray. The following selection attempts to include a range of interpretations and points of view (not all of which I agree with) to give readers some idea of the critical spectrum.

Assiter, Alison (1990), *Althusser and Feminism*. London: Pluto Press (includes chapter on Irigaray).

Bartkowski, Frances (1986), 'The question of ethics in French feminism'. *Berkshire Review*, 21, pp. 22–9.

Baruch, Elaine Hoffman and Serrano, Lucienne (1988), *Women Analyze Women in France, England and the United States*. London: Harvester Wheatsheaf.

Beauvoir, Simone de (1965), *The Prime of Life*. Harmondsworth: Penguin [first published 1960].

Benveniste, Emile (1966), *Problèmes de linguistique generale* 1. Paris: Gallimard. Trans. *Problems in General Linguistics*. Trans. M. E. Meek. Coral Gables, Fla.: University of Miami Press (1971).

Benveniste, Emile (1974), *Problèmes de linguistique générale* II. Paris: Gallimard.

Berg, Elizabeth L. (1982), 'The third woman'. *Diacritics*, 12 (2), pp. 11–20 [review of *Speculum* and *Amante marine*].

Berg, Maggie (1988), 'Escaping the cave: Irigaray and her feminist critics'. In Gary Wihl and David Williams (eds), *Literature and Ethics*. Toronto: University of Toronto Press.

Bernasconi, Robert and Critchley, Simon (eds) (1991), *Rereading Levinas*. Bloomington: Indiana University Press.

Bono, Paolo and Kemp, Sandra (eds) (1991), *Italian Feminist Thought*. Oxford: Blackwell.

Bowlby, Rachel (1983), 'The feminine female'. *Social Text*, 7, pp. 54–68.

Braidotti, Rosi (1986), 'The ethics of sexual difference: the case of Foucault and Irigaray'. *Australian Feminist Studies*, 3, pp. 1–13.

Braidotti, Rosi (1991), *Patterns of Dissonance*. Trans. Elizabeth Gould. Cambridge: Polity Press. [chapter on Irigaray].

Brennan, Teresa (ed.) (1989), *Between Feminism and Psychoanalysis*. London: Routledge.

Burke, Carolyn (1981), 'Irigaray through the looking glass'. *Feminist Studies*, 7 (2), pp. 288–306.

Burke, Carolyn (1987), 'Romancing the philosophers: Luce Irigaray'. *The Minnesota Review*, 29. Reprinted (1989) in Dianne Hunter, (ed.), *Seduction and Theory: Feminist Readings on Representation and Rhetoric*. Chicago: University of Illinois Press.

Butler, Judith (1990), *Gender Trouble: Feminism and the Subversion of Identity*. London: Routledge.

Cameron, Deborah (1990), *The Feminist Critique of Language: a reader*. London: Routledge.

Campioni, Mia and Braidotti, Rosi (1982), 'Mothers/Daughters/Feminists: the darkest continent'. *Refractory Girl*, 23, pp. 9–12.

Chodorow, Nancy (1978), *The Reproduction of Mothering: Psychoanalysis and the Sociology of Gender*. Berkeley: University of California Press.

Cicioni, Mirna (1989), ' "Love and respect, together": the theory and practice of *affidamento* in Italian feminism'. *Australian Feminist Studies*, 10, pp. 71–83.

Dallery, Arleen B. (1989), 'The politics of writing (the) body: *écriture féminine*'. In Alison M. Jaggar and Susan R. Bordo, (eds), *Gender/Body/Knowledge: feminist reconstructions of being and knowing*. New Brunswick and London: Rutgers University Press.

Eco, Umberto (1988), *Sémiotique et philosophie du langage*. Paris: Presses universitaires de France.

Eisenstein, Hester and Jardine, Alice (eds) (1980), *The Future of Difference*. Boston: G. K. Hall.

Favret-Saada, Jeanne (1977), 'Excusez-moi, je ne faisais que passer'. *Les Temps modernes*, 371, June, pp. 2089–2103.

Felman, Shoshana (1975), 'Women and Madness: the critical phallacy'. *Diacritics* (Winter), pp. 2–10 (includes review of *Speculum*).

Féral, Josette (1978), 'Antigone or the irony of the tribe'. *Diacritics* (Fall) pp. 2–14. [review of *Speculum* and *This Sex Which Is Not One*.].

Féral, Josette (1981), 'Towards a Theory of Displacement'. *Sub-Stance* 32, pp. 52–64.

Fuss, Diana J. (1989), 'Essentially speaking: Luce Irigaray's language of essence'. *Hypatia*, 3 (3) (Winter), pp. 62–80.

Fuss, Diana J. (1990), *Essentially Speaking*. London: Routledge.

Gallop, Jane (1982), *Feminism and Psychoanalysis: the daughter's seduction*. London: Macmillan.

Gallop, Jane (1983), '*Quand nos lèvres s'écrivent*: Irigaray's body politic'. *Romanic Review*, 74, pp. 77–83. Reprinted in *Thinking Through the Body*. New York: Columbia University Press (1988), pp. 92–100, 117–18.

Gearhart, Suzanne (1985), 'The scene of psychoanalysis: the unanswered questions of Dora'. In Charles Bernheimer and Claire Kahane, (eds), *In Dora's Case: Freud–Hysteria–Feminism*. London: Virago, pp. 105–27.

Girard, René (1977), *Violence and the Sacred*. Baltimore: Johns Hopkins University Press.

Godard, Linda (1985), 'Pour une nouvelle lecture de la question de la "Femme": essai à partir de la pensée de Jacques Derrida'. *Philosophiques*, 12 (1), (Spring), pp. 147–64.

Greimas, A (1966), *Sémantique structurale*. Paris: Larousse.

Greimas, A. J. and Courtés, J. (1979), *Sémiotique: dictionnaire raisonné de la théorie du langage*. Paris: Hachette.

Gross, Elizabeth (1986), 'Derrida, Irigaray and deconstruction'. In 'Leftwright', *Intervention*, 20, pp. 70–81.

Gross, Elizabeth (1986), 'Irigaray and sexual difference'. *Australian Feminist Studies*, 2, (Autumn), pp. 63–77, (review of *Speculum* and *This Sex Which Is Not One*).

Gross, Elizabeth (1986), *Irigaray and the Divine*. Sydney: Local Consumption Occasional Paper, no. 9.

Gross, Elizabeth (1986), 'Philosophy, subjectivity and the body'. In Carole Pateman and Elizabeth Gross, (eds), *Feminist Challenges*. Sydney: Allen & Unwin, pp. 125–43.

Grosz, Elizabeth (1988), 'Desire, the body and recent French feminism'. *Intervention*, 21–2, pp. 28–33.

Grosz, E. A. (1988), 'The hetero and the homo: the sexual ethics of Luce Irigaray'. *Gay Information*, 17–18, (March), pp. 37–44.

Grosz, Elizabeth (1989), *Sexual Subversions: three French feminists*. Sydney: Allen & Unwin.

Grosz, Elizabeth (1990), *Jacques Lacan: a feminist introduction*. London: Routledge [includes section on Irigaray and Lacan].

Hekman, Susan J. (1990), *Gender and Knowledge: elements of a postmodern feminism*. Boston: Northeastern University Press.

Hirsch, Marianne (1981), 'Mothers and daughters: a review essay'. *Signs*, 7 (1), pp. 200–222.

Holmlund, Christine (1989), 'I Love Luce: the lesbian, mimesis and masquerade in Irigaray, Freud and mainstream film'. *New Formations*, 9 (Winter), pp. 105–23.

Homans, Margaret (1986), 'Reconstructing the feminine'. *The Women's Review of Books*, 6 (March), pp. 12–13 [review of *Speculum* and *This Sex Which Is Not One*].

Jacobus, Mary (1986), *Reading Woman: essays in feminist criticism*. London: Methuen [chapters on Irigaray].

Jakobson, Roman and Halle, Morris (1956), *Fundamentals of Language*. The Hague: Mouton.

Jardine, Alice (1985), *Gynesis: Configurations of Woman and Modernity*. Ithaca: Cornell University Press.

Johnson, Pauline (1988), 'The dilemmas of Luce Irigaray', *Australian Feminist Studies*, 6 (Autumn), pp. 87–96.

Kearney, Richard (1988), *The Wake of Imagination: ideas of creativity in western culture*. London: Hutchinson.

Lauretis, Teresa de (1989), 'The essence of the triangle or, taking the risk of essentialism seriously'. *differences*, 1 (2), pp. 3–37.

Le Doeuff, Michèle (1989), *L'Etude et le rouet*. Paris: Seuil. Trans. (1991) *Hipparchia's Choice: an essay concerning women, philosophy, etc*. Trans. Trista Selous. Oxford: Basil Blackwell.

Leland, Dorothy (1989), 'Lacanian psychoanalysis and French feminism: toward an adequate political psychology'. *Hypatia*, 3 (3), (Winter), pp. 81–103.

Merleau-Ponty, Maurice (1962), *Phenomenology of Perception*. Trans. Colin Smith. London: Routledge & Kegan Paul [first published 1945].

Milan Women's Bookstore Collective (1990), *Sexual Difference: A Theory of Social-Symbolic Practice*. Bloomington: Indiana University Press.

Mitchell, Juliet and Rose, Jacqueline (eds) (1982), *Feminine Sexuality: Jacques Lacan and the Ecole Freudienne*. London: Macmillan.

Moi, Toril (1985), *Sexual/Textual Politics: Feminist Literary Theory*. London: Methuen.

Moi, Toril (1990), *Feminist Theory and Simone de Beauvoir*. Oxford: Basil Blackwell.

Moi, Toril (ed.) (1987), *French Feminist Thought*. Oxford: Blackwell.

Montefiore, Jan (1987), *Feminism and Poetry: Language, Experience, Identity in Women's Writing*. London: Pandora [includes section on Irigaray].

Mortensen, Ellen (1989) ' "Le Féminin" and nihilism: reading Irigaray with

Nietzsche and Heidegger', unpublished Ph.D. diss., University of Wisconsin-Madison.

Munster, Anna (1986), 'Playing with a different sex: between the covers of Irigaray and Gallop'. In E. A. Grosz, Terry Threadgold, David Kelly, Alan Cholodenko and Edward Colless (eds), *Futur*Fall: excursions into post-modernity*. University of Sydney: Power Institute of Fine Arts. pp. 118–27.

Nancy, Jean-Luc and Lacoue-Labarthe, Philippe (eds) (1981), *Les Fins de l'homme*. Paris: Galilée.

Nicholson, Linda J. (ed.) (1990), *Feminism/Postmodernism*. New York and London: Routledge.

Nye, Andrea (1988), *Feminist Theory and the Philosophies of Man*. London: Croom Helm [includes chapter on Irigaray].

Nye, Andrea (1989), 'The hidden host: Irigaray and Diotima at Plato's *Symposium*'. *Hypatia*, 3 (3), (Winter), pp. 45–61.

Nye, Andrea (1989), 'The voice of the serpent: French feminism and philosophy of language'. In Ann Garry and Marilyn Pearsall, (eds), *Women, Knowledge and Reality: explorations in feminist philosophy*, Boston and London: Unwin Hyman, pp. 233–49.

Plaza, Monique (1978), ' "Phallomorphic power" and the psychology of "woman" '. Trans. Miriam David and Jill Hodges. *Ideology and Consciousness*, 4 (Autumn), pp. 4–36.

Reineke, Martha J. (1987), 'Lacan, Merleau-Ponty and Irigaray: reflections on a specular drama'. *Auslegung: a journal of philosophy*, 14 (Winter), pp. 67–85.

Rich, Adrienne (1977), *Of Woman Born: motherhood as experience and institution*. London: Virago [first published 1976].

Roudinesco, Elisabeth (1990), *Jacques Lacan & Co*. London: Free Association.

Rowe, John Carlos (1985–6), ' "To live outside the law, you must be honest": the authority of the margin in contemporary theory'. *Cultural Critique*, 2. pp. 35–70.

Schneidermann, Stuart (1983), *Jacques Lacan: death of an intellectual hero*. Cambridge, Mass.: Harvard University Press.

Schor, Naomi (1989), 'This essentialism which is not one: coming to grips with Irigaray'. *differences*, 1 (2), pp. 38–58.

Schwarzer, Alice (1984), *Simone de Beauvoir Today: conversations 1972–1982*. London: Chatto and Windus.

Silverman, Kaja (1988), *The Acoustic Mirror: the female voice in psychoanalysis and cinema*. Bloomington: Indiana University Press [includes chapter on Irigaray].

Smith, Paul (1988), *Discerning the Subject*. Minneapolis: University of Minnesota Press [includes chapter on Irigaray].

Spender, Dale (1980), *Man Made Language*. London: Routledge & Kegan Paul.

Sprengnether, Madelon (1990), *The Spectral Mother: Freud, feminism and psychoanalysis*. Ithaca: Cornell University Press [includes discussion of Irigaray].

Stanton, Domna C. (1986), 'Difference on Trial: a critique of the maternal metaphor in Cixous, Irigaray and Kristeva'. In Nancy K. Miller, (ed.), *The Poetics of Gender*. New York: Columbia University Press, pp. 157–82.

Stephenson, Katherine (1987), 'Luce Irigaray's "L'Ordre sexuel du discours': a comparative English study on sexual differentiation in language use'. In *Semiotics*, University Press of America, pp. 257–66.

Threadgold. Terry (1988), 'Language and Gender'. *Australian Feminist Studies*, 6 (Autumn), pp. 41–70.

Turkle, Sherry (1979), *Psychoanalytic Politics: Jacques Lacan and Freud's French Revolution*. London: Burnett Books.

Wenzel, Hélène (1986), Interview with Simone de Beauvoir, *Women's Review of Books*, 3 (6).

Whitford, Margaret (1991), *Luce Irigaray: philosophy in the feminine*. London: Routledge.

Index

Index

Index